MW00477774

Advanced Introduction to Law and Development

Elgar Advanced Introductions are stimulating and thoughtful introductions to major fields in the social sciences and law, expertly written by some of the world's leading scholars. Designed to be accessible yet rigorous, they offer concise and lucid surveys of the substantive and policy issues associated with discrete subject areas.

The aims of the series are two-fold: to pinpoint essential principles of a particular field, and to offer insights that stimulate critical thinking. By distilling the vast and often technical corpus of information on the subject into a concise and meaningful form, the books serve as accessible introductions for undergraduate and graduate students coming to the subject for the first time. Importantly, they also develop well-informed, nuanced critiques of the field that will challenge and extend the understanding of advanced students, scholars and policy-makers.

Titles in the series include:

International Political Economy
Benjamin J. Cohen

The Austrian School of Economics
Randall G. Holcombe

Cultural Economics
Ruth Towse

Law and Development
Michael J. Trebilcock and Mariana Mota Prado

International Conflict and Security Law
Nigel D. White

Comparative Constitutional Law
Mark Tushnet

International Human Rights Law
Dinah L. Shelton

Advanced Introduction to

Law and Development

MICHAEL J. TREBILCOCK

*University Professor and Chair in Law and Economics,
Faculty of Law, University of Toronto, Canada*

MARIANA MOTA PRADO

Associate Professor, Faculty of Law, University of Toronto, Canada

Elgar Advanced Introductions

Edward Elgar
Cheltenham, UK • Northampton, MA, USA

Published by
Edward Elgar Publishing Limited
The Lypiatts
15 Lansdown Road
Cheltenham
Glos GL50 2JA
UK

Edward Elgar Publishing, Inc.
William Pratt House
9 Dewey Court
Northampton
Massachusetts 01060
USA

A catalogue record for this book
is available from the British Library

Library of Congress Control Number: 2014938805

ISBN 978 1 78347 338 0 (cased)
ISBN 978 1 78347 339 7 (paperback)
ISBN 978 1 78347 340 3 (eBook)

Typeset by Servis Filmsetting Ltd, Stockport, Cheshire
Printed and bound in Great Britain by T.J. International Ltd, Padstow

Contents

Abbreviations

BITs	bilateral investment treaties
DRC	Democratic Republic of Congo
EITI	Extractive Industries Transparency Initiative
FDI	foreign direct investment
GDI	gross domestic investment
GDP	gross domestic product
GNI	gross national income
GNP	gross national product
GSP	Generalized System of Preferences
HDI	Human Development Index
IIAs	international investment agreements
ILO	International Labour Organization
IMF	International Monetary Fund
IRAs	independent regulatory agencies
ISI	import substitution industrialization
LDCs	less-developed countries
MAI	multilateral agreement on investment
MDGs	Millennium Development Goals
MFN	Most-Favoured Nation
MNCs	multinational companies
MPI	Multi-dimensional Poverty Index
NGOs	non-governmental organizations
NIE	New Institutional Economics
NPM	New Public Management
NSE	New Structural Economics
ODA	official development assistance
OECD	Organisation for Economic Co-operation and Development
PPPs	public-private partnerships
PTAs	Preferential Trade Agreements
SARAs	semi-autonomous revenue agencies
SDT	special and differential treatment
SME	small and medium-sized enterprise
SOEs	state-owned enterprises

SPVs	Special Purpose Vehicles
UNDP	United Nations Development Programme
WGI	World Governance Indicators
WTO	World Trade Organization

Introduction

"Law and Development" is a term used to describe attempts to understand the relationship between legal systems and legal institutions and a wide variety of development outcomes. Hence, this book will mostly focus on the question of what kind of law and legal arrangements are perceived (correctly or not) to produce development. Before that, however, it is necessary to understand what we mean by development, a topic that has generated heated academic and policy debates. Different conceptions of development are discussed in the first chapter. The following chapters turn to a discussion about causal connections between legal and non-legal variables and development outcomes. The first chapter sets the context for a detailed analysis of the design of political, bureaucratic, private and international legal institutions, inquiring into when and how they may be relevant for development.

The book is inspired by our previous joint work, *What Makes Poor Countries Poor? Institutional Determinants of Development* (Edward Elgar, 2011). Indeed, the structure of the book largely follows the structure of our previous publication. There are, however, important and substantive differences between the two.

First, this book does not try to propose an argument or take sides in certain academic debates. Instead, it provides a concise map of the field for a reader who has little to no familiarity with the topic and is searching for an accessible introduction. This should make the book very useful as a textbook for courses and seminars, especially if complemented by the more in-depth coverage of the academic literature and policy debates addressed in our previous book.

Second, our analysis is significantly more concise in this volume, providing for a quicker read. The cost of such conciseness is, of course, the inevitable and necessary simplifications and omissions. Therefore, we recommend our other book as a useful complement to this short volume.

Third, the book has significantly more material on gender and development than our previous work. This is not only an important topic in the field, but it is probably the topic that poses some of the biggest challenges for institutional conceptions of development. Thus, we have decided to address the omission in our first volume by adding a chapter on this topic.

In writing this book, we gratefully acknowledge the research assistance of Lindsey Carson, Susannah Leslie, Joanna Noronha and Kristen Pue, and the logistical assistance of Nadia Gulezko.

PART I

CONCEPTUAL FOUNDATIONS

1   Defining development

What is development? In some respects, this question is related to philosophical debates of what constitutes the good life and dates back at least to the ancient Greeks. It is not the purpose of this chapter to provide an intellectual history of moral and political philosophy from the ancients onwards, or to espouse and defend any fully elaborated conception of the good life. Instead, this chapter identifies some prominent strands in post-war debates over the ends of development.[1]

1.1   Development as economic growth: GDP (or GNI) per capita

Development has been historically associated with wealth, in other words, the richest countries would be viewed as more developed than poor ones. Under this conception, wealth is measured by a country's gross domestic product (GDP) or gross national income (GNI) These measures indicate the total amount of resources a country has, and allows us to compare the size of countries' economies. For instance, the United States and China are the largest economies in the world if measured by their GDPs.[2]

The GDP alone is not enough to classify countries as developed or developing, however. The aggregate level of wealth in a country can be a significant amount of money or not, depending on the size of its population. For instance, China is the second largest economy in the world, after the United States. Current predictions indicate that China is likely to surpass the United States in the next few years, becoming

---

1 See generally H.W. Arndt, *Economic Development: The History of an Idea* (Chicago, IL: University of Chicago Press, 1989); G. Meier, *The Biography of a Subject: An Evolution of Development Economics* (Oxford University Press, 2004).

2 World Bank, "GDP (current US$)", available at http://data.worldbank.org/indicator/NY.GDP. MKTP.CD (accessed 11 October 2013).

then the largest economy in the world. However, if we divide the GDP of each country by their population, we find that the United States is significantly richer than China, with US$49,965 of GDP per capita, compared to China's US$6,168.[3] This is why a country's wealth is often measured by the GDP per capita.

GDP per capita has been central to much thinking in development economics in the post-war period, as reflected in the World Bank classification of countries into four income tranches: high income, middle income, low-middle income, low income. Low-income countries are defined as having a per capita gross national income in 2012 of US$1,035 or less; lower-middle income countries have incomes between US$1,036 and US$4,085; upper-middle income countries have incomes between US$4,086 and US$12,615; and high-income countries have incomes of US$12,616 or more.[4]

This measurement reflects a particular concept of development, centred around economic wealth, and it is also associated with policies designed to promote economic growth. There has been much resistance to such a conception of development and to growth policies, as we discuss in the next section. Even if one embraces such criticisms, however, economic growth should still be regarded as relevant in a development context, if the data is accurate.[5] To illustrate this point, it is useful to differentiate economic growth from two related concepts: poverty and inequality.

To understand the relationship between economic growth and poverty, take the case of the Democratic Republic of Congo (DRC), with a GDP per capita of US$272 in 2012.[6] This is one of the poorest countries in the world, despite its enormous mineral wealth. Similarly to other countries, such as the United States and Brazil, in the DRC income is not equally distributed: some people are extremely rich (for example,

---

3 World Bank, "GDP per capita (current US$)", available at http://data.worldbank.org/indicator/ NY.GDP.PCAP.CD (accessed 11 October 2013).

4 World Bank, "Country Classification, Data and Statistics", available at http://data.worldbank.org/ about/country-classifications (accessed 11 October 2013).

5 M. Jerven, *Poor Numbers: How We Are Misled by African Development Statistics and What to Do about It* (Ithaca, NY: Cornell University Press, 2013). (Showing that many African nations lack the capacity to produce reliable data. As a consequence, policies guided by these numbers can be misguided).

6 World Bank, "World DataBank", available at http://databank.worldbank.org/data/views/reports/ tableview.aspx (accessed 25 October 2013).

the former long-time ruler, now deceased, Mobutu), whereas 46.5 per cent of the population lives in poverty.[7] However, even if internal incomes were somehow equally distributed, the average per capita income would still be US$272. This means that each citizen would live on less than a dollar a day, despite the fact that the country would no longer face inequality problems. This extreme example shows that increasing GDP per capita by promoting economic growth can be an important instrument in eliminating poverty and therefore promoting economic development. Asian countries, especially China, offer illustrative examples of how economic growth can help reduce poverty. It is estimated that more than 500 million people were lifted out of poverty in China in the last three decades, due to high rates of economic growth.[8]

This raises an important policy question: could we eliminate poverty by simply giving poor people money coming from other countries? Many believe that this type of external redistributive programme (known as Official Development Assistance, or Foreign Aid) can help solve the problem of poverty in developing countries. However, as we will discuss in greater detail in Chapter 14, there are reasons to be sceptical. One reason is that the amount of aid currently allocated to developing countries is not remotely sufficient to eliminate poverty. For instance, the total amount of aid sent to developing countries in a year is normally a little above US$100 billion.[9] This is the annual expenditure budget of one single Canadian province, Ontario. Today there are around 1 billion people in the world living in absolute poverty, while there are around 13 million people living in Ontario. Thus, it is hard to think aid will solve the problem unless the amount of these transfers was dramatically increased.

The concept of poverty should not be confused with inequality. A country can have high rates of inequality while maintaining low levels of extreme poverty. An illustrative example is the United States. There

---

7 World Bank, "World DataBank, Poverty headcount ratio at national poverty line (percentage of population)", available at http://databank.worldbank.org/data/views/reports/tableview.aspx?isshared=true&ispopular=series&pid=16. (accessed 11 October 2013). (This figure is for 2011).

8 World Bank, "China Overview", available at www.worldbank.org/en/country/china/overview (accessed 11 October 2013).

9 World Bank, "Net bilateral aid flows from DAC donors, Total (current US$)", available at http://databank.worldbank.org (accessed 25 October 2013). Net bilateral aid flows from DAC donors are the net disbursements of official development assistance (ODA) or official aid from the members of the Development Assistance Committee (DAC).

are cases, however, in which the inequality exists alongside (and may be one of the causes of) extreme poverty. For instance, Brazil has a high rate of inequality,[10] with the richest 20 per cent of the population accruing around 60 per cent of Brazil's income compared to only 3 per cent by the poorest 20 per cent.[11] This means that the GDP per capita indicated earlier is far from representing how the income is distributed among the population. Moreover, 6.1 per cent of the Brazilian population lives in extreme poverty.[12]

While economic growth can help increase GDP per capita, as illustrated by the example of the DRC, it may not help reduce poverty, as exemplified historically by the Brazilian case. That country had spectacular rates of economic growth in the 1960s and 1970s (averaging 7.33 per cent).[13] However, this economic growth was not distributed to the lower echelons of the population, being largely concentrated in the upper classes. This means that GDP per capita increased during this period, but both inequality and absolute poverty increased as well. Therefore, one may say that there was growth without development. China has recently started to see a rise in economic inequality, which may raise similar concerns.

Due to these limitations (and other criticisms not discussed here), in recent decades dissatisfaction with such a narrow conception of development has been strongly manifested in a number of quarters. At a conceptual level, the primacy of per capita income as an index of a country's state of development and maximization of rates of economic growth (and hence per capita income) as the primary end of development has been challenged by Amartya Sen, Nobel Laureate in Economics, as we discuss in section 1.3 below.

---

10 See World Bank, "Inequality and Economic Development in Brazil" (Washington, DC: The World Bank, 2004), available at http://www-wds.worldbank.org/servlet/WDSContentServer/WDSP/IB/2004/10/05/000012009_20041005095126/Rendered/PDF/301140PAPER0Inequality0Brazil.pdf (accessed 28 April 2014).

11 World Bank, "World DataBank", available at http://databank.worldbank.org/data/views/reports/tableview.aspx# (accessed 25 October 2013).

12 World Bank, "Poverty headcount ratio at $1.25 a day (PPP) (percentage of population)", available at http://data.worldbank.org/indicator/SI.POV.DDAY/countries (accessed 11 October 2013). (These figures are from 2009).

13 R. Adrogue, M. Cerisola and G. Gelos, "Brazil's Long-Term Growth Performance – Trying to Explain the Puzzle" (2006) IMF Working Paper WP/06/282 at 3.

1.2   Development as lack of poverty: the Multi-dimensional Poverty Index

Recently, there has been an increased focus on poverty. This new focus has had its merits, but it has also had its shortfalls. One is the fact that poverty has been primarily defined in economic terms. Absolute poverty, for example, is currently defined by the World Bank as an individual living on less than 1.25 dollars a day.[14] This narrow definition raises the same type of concerns directed at the aggregate measures of a country's wealth, such as GDP per capita. For instance, an individual whose income is less than a dollar a day may live in a country where there is an active welfare state with a vast network of support services. This stands in sharp contrast with an individual whose income is similar to the first one, but s/he is also deprived of any type of governmental assistance.

In an attempt to capture these other dimensions of poverty that are not captured by measurements of individual income, the Oxford University's Oxford Poverty and Human Development Initiative (OPHI) joined the United Nations Development Programme (UNDP) Human Development Report Office to create a new index to indicate the nature and quantify the extent of poverty. It is called the MPI, or Multi-dimensional Poverty Index.[15] The MPI examines a range of deprivations by using ten indicators at the household level (such as child mortality, years of schooling, and access to water, sanitation and electricity). This multi-dimensional approach to poverty reveals not only how many people are poor but also the nature and intensity of their poverty, which is relevant for policy design.[16]

The percentage of people living in poverty according to the MPI is higher than the percentage of people living on less than US$2 a day in 43 countries and lower than those living on less than US$1.25 a day in 25 countries. For example, in Ethiopia, 90 per cent of the population are MPI poor compared to 39 per cent classified as living in extreme

---

14 M. Ravallion, S. Chen and P. Sangraula, "Dollar a Day Revisited" (Washington, DC: The World Bank, 2008), available at http://www-wds.worldbank.org/external/default/WDSContentServer/IW3P/IB/2008/09/02/000158349_20080902095754/Rendered/PDF/wps4620.pdf (accessed 28 April 2014).

15 This new index has featured in the UNDP, Human Development Reports since 2010. See 2013 UNDP Human Development Report, available at http://hdr.undp.org/en/media/HDR_2013_EN_complete.pdf (accessed 28 April 2014).

16 S. Alkire and M.E. Santos, "Acute Multidimensional Poverty: A New Index for Developing Countries" (2010) OPHI Working Paper No. 38 at 7.

poverty; on the other hand, in Tanzania, 89 per cent of people live in extreme income poverty but only 65 per cent are MPI poor. This index captures access to key services such as sanitation and water in a more direct fashion, so the picture of deprivation seems to be a more accurate one: in some countries, services are available for free, while in others they are out of reach even for working people with an income.[17]

1.3   Development as freedom: Human Development Index

In a widely celebrated book, *Development as Freedom*, Amartya Sen accepts that policies and institutions that increase per capita incomes by increasing economic growth are instrumental in promoting development. However, he argues that economic growth is not the ultimate end of development. In his view, the ends of development should be focused on promoting individual freedom, in the sense of enhancing the ability of individuals to choose to live lives that they have reason to value.[18]

For Sen, freedom in various dimensions (political freedoms, economic facilities, social opportunities, transparency guarantees and protective security) constitutes both the means and ends of development. These freedoms are complementary, mutually reinforcing, and promote more robust forms of individual agency and expand human capabilities, opportunities and functioning. In this context, economic growth is important for what it enables individuals, and the communities and societies of which they are members, to achieve. However, economic growth is not the only means of promoting development.

Sen shows that one's choices and possibilities are not only limited or reduced by lack of money, but they can also be reduced by a shorter lifespan, for example. A comparison between the life expectancy of African-Americans in the United States, and citizens of the state of Kerala, in India, and China is illustrative. African-Americans have a higher GDP per capita, but a shorter life expectancy than their counterparts in these other countries. The example illustrates that it is not

---

17 S. Alkire and M.E. Santos, "Multidimensional Poverty Index: 2010 Data. Research Brief" (July 2010) Oxford Poverty and Human Development Initiative, available at http://www.ophi.org.uk/wp-content/uploads/OPHI-MPI- Brief.pdf (accessed 28 April 2014), at 4.

18 A. Sen, *Development as Freedom* (New York, NY: Knopf, 1999). See also M.C. Nussbaum, *Creating Capabilities: The Human Development Approach* (Cambridge, MA and London: Belknap-Harvard University Press, 2011).

fully clear whether being richer, but having a shorter life would be everyone's preferable option. Everyone would prefer to be richer, if everything else was held constant. Conversely, we all would prefer to live longer, all else equal. However, choice becomes much more complicated if the price for greater wealth is a shorter lifespan; or if living longer implies living with chronic destitution and suffering.

Partly reflecting Amartya Sen's concept of development, the UNDP, in an annual series of Human Development Reports dating back to 1990,[19] has constructed a Human Development Index (HDI) based on three ends of development: longevity, as measured by life expectancy at birth; knowledge, as measured by a weighted average of adult literacy and mean years of schooling; and standard of living, as measured by per capita income.[20] While there is a strong positive correlation between per capita income and health and education status, this correlation is not perfect or tight. Rankings of developing countries often change significantly, either upwards or downwards, when health and education variables are incorporated along with a per capita income variable in this index.

Despite moving away from a strictly economic concept of development, the HDI is mostly based on quantifiable variables, which can be measured periodically, and allow frequent comparison between different countries and their levels of development. In this respect, it is similar to income measures of GDP per capita.[21] The difference is that the multiplicity of variables in this index makes it harder to draw clear-cut lines that distinguish developed from developing countries, such as the lines drawn by the World Bank between low, middle and high income countries. For example, Vietnam, Chile and Cuba fare better on health and education (and in the overall HDI ranking) than other countries with the same level of income, whereas Bahrain, Angola and the United States do worse on health and education rankings than other countries with the same level of income.[22]

---

19 UNDP, "Origins of the human development approach" in *Human Development Reports*, available at http://hdr.undp.org/ en/humandev/origins/ (accessed 15 May 2009).

20 UNDP, "The Human Development Index (HDI)" in *Human Development Reports*, available at http://hdr.undp.org/en/statistics/indices/hdi/ (accessed 15 May 2009).

21 For a critique of these measures as the basis for an agenda for public policy-making, see K. Rittich, "Governing by Measuring: the Millennium Development Goals in Global Governance" in H. Ruiz-Fabri, R. Wolfrum and J. Gogolin (eds), *Select Proceedings of the European Society of International Law*, Vol. 2, 463 (Oxford, UK: Hart Publishing, 2010).

22 UNDP, "The Human Development Index (HDI)" in *Human Development Reports*, available at http://hdr.undp.org/en/reports/ (accessed 28 April 2014). These discrepancies have

1.4   Sustainable development

Another example of efforts to use more comprehensive measures to assess a country's level of development is exemplified by the eight Millennium Development Goals (MDGs) adopted in September 2000 by 189 members of the United Nations. The goals include eradication of extreme poverty and hunger, gender empowerment, and sustainable development, among others.[23] In addition to defining these eight goals, the member countries of the United Nations also committed to a set of targets to be achieved by 2015 and defined indicators to monitor progress in achieving each of these goals.[24] For example, goal number one is to eradicate extreme poverty and hunger, while the target is to halve the proportion of people living on less than 1 dollar a day and those who suffer from hunger by 2015.

Like measures of GDP per capita, the MDGs are also embedded within a concept of development – one that might be multi-faceted and less simplistic than GDP per capita, but still reveal a notion of what is development. The MDGs have at least two novelties: a concern with gender equality, and a concern with environmental sustainability. These are two concerns that have gained a great deal of prominence in

---

persisted since 1990. See also UNDP, "Defining and Measuring Human Development", *Human Development Report* (1990) at 14–16, available at http://hdr.undp.org/en/media/hdr_1990_en_front.pdf (accessed 28 April 2014).

23 These goals are: 1. Eradicate extreme poverty and hunger. 2. Achieve universal primary education. 3. Promote gender equality and empower women. 4. Reduce child mortality. 5. Improve maternal health. 6. Combat HIV/AIDS, malaria and other diseases. 7. Ensure environmental sustainability. 8. Develop a global partnership for development.

24 The 2015 Targets are 1. Halve the proportion of people living on less than 1 dollar a day and those who suffer from hunger. 2. Ensure that all boys and girls complete primary school. 3. (Target for 2005) Eliminate gender disparities in primary and secondary education (preferred). (Target for 2015) Eliminate gender disparities at all levels. 4. Reduce by two-thirds the mortality rate among children under five. 5. Reduce by three-quarters the ratio of women dying in childbirth. 6. Halt and begin to reverse the spread of HIV/AIDS and the incidence of malaria and other major diseases. 7. (General target) Integrate the principles of sustainable development into country policies and programmes and reverse the loss of environmental resources. (Target for 2015) Reduce by half the proportion of people without access to safe drinking water. (Target for 2020) Achieve significant improvement in the lives of at least 100 million slum dwellers. 8. Develop further an open trading and financial system that includes a commitment to good governance, development and poverty reduction – nationally and internationally; Address the special needs of the least developed countries and those of landlocked and small-island developing states; Deal comprehensively with the debt problems of developing countries; Develop decent and productive work for youth; In cooperation with pharmaceutical companies, provide access to affordable essential drugs in developing countries; In cooperation with the private sector, make available the benefits of new technologies – especially information and communication technologies.

the development field recently, and we will dedicate an entire chapter to the former,[25] while discussing the latter here.

Preserving the environment can be conceived as an end in itself, but in the development field it is often conceived as a means to protect the interests of future generations. While the use of natural resources may promote growth and help current generations, if such use causes the depletion of such resources, it will deprive future generations of basic sustenance, condemning them to live in poverty. This concern is often captured in the concept of sustainable development, which is "development that meets the needs of the present without compromising the ability of future generations to meet their own needs".[26] The idea of sustainable development has been captured by a new measurement of wealth, called Green GDP. This index accounts for economic growth, but it discounts the environmental costs of such growth by discounting loss of biodiversity and costs caused by climate change from the conventional GDP.[27]

In an attempt to address the environmental sustainability challenge, a series of achievable environmental goals were established in 1992. Agenda 21, formulated during the United Nations Conference on Environment and Development (Rio Summit), is a non-binding action plan to promote sustainable development and it has been adopted by international and multi-lateral organizations, as well as national governments.[28] Despite these efforts, sustainable development still seems to remain a formidable challenge. Jeffrey Sachs offers alarming predictions if the current rates of population and economic growth are maintained. The global population is likely to rise to 9.2 billion in 2050, an increase of 40 per cent. If the world's average income per person rises four-fold over this period, the gross world product will increase 6.3 times. This increased economic activity will require even more resources in what Sachs considers "an already crowded planet".[29]

---

25 See Chapter 8.

26 *Report of the World Commission on Environment and Development.* G.A. Res 42/187, UN Doc. A/RES/42/187 (1987).

27 J. Stiglitz, A. Sen and P.J.-P. Fitoussi, "Report by the Commission on the Measurement of Economic Performance and Social Progress" (2008) Commission on the Measurement of Economic Performance and Social Progress, available at http://www.stiglitz-sen-fitoussi.fr/en/index.htm (accessed 28 April 2014).

28 "Agenda 21: Programme of Action for Sustainable Development" U.N. GAOR, 46th Sess., Agenda Item 21, UN Doc A/Conf.151/26 (1992), available at http://sustainabledevelopment.un.org/index.php?page=view&nr=23&type=400&menu=35 (accessed 28 April 2014).

29 J. Sachs, *Common Wealth* (New York, NY: The Penguin Press, 2008) at 22–3.

Independent of the accuracy of these predictions, the 2003 World Development Report shows that the current use of natural resources is already creating strains for people around the world, and the problem has been particularly acute in developing countries. First, many cities already have unhealthy levels of air pollution. The World Bank estimates that in 1,445 cities in the world the population suffers from exposure to concentration of dust particles, or total suspended particles (TSP) above traditional guidelines of 90 micrograms μ/m. Second, fresh water is also growing increasingly scarce. The World Bank estimates that one-third of the world's people live in countries that are already experiencing moderate to high water shortages due to rising consumption. Moreover, excess nitrogen (from fertilisers, human sewage, and combustion of fossil fuels) has created excess nutrients in lakes, rivers, and coastal waters and reduced soil fertility. Third, soil degradation has caused productivity losses. The extent of such degradation, according to the World Bank, is significant: "nearly 2 million hectares of land worldwide (23 per cent of all cropland, pasture, forest, and woodland) have been degraded since the 1950s. About 39 per cent of these lands are lightly degraded, 46 per cent moderately degraded, and 16 per cent so severely degraded that the change is too costly to reverse". Fourth, the stock of forests, biodiversity and fisheries is in rapid decline. Deforestation is concentrated in developing countries, which have lost nearly 200 million hectares of forest between 1980 and 1995. In contrast, forest cover in industrial countries is either stable or increasing. Deforestation has a negative impact on biodiversity, but so do other types of human activity. For instance, some suggest that 20 per cent of all endangered species are threatened by non-native species introduced by human activity. As to fisheries, "about 58 per cent of the world's coral reefs and 34 percent of all fish species are at risk from human activities. 70 percent of the world's commercial fisheries are fully exploited or overexploited and experiencing declining yields". Climate change poses especial risks to low-lying developing countries from rising sea levels, and other developing countries from prolonged droughts, torrential rains, tsunami and other extreme weather events. In sum, the world's current use of natural resources is not consistent with sustainable growth over the long term.[30]

---

30 World Development Report 2003, "Sustainable Development in a Dynamic Economy" (Washington, DC: The World Bank, 2003), available at www.dynamicsustainabledevelopment.org (accessed 28 April 2014).

What are the possible solutions? While some have suggested that economic growth is antithetical to preservation of environmental resources, in 2010, two high-profile publications argued that growth and environmental protection can be reconciled.

In *The Plundered Planet*, Paul Collier argues that the exploitation of natural resources is often conceived of as antithetical to the interests of future generations who will be deprived of those resources. However, he argues that if these resources are used to promote growth and benefit society at large, the exploitation of those resources can actually be in the interest of both current and future generations. This is what Collier calls "pragmatic environmentalism": sometimes it is better for resources to be preserved, but sometimes it is better for them to be explored and used to promote development. For this to be achieved, he suggests using foreign aid to finance surveys to assess what these countries have (to avoid selling natural resources without knowing) and a natural resources charter with strong rules to guarantee that the exploitation of natural resources will benefit the entire population of a developing country (as opposed to benefiting a small local elite and multinational corporations).[31]

Along the same lines, the 2010 World Development Report, entitled *Development and Climate Change* advocated incorporating environmental concerns in policies to promote economic growth. The political battles around the signature of the Kyoto protocol, however, may suggest that there will be strong political resistance to this agenda. Developing countries claim that the current developed countries have accumulated wealth by depleting resources, and are responsible for most greenhouse gases. Thus, it would not be fair to countries that are currently developing their economies to be deprived of similar benefits from economic growth.[32]

1.5   Development as quality of life: the National Happiness Index

A movement to redefine development based on well-being supported the development of the Gross National Happiness (GNH) Index.

31 P. Collier, *The Plundered Planet: How to Reconcile Prosperity with Nature* (London: Allen Lane, 2010).

32 M. Trebilcock, *Dealing with Losers: The Political Economy of Policy Transitions* (New York, NY: Oxford University Press, 2014).

Spearheaded by the King of Bhutan, the index includes nine domains: psychological well-being, health, education, time use, cultural diversity and resilience, good governance, community vitality, ecological diversity and resilience, and living standards. These domains are considered conditions of a "good life" and are measured by 33 indicators.[33]

While initially supported only by a few academics and the government of Bhutan, the concept has gained international attention recently. In 2011, the United Nations approved a resolution entitled "Happiness: Towards a Holistic Approach to Development".[34] Sponsored by Bhutan, the resolution states that "happiness is [a] fundamental human goal and universal aspiration; that GDP by its nature does not reflect the goal; that unsustainable patterns of production and consumption impede sustainable development; and that a more inclusive, equitable and balanced approach is needed to promote sustainability, eradicate poverty, and enhance well-being and profound happiness". This resolution was followed by two World Happiness Reports, published in 2012 and 2013, which measured the overall happiness in different countries and ranked them against each other.[35] Alongside its recognition at the United Nations, in 2013 the Organisation for Economic Co-operation and Development (OECD) issued guidelines for an international standard for the measurement of well-being, largely subscribing to the concerns that have driven the creation of the happiness index.[36]

Despite increasing recognition, the concept and the index have not been immune from criticisms. One is that it is not possible to measure people's happiness, as it is a volatile emotion that is constantly changing through the day. This would challenge not only the feasibility but also the usefulness of measuring happiness. The authors of the World Happiness Report promptly dismiss these concerns by indicating that they are capturing people's satisfaction with their lives overall, which, according to them, is more stable and permanent, than a person's mood on a particular day.

---

33 The Centre for Bhutan Studies, "Bhutan GNH Index", available at http://www.grossnationalhappiness.com/articles/ (accessed 28 April 2014).

34 G.A. Res. 65/309, UN Doc. A/RES/65/309. (2011).

35 J. Halliwell, R. Layard and J. Sachs (eds), *World Happiness Report* (New York, NY: Earth Institute, 2012) commissioned for the United Nations Conference on Happiness (April 2012); J. Helliwell, R. Layard and J. Sachs, *World Happiness Report 2013* (New York, NY: Earth Institute, 2013).

36 OECD, "OECD Guidelines on Measuring Subjective Wellbeing" (2013), available at http://www.oecd.org/statistics/guidelines-on-measuring-subjective-well-being.htm (accessed 28 April 2014).

Another criticism pertains to the methodology used to collect this data. Robert and Edward Skidelsky in a book entitled *How Much is Enough? Money and the Good Life* argue that the material conditions for the good life already exist in our world (health, respect, friendship, leisure and other non-material goods), but the continuous and blind pursuit of economic growth has been an obstacle to achieving it. Despite subscribing to the concerns that informed the creation of the GNH Index, they express considerable scepticism as to the robustness of methodologies for measuring happiness and for making comparisons across societies.[37]

1.6 Cultural relativism: challenging the notion of development

So far, we have discussed conceptions of development that reflect different interpretations of what is required to achieve human well-being. Despite their divergences, these conceptions have one thing in common: they assume that there is a universal conception of the good life (the ends of development). In contrast to the views presented here, some authors argue that societies have diverse, culturally defined conceptions of "the good life" and how one goes about achieving it. This perspective asserts that different societies have different values and these differences should be respected: there are no grounds for judging that the values of some societies are better than others.

The most radical versions of this argument claim that everything is culturally defined, questioning the validity of the entire development enterprise. For example, Arturo Escobar argues for the preservation of indigenous culture and against the use of Western (or any) standards as a benchmark, and claims that the imperialistic nature of the development discourse makes it comparable to discourses of colonization.[38] The idea that there is an incompatibility between Western and other cultures may assume a static and perhaps immutable view of culture, which presupposes that we cannot intentionally and purposively change culture. A stronger version of this argument claims that

---

37 R. Skidelsky and E. Skidelsky, *How Much is Enough? Money and the Good Life* (New York, NY: Other Press LLC, 2012).

38 A. Escobar, "Introduction: Development and the Anthropology of Modernity" in *Encountering Development: The Making and Unmaking of the Third World* (Princeton, NJ: Princeton University Press, 1995) at 3–20.

"culture is destiny", that with or without intentional attempts to do so, culture will not change.

In contrast to those who use a concept of culture to challenge conceptions of development, there are theorists who question the notion of culture as defined in the development literature. Scholars such as Tatsuo question Western representations of the First and Third Worlds that try to establish clear lines to separate them. Tatsuo claims, for instance, that most of the debate about development and culture is built upon false dichotomies that separate Western cultures from other cultures.[39] If we abandon these dichotomies, Tatsuo argues, the tension and incompatibility between liberal democracy and "Asian culture" largely disappears. A similar argument is developed by Amartya Sen in his book *Identity and Violence*.[40] According to him, identities have been often defined by singling out one aspect of a person's life, such as religion, when in fact a person may identify more strongly with other aspects of his or her character. Sen claims that the miniaturization of identities has created polarization between different ethnic and religious groups, and has been a source of ethnic and religious conflict around the world.

1.7   Conclusion

Focusing narrowly on economic growth as an end in and of itself – abstracting from what it enables members of a society, individually or collectively, to achieve (perhaps, as Sen would argue, in terms of enhanced human capabilities and functioning) – would be to accord economic growth a primacy in the conception of the ends of development that it cannot sustain. Nevertheless, it is important to recognize the opposing danger: the ends of development may become so diffuse that "one sometimes wonders whether it now stands for anything more substantial than everyone's own utopia".[41]

39 I. Tatsuo, "Liberal Democracy and Asian Orientalism" in J. Bauer and D. Bells (eds), *The East Asian Challenge for Human Rights* (Cambridge, UK: Cambridge University Press, 1999).

40 A. Sen, *Identity and Violence: The Illusion of Destiny* (New York, NY: Norton, 2006).

41 Arndt, *supra* note 1, at 165.

2   Determinants of development

While the previous chapter discussed the ends of development, this chapter will focus on the means to achieve those ends, in other words, what causes development. Debates about the means of development have often reflected as much diversity of viewpoints as debates over the ends. In this chapter we provide a brief overview of a wide variety of theories regarding the means of development. At the risk of over-simplifying their differences, we have grouped these theories under three major headings: (1) economic theories, (2) cultural theories, and (3) geographic theories.

While these theories offer different and often conflicting explanations about why certain societies became rich, while others have remained or become poor, they have one common feature: they ignore or reject the idea that institutions are important for development (an idea that will be explored at greater length in Chapter 3). Ignoring or rejecting the idea that institutions matter for development challenges the idea that law or legal institutions can help promote certain development outcomes. To counter this argument, at the end of this chapter we offer a critical analysis of the often ignored institutional dimensions of these theories, which are often embedded in their policy implications.

2.1   Economic theories of development

Over the post-war period, various schools of thought concerned with economic growth have come into and out of favour, including: capital fundamentalism; *dirigiste* central planning; neo-Marxist dependency theory; the Washington Consensus (the neoclassical model or market fundamentalism); endogenous growth theories; and eclectic combinations of all of the foregoing.

According to theories known as "capital fundamentalism" or the "linear stages of growth approach", countries need to mobilize domestic savings and foreign investment to generate sufficient investment to accelerate GDP growth. Linear stages of growth theory was a branch of modernization theory, which conceived of developing countries as backward societies that must be brought into modern civilization through the evolutionary process of industrialization and economic development. The dominant theory of development in the 1950s and 1960s, its basic assumption was that there were pre-defined stages through which every country must proceed in order to achieve economic development, and developing nations could be located at a particular stage based on national growth and investment rates.[1] Thus, the most crucial need of developing countries was capital. However, some developing countries had very low rates of new capital formation, and were not able to save the resources required (15 to 20 per cent of GDP) to promote economic development. In this context, foreign aid (and to some extent foreign direct investment) were proposed as a solution to the savings gap.[2]

The linear stages approach to development was replaced in the 1970s with two other competing theories: structural change and international dependence theories. In contrast to linear stages theory, these two sets of theories went beyond economic policies, addressing the need for political and social change in order to foster development.

Structural change theories argued that economic growth required that "underdeveloped economies transform their domestic economic structures from a heavy emphasis on traditional subsistence agriculture to a more modern, more urbanized, and more industrially diverse manufacturing and service economy". This transformation required the state to implement policies to foster industrialization and mechanization of the agricultural sector, to provide a strong educational system to train the work force and enable rural workers to move to industrial sectors, and to undertake urban planning and make infrastructure investments to accommodate the growth of urban centres.[3]

Dependency theories were primarily conceived in developing nations (especially in Latin America), and emerged largely in response to mod-

---

1 W.W. Rostow described the stages as follows: (a) traditional society; (b) pre-conditions for take-off into self-sustaining growth; (c) take-off; (d) the drive to modernity or maturity; (e) the age of high mass consumption. W.W. Rostow, *The Stages of Economic Growth: A Non-Communist Manifesto* (Cambridge, UK: Cambridge University Press, 1960), chapter 2.

2 M. Todaro and S. Smith, *Economic Development* (Boston, MA, San Francisco, CA, New York, NY: Addison Wesley, 2012, 11th edn) at 110–14.

3 *Ibid.*, at 115.

ernization theory and the capital fundamentalists' overly simplistic understanding of economic development. Dependency theories looked to external and historical influences of colonial or economic power as central to the state of domestic economic development. The basic claim of these theories was that the international economic order is polarized and entails a relationship of dependence between the industrial centre and an agrarian periphery.[4]

Dependency theorists argued that developing countries who were exporters of basic agricultural products, for which demand was inelastic, suffered deteriorating terms of trade relative to imported manufactured goods, for which demand was more elastic (sensitive to price). They also argued that foreign direct investment was often concentrated in "enclave" projects such as mining, with few positive spillovers to the broader economy and often negative spillovers in terms of environmental degradation and displacement of local residents. Also, these investments generated less than optimal revenues for host countries because of corrupt relationships between foreign investors and host country officials. This combination of factors was argued to impede the development of an indigenous manufacturing sector and would lead to truncated economies where developing countries were largely "hewers of wood and drawers of water".

The neoclassical (or neoliberal) counter-revolution replaced the structural change and dependency theories, becoming the dominant paradigm in development theory in the 1980s and 1990s. The neoclassical model assumed that free markets could promote an efficient allocation of economic resources by creating efficient pricing signals, thus being labelled "market fundamentalism".

This model assumed that the state was often the source of the problem rather than the solution to challenges of development. In the late 1980s, the neoliberal theory was embodied in a set of policy prescriptions that became known as the "Washington Consensus". The central tenets of the Consensus were: macro-economic stability (fiscal discipline, tax reforms and reductions in public expenditures), liberalization (open trade and market deregulation), privatization, and policies to attract foreign direct investment (FDI) and stimulate private entrepreneurship (reduction of tax and regulatory burdens, availability of credit for private investors, and fostering of competition within sectors).

---

4 *Ibid.*, at 122.

Endogenous growth theory developed in response to the inability of the neoclassical model to explain rates of technological change and productivity growth, as well as the variable long-term growth rates experienced by different countries.[5] In contrast with neoclassical theories, endogenous theories of growth emphasize that "economic growth is an endogenous outcome of an economic system, not the result of forces that impinge from outside".[6] Endogeneity, in economics, refers to the fact that variables in a certain model are not independent – that is, changes in one variable will produce changes in another variable, and vice versa. Endogenous theories of growth thus claim that these variables, such as technological change, are not independent: they impact on growth, which in turn impacts on them. Technological change is an outcome of public and private investments in education (human capital), infrastructure, and research and development in knowledge-intensive industries.[7] This knowledge is a public good that can be re-used by other producers, leading to knowledge spillovers, which generate growth because productivity increases as knowledge is accumulated and disseminated. This theory explains why many developed countries continue to experience high or increasing levels of growth, as "the more you learn, the faster you learn things".[8]

Another response to the failure of neoclassical theories is the New Structural Economics (NSE). Similarly to structural theories, the NSE associates development with the structure of a country's economy, specially the industrial sector. However, it suggests that the industrial structure of a country is "endogenous to its endowment structure", in other words, a country's resources (land, population, skills, capital, natural resources, and so on.) should determine the country's comparative industrial advantage. The prediction is that economic growth will take place if countries invest in their natural or latent comparative advantages. Thus, governments need to design industrial policy that facilitates the development of those industries which can produce

---

5 S. Ghatak, *Introduction to Development Economics* (London, New York, NY: Routledge, 2003, 4th edn) at 58. For extensive critiques of neoliberal theories of development, see H.-J. Chang and I. Grabel, *Reclaiming Development: An Alternative Economic Policy Manual* (London, New York, NY: Zed Books, 2004) and E. Reinert, *How Rich Countries Got Rich ... And Poor Countries Stay Poor* (London: Constable and Robinson, 2007).

6 P.M. Romer, "The Origins of Endogenous Growth" (1994) 8 *Journal of Economic Perspectives* at 3–22.

7 Todaro and Smith, *supra* note 2, at 150.

8 J.M. Cypher and J.L. Dietz, *The Process of Economic Development* (London, New York, NY: Taylor and Francis, 2008, 3rd edn) at 249.

most effectively, while at the same time providing space for market forces to lead the process of technological innovation.[9]

2.2   Cultural theories of development

The word culture does not have a singular or universal meaning, and can be used to describe a wide array of societal forces, such as formal and informal norms of behaviour, religious beliefs, informal codes of conduct, social habits and attitudes, or the existing value systems that prevail in a particular society. Despite these ambiguities, or perhaps because of them, the term has wide currency in development theory.

Some theorists believe that culture is at the very core of conceptions of development and, as a consequence, only cultural reforms can promote development. For instance, in *The Wealth and Poverty of Nations: Why Some Are So Rich and Some So Poor*, Davis Landes concludes: "if we learn anything from the history of economic development, it is that culture makes all the difference".[10] This school of thought dates back to the work of German sociologist Max Weber, in his book *The Protestant Ethic and the Spirit of Capitalism*, where he argued that Protestantism fostered values (hard work, thrift, material progress) that operated as an important underpinning of a successful capitalist economy.[11]

According to some theorists, the main implication of the idea that culture matters for development is that universal conceptions of development cannot be realized unless the culture of developing societies mimics the culture of developed nations, which are more congenial to development objectives. Harrison argues, for instance, that some societies have a progress-resistant cultural outlook that will prevent development unless they change these cultural traits.[12] This discourse suggests that there is something universal that all societies should aspire to (rationalism, human rights, democracy, and so on.) and assumes that there are societies that are at more advanced stages

---

9 J.Y. Lin, *The Quest for Prosperity: How Developing Economies Can Take Off* (Princeton, NJ: Princeton University Press, 2012).

10 D. Landes, *The Wealth and Poverty of Nations: Why Some Are So Rich and Some So Poor* (New York, NY: W.W. Norton and Company 1999) at 516.

11 M. Weber, *The Protestant Ethic and the Spirit of Capitalism*, translated by Talcott Parsons (New York, NY: Scribner's, 1930).

12 L.E. Harrison, *The Central Liberal Truth* (New York, NY: Oxford University Press, 2006); L. Harrison and S. Huntington, *Culture Matters* (New York, NY: Basic Books, 2000).

of their evolution, and that they should serve as models to laggard societies. In other words, Harrison can be accused of formulating a revamped version of modernization theory.

A more recent version of this theory identifies personality traits of successful individuals (a deep-seated belief in their exceptionality, insecurity, and impulse control), and claims that some cultural groups have more effective mechanisms for instilling these traits than others. Although this claim is not used to explain the development outcome of countries, it is used to analyse why some cultural groups experience exceptional upward social mobility in the United States, in contrast to others.[13]

Culture can also be understood in the light of Amartya Sen's distinction between the ends and the means of development. Cultural freedom can be conceived as a goal of the development process if one believes that the opportunity to engage in cultural activities is part of the basic freedoms that constitute development. In turn, culture can be conceived as a means to an end, viewed as a necessary component of the process that generates economic gains or increased freedom of choice.[14]

An example of the latter view is the new institutional economists, who follow for the most part Douglass North's definition of institutions:

> Institutions are the rules of the game of a society, or, more formally, are the humanly devised constraints that structure human interactions. They are composed of formal rules (statute law, common law, regulation), informal constraints (conventions, norms of behaviour and self-imposed codes of conduct), and the enforcement characteristics of both.[15]

Most of what we refer to as culture is encompassed by what North calls "informal institutions". However, institutional economists do not go much beyond acknowledging that culture influences human behaviour. It is not clear how, when and why it does so. The result is that

---

13 A. Chua and J. Rubenfeld, *The Triple Package: How Three Unlikely Traits Explain the Rise and Fall of Cultural Groups in America* (New York, NY: The Penguin Press, 2014).

14 A. Sen, "How does Culture Matter?", in V. Rao and M. Walton (eds), *Culture and Public Action* (Stanford, CA: Stanford University Press: 2004) at 39.

15 D. North, "The New Institutional Economics and Third World Development" in J. Harris, J. Hunter and C.M. Lewis (eds), *Economics and Third World Development* (London: Routledge, 1995).

culture is often treated as a black box in institutional analyses. We do not know if formal institutions can change culture and vice versa. And if these changes are possible, we do not know when and under which circumstances they are likely to take place.[16]

This poses a major challenge for the advancement of our understanding of the problem of development. While institutional theories of development have become prominent in development discourse (see Chapter 3), without a thorough assessment of the role that culture plays in institutional stability and institutional change, reforms may have either limited success or unintended results. Culture is an important factor that is currently largely missing in the institutional reform puzzle. The question, as Amartya Sen cautions, is not *whether*, but *how* we incorporate the cultural dimension in development practice:

> The importance of culture cannot be instantly translated into ready-made theories of cultural causation. It is evidently too easy to jump from the frying pan of neglecting culture into the fire of crude cultural determinism. The latter has caused much harm in the past (and has even encouraged political tyranny and social discrimination), and it continues to be a source of confusion which can seriously mislead assessment and policy in the contemporary world.[17]

2.3   Geographic theories of development

A third group of theories claims that development is largely dependent on the geographic location and condition of a country. These theories diverge, however, in their explanation of why geography matters, and whether it has a direct or indirect effect on development.

Several basic claims are made to support the idea that geography can directly impact on a country's development.

The first basic claim is based on climate: tropical countries are more likely to be underdeveloped. Some scholars believe that tropical climates impact on productive economic activity, especially agriculture, because of the fragility and low fertility of tropical soils, high prevalence of crop pests and parasites, high evaporation and unstable supply of

---

16 D. Acemoğlu and S. Johnson, "Unbundling Institutions" (2005) 113 *Journal of Political Economy* 5.
17 Sen, *supra* note 14, at 55.

water, as well as ecological conditions favourable to infectious human diseases.[18] Others claim that tropical climates inhibit work because of hot weather and humidity,[19] or the abundance of easily obtainable, non-agriculturally produced food, which reduces the need to work hard and so creates a culture of idleness.[20]

The second claim is based on location: landlocked countries face significant barriers to engaging in trade, and are therefore significantly deprived of the economic benefits derived from international or inter-regional commercial activity.[21] This can create a poverty trap whereby development prospects are limited because landlocked countries face impediments to integrating into the global economy, a problem which is particularly severe where the landlocked country's coastal neighbour has not invested sufficiently in the infrastructure necessary to allow its neighbour to transport goods to the coast where they can be traded inter-continentally. Paul Collier describes these landlocked countries as "hostages to their neighbours", especially where instability or violence restricts access to trade routes.[22]

The third claim is based on natural endowments. While natural wealth can positively impact on a country's development outlook, this is not necessarily the case: the phenomenon of the "resource curse" has shown that under certain circumstances abundance of natural resources will not lead to growth. It will, instead, foster rent seeking and corruption, and may lead to an increased likelihood of civil conflict resulting from disputed resource ownership.[23]

Engerman and Sokoloff make an alternative geographic claim supporting the idea that geography has an indirect effect on development by influencing the emergence of strong or weak institutions. This theory

---

18 D.E. Bloom and J.D. Sachs, "Geography, Demography, and Economic Growth in Africa" (1998) 29 *Brookings Papers on Economic Activity* at 207–96; J.D. Sachs, "Tropical Underdevelopment" (2000) Centre for International Development at Harvard University, Working Paper No. 57.

19 Landes, *supra* note 10.

20 W. Easterly and R. Levine, "Tropics, Germs, and Crops: How Endowments Influence Economic Development" (2003) 50 *Journal of Monetary Economics* 1, at 7 (citing Machiavelli).

21 J. Sachs and A. Warner, "Economic Reform and the Process of Global Integration", in W.C. Brainard and G.L. Perry (eds), *Brookings Papers on Economic Activity* (Washington, DC: Brookings Institution Press, 1990).

22 P. Collier, *The Bottom Billion* (Oxford: Oxford University Press, 2007) at 55.

23 R.M. Auty (ed.), *Resource Abundance and Economic Development* (Oxford and New York, NY: Oxford University Press, 2001). See also M. Ross, "Does Oil Hinder Democracy?" (2001) 53:3 *World Politics* at 325–61.

points to certain resource endowments as creating high levels of inequality of wealth, human capital and political power (for example, plantation agriculture versus family farms), which work against the development of strong institutions. Instead of fostering developmentally beneficial institutions, high levels of inequality allow the growth of "institutional structures that greatly advantage members of elite classes".[24]

Another argument based on natural resources focuses on germs and crops. Diamond, in his book *Guns, Germs and Steel: The Fates of Human Societies*, shows that some nations, including European nations, developed resistance to germs acquired from farm animals, whereas others, such as colonized nations, did not have farm animals and therefore did not develop such resistance.[25] The spread of these germs at the time of colonization negatively impacted the development prospects of colonized nations. Also, regions such as Africa had germs that restricted the use of farm animals, undermining their productivity. Further, some regions had plant species that could be easily domesticated into high-yielding food crops, such as grains. In contrast, other regions did not have species that would lend themselves so easily to cultivation.

Economic geography is still another theory of development, which focuses on economic models of the geography of development, looking at why economic development takes place in a certain area rather than another, despite the lack of relative geographic advantages. This differs from the approaches explained above, which use the physical geographic traits of a country to explain a history of underdevelopment. Economic geography seeks to explain such phenomena as the "division of the world into industrial and nonindustrial countries, the emergence of regional inequality within developing countries, and the emergence of giant urban centers".[26] The theory focuses on a combination of the forces of change and necessity producing one of many possible equilibria, which benefits a particular place over another. The World Development Report (2009) produced by the World Bank examines geographic disparities in wealth by utilizing three explanatory

24 S.L. Engerman and K.K.L. Sokoloff, "Factor Endowments, Inequality, and Paths of Development among New World Economies" (2000) 14:3 *Journal of Economic Perspectives* at 217–32.

25 J. Diamond, *Guns, Germs, and Steel: The Fates of Human Societies* (New York, NY: W.W. Norton and Co, 1997).

26 P. Krugman, "The Role of Geography in Development" (1999) 22:2 *International Regional Science Review* at 147.

concepts from economic geography: density (a local measure of human concentration); distance (a national measure of distance to hubs of economic activity, in other words, transport costs); and division (an international measure of economic integration and the impermeability of economic borders).[27] The Report concludes that three spatial transformations, "higher densities, shorter distances, and lower divisions", are necessary for development to occur.

One of the most prominent proponents of geographic theories of development is Jeffrey Sachs. He claims that barriers to development include three features that are intrinsically connected to a country's geography:

1. transportation costs (which can be especially high for landlocked countries);
2. diseases (an acute problem in the tropics, where infectious diseases may deter investment); and
3. poor soil fertility (which can be caused partly by torrential rains, such as those that occur in equatorial regions).[28]

Other authors provide a great deal of evidence that poor institutions, rather than geography, are the fundamental cause of underdevelopment (Chapter 3). Some of these institutionalists include geographic factors as a secondary cause of a country's level of development.

Daron Acemoğlu, Simon Johnson and James A. Robinson are among the many authors who support the idea that geographic factors play only an indirect role in development by affecting a country's institutions. They argue that geographic factors influenced the types of institution that were implemented by colonizers: in regions with inhospitable climates, colonizers established extractive institutions to exploit natural resources (extractive societies); in regions with hospitable climates, colonizers created settler societies, which developed strong institutions (neo-Europes). Acemoğlu, Johnson and Robinson's argument differs from Sachs' argument in that they conclude that geography has only an indirect effect on a country's level of develop-

27 World Development Report 2009, "Reshaping Economic Geography" (Washington, DC: The World Bank, 2009), available at http://web.worldbank.org/WBSITE/EXTERNAL/EXTDEC/ EXTRESEARCH/EXTWDRS/0,,contentMDK:23062295~pagePK:478093~piPK:477627~theSit ePK:477624,00.html (accessed 28 April 2014).

28 J. Sachs, "Institutions Matter, But Not for Everything: The Role of Geography and Resource Endowments in Development Shouldn't be Underestimated" (2003) *Finance and Development* 38.

ment: development is determined by the institutional environment, which was historically affected by geography.[29]

2.4   Institutional dimensions of theories of development

Theories claiming that institutions are central to promote development have become very prominent in the past two decades. Their importance justifies devoting a separate chapter to them (Chapter 3). This section will preface that discussion by showing that the non-institutional theories discussed earlier have strong institutional assumptions implicit in their analyses. Most of these theories simply assumed the relevant institutional capacity to implement the (highly divergent) policies that each theory espoused.

Economic theories of development predominant in the past either disregarded the nature and quality of a developing country's domestic institutions or, alternatively, simply assumed that a country possessed the institutional capacity to implement the theories of development in question.[30] As Pranab Bardhan has noted: "in this [traditional development] literature the state was often left floating in a behavioral and organizational vacuum, making it easy to be used for a blanket endorsement of indiscriminate state intervention". For instance, in early post-war development, capital fundamentalism proposed a state-centred approach to promoting savings and investments through state-created tax incentives for both private savings and investment in production by private companies, and high levels of investment in state-owned companies.[31] Thus, the "capital fundamentalists" assumed a functioning state, bureaucracy, tax system, and other institutional features of an operational economy, but they did not address the problem of how to acquire these institutions.[32]

Similar to "capital fundamentalism", the linear stages theories also had institutional implications for promoting political and social change

---

29 D. Acemoğlu, S. Johnson and J. Robinson, "The Colonial Origins of Comparative Development: An Empirical Investigation", 91 *American Economic Review* at 1369–401.

30 P. Bardhan, "Symposium on the State and Economic Development" (1990) 4 *Journal of Economic Perspectives* 3, 3–7.

31 M. Trebilcock, "What Makes Poor Countries Poor? The Role of Institutional Capital in Economic Development" in E. Buscaglia, W. Ratliff and R. Cooter (eds), *The Law and Economics of Development* (Greenwich, CT: JAI Press, 1997) at 17.

32 Bardhan, *supra* note 30, at 3–7.

that were not addressed directly by their theoretical models. Structural theories also had assumptions about industrialization and urbanization policies that largely ignored the complex institutional framework that is required to enable the state to perform all these functions.

Dependency theories also had important institutional connections that were not addressed in their models. To eliminate dependency, some theorists advocated aggressive economic nationalism[33] grounded in import substitution industrialization (ISI), with high levels of tariff protection to restrict the flow of imports and to promote the development of local industries.[34] ISI policies assume a major role for the state, especially in making investments in infrastructure (transportation, energy and telecommunications) and in fostering industrialization in capital-intensive industries (the commanding heights of the economy). These economic theories, however, did not explore the fact that heavy state intervention in the economy assumes at least an efficient and competent bureaucracy and a functional executive branch. Moreover, the policies prescribed required effective laws and regulations, such as the tariffs and exchange controls on which the ISI model depended. Despite being central to dependency theories, these institutional connections were largely unexplored in the academic literature.

Similarly, neoliberal theories largely ignored the central role of the state – not in directly promoting development, but instead in providing the pre-conditions for markets to operate. Markets depend on a functioning legal system and effective regulation of capital markets, banking sectors, competition policies, the trade system, tax collection, and investment in infrastructure, healthcare and education, and so on. The lack of attention to these institutional connections has been perceived to be one of the central reasons why many of these policies failed.[35]

Endogenous growth theory leads to an important policy implication: there is room for state intervention to create incentives for accumulation of knowledge (human capital) and technological progress. Private

---

33 B. Tamanaha, "The Lessons of Law-and-development Studies" (1995) 89:2 *American Journal of International Law* at 478.

34 J. Coatsworth, "Structures, Endowments and Institutions in the Economic History of Latin America" (2005) 40:3 *Latin America Research Review* at 126.

35 D. Rodrik, "Goodbye Washington Consensus, Hello Washington Confusion? A Review of the World Bank's Economic Growth in the 1990s: Learning from a Decade of Reform" (2006) 44:4 *Journal of Economic Literature*, 973–87.

organizations are likely to under-invest in human capital generation, as some of the benefits from this expenditure are externalities that benefit society at large but are not captured by the private organizations bearing the costs. Therefore, government is advised to subsidize this gap between private investment and the socially optimal level of investment in human capital formation, research and training.[36] Among economic theories of development, endogenous growth theory is perhaps the one that has most explicitly acknowledged the role of institutions in promoting economic development. However, they do not provide any insight into how to improve them.

Cultural and geographic theories of development similarly tend to marginalize the importance of the character and quality of a country's institutions in advancing its development goals. Cultural theories tend to stress deeply embedded cultural beliefs and practices as a determinant of development (while being vague about or how these have evolved and might be changed).[37] Geographic theories, in turn, tend to emphasize natural endowments as a key determinant of development.

As Amartya Sen argues, culture can interact with the ends and means of development in indirect ways, which have important policy implications. As to ends, culture strongly influences value systems, affecting what a given society will consider to be "a good life", therefore impacting upon what a society considers to be the ultimate end of the development process, as discussed in Chapter 1. As to means, culture may be a relevant consideration when designing effective strategies to reach development goals. Culture can influence economic, political and social behaviour in substantial ways. In economic terms, culture can influence levels of entrepreneurship, willingness to take risks, and business ethics. In political terms, culture can impact on the frequency and quality of public discussion, civic interaction and engagement in deliberative processes. In social terms, culture can determine levels of solidarity and trust, as well as educational attainment, marital patterns, or expectations about others' behaviour. Thus, on this view, reforms that try to influence economic behaviour should take into account specific cultural characteristics that guide economic behaviour in particular societies. Similarly, attempts to promote political

36 Cypher and Dietz, *supra* note 8, at 249.
37 See for example, A. Licht, C. Goldschmidt and S. Schwartz, "Culture Rules: The Foundations of the Rule of Law and other Norms of Governance" (2007) 35 *Journal of Comparative Economics* at 659–88.

reforms, such as implementing a liberal democracy, must acknowledge that political behaviour is influenced by culture, and that the same political institutions might not function in the same way in different cultural contexts.[38] One of the conclusions that can be drawn from the influence of culture on human behaviour is that development policies need to be adjusted to divergent cultural contexts, and it is unlikely that one will be able to design a universal blueprint for all developing countries.

However, as Sen argues, culture is not the only factor that influences human behaviour. Thus, there is room to develop some common strategies that transcend cultural divides. Despite cultural differences, many societies share important commonalities. Heterogeneous beliefs and practices will often exist within a given culture, and these dissenting voices can play an important role in questioning the maintenance and permanence of certain entrenched cultural traits. Finally, culture is dynamic, making it difficult to draw conclusive distinctions between societies. Cultural change may occur endogenously, or may be linked to external forces arising from interaction with other cultures.[39] In other words, culture is not destiny. Policy-makers should be mindful of cultural factors when designing development policies, but no society should be viewed as a prisoner of its existing cultural context.

There is a general consensus that the quality of institutions determines whether or not a country will be able to utilize resource wealth to become rich.[40] Sachs acknowledges the importance of economic policy and institutions – such as trade openness, fiscal rectitude, and the rule of law – for development, but he believes that "for much of the world, bad climates, poor soils and physical isolation are likely to hinder growth whatever happens to policy".[41] Thus, tropical countries cannot eliminate poverty by simply promoting good economic policies or institutional reforms. According to Sachs, the poverty trap can be overcome by investing in infrastructure to reduce transportation costs, in agricultural technology to increase productivity, and in improved healthcare services and treatment to reduce the burden of tropical diseases. To enable these investments, he argues that the developed world should increase foreign aid to poor countries, especially in Africa.

---

38 Sen, *supra* note 14 at 42–3.
39 *Ibid.*, at 43–4.
40 Collier, *supra* note 22.
41 J. Sachs, "The Limits of Convergence: Nature, Nurture and Growth" (14 June 1997) *The Economist*.

Once geographical barriers to development are addressed, institutions then become relevant.[42]

However, Sachs' proposals do not eliminate the institutional question. It is unlikely that a country can implement the ambitious policies Sachs calls for without well-functioning institutions. Regardless of the specific policy arrangements, strong institutions are necessary for government policies to provide the necessary framework for effective development.

2.5 Conclusion

This chapter has surveyed the development theories of the past 60 years, and highlights their implications for institutional questions and institutional reform. There has been much controversy and criticism of development theory, spurring continuous debate in this field of study. However, there now seems to be a general consensus that institutions play an important role in promoting development. Contrary to common arguments for less state intervention in the economy, most scholars agree that it is the *quality* of state intervention that matters, not necessarily its quantity. The quality of intervention, in turn, is now recognized as a function of the quality of a state's institutions. The focus of this perspective is on how a state should organize itself through its political, bureaucratic, administrative and legal institutions to advance its development goals. We describe this perspective in more detail and the challenges it raises in the following chapters.

---

42 J. Sachs, *The End of Poverty* (New York, NY: The Penguin Press, 2005).

3   Institutional theories of development

3.1   Introduction

Beginning in the early 1990s, an institutional perspective on development has become increasingly prominent in development thinking, captured in the mantra "institutions matter", or "governance matters". This perspective views the quality of a country's domestic institutions as a major determinant of its development prospects.

The idea that institutions matter for development has both a theoretical and empirical genesis. The theoretical genesis of institutionally focused development theories is based on a number of assumptions and arguments developed by a school of thought called the New Institutional Economics (NIE). The basic assumption of NIE is that people are rational actors who respond to incentives, and these incentives are influenced, if not determined, by institutions that induce individuals and organizations to engage in productive activities – or the converse. According to Douglass North, one of the pioneers of the field of NIE, "the institutional framework dictates the kinds of skills and knowledge perceived to have the maximum pay-off...If the institutional matrix rewards piracy (or more generally redistributive activities) more than productive activity, then learning will take the form of learning to be better pirates".[1] The empirical genesis or support for institutional theories of development is predominantly based on cross-country quantitative studies that show strong correlations between institutional quality and growth and development around the world. Some studies make the stronger claim that empirical evidence also supports causation from institutional quality to development.

---

1 D. North, "The New Institutional Economics and Third World Development", in J. Harris, J. Hunter and C.M. Lewis (eds), *Economics and Third World Development* (London: Routledge, 1995) at 17; see more generally, D. North, *Institutions, Institutional Change, and Economic Performance* (Cambridge, UK: Cambridge University Press, 1990).

The institutional perspective on development is, at least superficially, compelling because it appears to identify important determinants of development that are, in principle, within each country's control. Thus, governments (and societies) should no longer consider themselves captive to factors such as history, culture, climate, geography, natural resource endowments, or the international economic system. According to this perspective, lawyers – who often conceive of themselves as institutional designers – should become important contributors to the development enterprise.

Reflecting the influence of this perspective, over the past two decades there has been a massive surge in development assistance for institutional reform projects in many developing and transition economies. These reform initiatives have been very expansive in scope, ranging from reforms of political institutions, various institutional elements of public administration, legal institutions (such as courts, police and prosecutorial services, correctional services, and legal educational institutions), and many areas of substantive law, especially commercial law such as corporate law, bankruptcy law, tax law and property rights. Many of these latter areas of law have been highlighted in a recent series of World Bank "Doing Business" Reports, which identify substantive and institutional impediments to business formation and expansion in both developed and developing countries.[2]

The institutional perspective on development raises a number of key questions, which are briefly addressed in this chapter.

3.2   What is an institution?

The term, as used in both the theoretical and empirical literature on institutional theories of development, exhibits significant ambiguity. For example, Douglass North defines institutions as follows: "Institutions are the rules of the game of a society, or, more formally, the humanly devised constraints that structure human interactions. They are composed of formal rules (statute law, common law, regulation), informal constraints (conventions, norms of behaviour, and

---

2 International Finance Corporation and The World Bank, "Doing Business Report Series", available at http://www.doingbusiness.org/reports (accessed 28 April 2014). See R. Cooter and H.-B. Shäffer, *Solomon's Knot: How Law Can End the Poverty of Nations* (Princeton, NJ: Princeton University Press, 2011).

self-imposed codes of conduct), and the enforcement characteristics of both".[3]

At least from a lawyer's perspective this is an odd definition of institutions. Beyond a country's constitution, lawyers do not think of institutions as the rules of the game. For example, the legally prescribed speed limit on a given highway is not considered to be an institution but rather a legal rule promulgated by one set of institutions, enforced by another, and in the event of disputes, adjudicated by yet another. Moreover, by including informal constraints (cultural conventions, norms of behaviour, and self-imposed codes of conduct) in this definition of institutions, the concept of institutions becomes so all-encompassing that it includes almost any conceivable factor that may influence human behaviour and hence risks losing any operational content.

As we have suggested in our previous book, an alternative definition of institutions that may be more attractive to lawyers is "those organizations (formal and informal) that are charged or entrusted by a society with making, administering, enforcing or adjudicating its laws or policies".[4]

3.3   Do institutions matter?

At one level, this question invites an intuitive or axiomatic response. A central characteristic of "failed states" is that few or none of the basic functions of the state are performed with even a minimal level of effectiveness, including such fundamental functions as maintaining some semblance of law and order, preventing mass starvation, and avoiding gross repression of or violence towards many segments of the population. "Failed states" are characterized as such precisely because they lack functioning public institutions.

Beginning in the late 1990s, led by the Governance Group at the World Bank, systematic cross-country econometric analyses of the impact of institutional quality on development outcomes have been undertaken. The World Bank's Worldwide Governance Indicators Project,[5] which

---

3 North, *supra* note 1.

4 M. Trebilcock and M.M. Prado, *What Makes Poor Countries Poor? Institutional Determinants of Development* (Cheltenham, UK and Northampton, MA, USA: Edward Elgar, 2011) at 27–8.

5 The World Bank Group, "Worldwide Governance Indicators", available at http://info.worldbank. org/governance/wgi/index.aspx#home (accessed 28 April 2014).

is regularly updated and now covers 215 economies, involves compiling a large number of subjective measures of institutional quality obtained from either polls of country experts or surveys of residents and grouping them into six clusters: 1) voice and accountability; 2) political stability; 3) government effectiveness; 4) regulatory quality; 5) rule of law; and 6) control of corruption.

The authors of these governance studies have created indices that measure institutional quality along each of these six dimensions as well as a composite governance index designed to measure the overall quality of governance in a society. They then regress three measures of development – per capita GDP; infant mortality; and adult literacy – on these indices and find strong correlations (and indeed strong causal relationships) between each of these indices of institutional quality, as well as a composite index, and their measures of development. Some of their findings are quite dramatic. For example, an improvement in the rule of law by one standard deviation from the current levels in the Ukraine to those middling levels prevailing in South Africa would lead to a four-fold increase in per capita income in the longer run.

A more recent study by Rodrik, Subramanian and Trebbi estimates the respective contributions of institutions, geography and international trade in determining income levels around the world.[6] The authors use a number of measures of institutional quality that capture the protection afforded to property rights as well as the strength of the rule of law. The authors find that the quality of institutions "trumps" everything else. For example, the authors conclude that an increase in institutional quality of one standard deviation, corresponding roughly to the difference between measured institutional quality in Bolivia and South Korea, produces a two log-points rise in per capita incomes, or a 6.4-fold difference, which, not coincidentally, is also roughly the income difference between the two countries.

However, these empirical findings have not gone unchallenged. A major methodological challenge is the problem of causation. Correlation does not necessarily imply causation: showing that all or most rich countries have good institutions does not prove that they are rich because they have good institutions. Indeed it is possible to argue that increased wealth causes the development of strong institutions,

---

6 D. Rodrik, A. Subramanian and F. Trebbi, "Institutions Rule: The Primacy of Institutions Over Geography and Integration in Economic Development" (2004) 9 *Journal of Economic Growth* 131.

rather than the reverse. In this vein, Glaeser, La Porta, Silanes and Schleiffer argue, based on cross-country econometric evidence, that a) human capital is a more basic source of growth than institutions, and b) growth causes good institutions, because poor countries escape from poverty through good policies, often pursued by dictators, and these countries only subsequently improve their political and related institutions.[7] To cite specific examples, economic take-off in countries such as South Korea, Taiwan and (more arguably) Singapore, was initiated by relatively authoritarian governments that over time, as levels of economic prosperity increased, evolved into softer forms of authoritarianism and, at least in some cases, fully-fledged democracies with a reasonably robust commitment to the rule of law.[8]

3.4 Which institutions matter?

A recently widely-acclaimed book by Acemoğlu and Robinson, *Why Nations Fail*,[9] drawing on panoramic examples across recorded history, argues that societies that are more inclusive economically and politically have higher growth rates than exclusionary societies dominated by small, powerful elites. In a similar vein, a recent book by North, Wallis and Weingast, *Violence and Social Orders*,[10] argues that limited-access social orders dominate most of recorded history and very few societies have successfully evolved from limited-access orders to open-access orders, where access to economic opportunities and political influence is broadly available. While these influential books provide general guidance as to what developing countries should be aspiring to, there is still much uncertainty regarding feasible reform strategies.

Much of the recent scholarship espousing an institutional perspective on development is relatively vague as to a) which institutions matter to development, and b) within classes of institutions (for example, political, bureaucratic or legal) which institutional characteristics

---

7 E. Glaeser, R. La Porta, F. Lopez-de-Silanes and A. Shleifer, "Do Institutions Cause Growth?" (2004) 9 *Journal of Economic Growth* 271.

8 See also R. Gilson and C. Milhaupt, "Economically Benevolent Dictators: Lessons for Developing Countries" (2001) *American Journal of Comparative Law* 227.

9 D. Acemoğlu and J. Robinson, *Why Nations Fail: The Origins of Power, Prosperity, and Poverty* (New York, NY: Crown Publishing, 2012).

10 D. North, J.J. Wallis and B. Weingast, *Violence and Social Orders: A Conceptual Framework for Interpreting Recorded Human History* (New York, NY: Cambridge University Press, 2010).

are conducive or antithetical to development. As Mary Shirley and other scholars have pointed out, cross-country econometric measures provide little operational guidance to policy reformers because of the level of abstractness employed in defining institutional variables.[11] Moreover, it is important to note that much of the recent institutional literature concludes that a host of context-specific factors determine optimal institutional characteristics within classes of institutions. For example, even amongst developed countries, the organization of their political systems, public administrations and legal systems vary enormously across a wide range of dimensions, so that even if one believes that institutional quality is an important determinant of a country's development prospects, there is clearly no single optimal blueprint for the design of these institutions. Moreover, the inter-relationships between public sector and private sector institutions vary greatly across even developed countries and more so across developing countries, as reflected in the literature on "varieties of capitalism".[12]

The "varieties of capitalism" approach was developed by scholars of comparative political economy, and focuses primarily on developed economies. Proponents classify countries as either "liberal market economies" (for example, the United States) or "coordinated market economies" (for example, Germany). The varieties of capitalism literature offers a sophisticated theory of institutional change, showing how institutions co-evolve with patterns of economic activity. For example, Hall and Soskice argue that the two ideal types of economies represent alternative ways of coordinating interactions among firms, employees, investors, consumers, shareholders, and so on. Those interactions are shaped by local institutions and end up influencing, if not determining, macro-economic policies and the overall structure of the economy. The relevant "institutions" include both rules enshrined in the formal legal system and informal rules such as shared expectations of appropriate behaviour shaped by common experiences. A key claim is that nations will tend to develop complementary institutions, meaning institutions that increase the returns from one another. While Hall and Soskice analysed primarily OECD countries, the framework has been used to analyse developing countries as well, although scholars have suggested

---

11 M. Shirley, *Institutions and Development* (Cheltenham, UK and Northampton, MA, USA: Edward Elgar, 2008).

12 See P. Hall and D. Soskice, *Varieties of Capitalism: The Institutional Foundations of Comparative Advantage* (New York, NY: Oxford University Press, 2001).

alternative models such as "hierarchical market economies" in Latin America,[13] and "dependent market economies" in Eastern Europe.[14]

This approach shares with the NIE the assumption that institutions determine economic outcomes. A distinctive feature is the emphasis on institutional interdependencies, i.e., the idea that both the structure and performance of any set of formal institutions is likely to be shaped by the broader institutional context in which they operate. This implies that it is impossible to foresee the consequences of adopting particular institutions, or whether those institutions are optimal in any sense, without accounting for the full complexity of institutional interdependencies.

3.5 Why are some countries afflicted with persistently bad institutions?

While it may be difficult to define a single optimal set of institutional arrangements, it may at least be possible to identify, from a broader social perspective, unambiguously bad or dysfunctional institutions (as in the case of "failed states"), where countries afflicted with such persistently bad or dysfunctional institutions are (in Mancur Olson's words) "leaving big bills on the sidewalk".[15] However, this raises the question of why would societies persist in such myopic or self-destructive behaviour, particularly in an era where mass communication technologies make information highly accessible at low cost, so that many members of these societies should be, and probably are, aware of the fact that alternative institutional arrangements in other countries appear to generate dramatically superior development outcomes. So why do bad institutions persist?

According to North, the reason is the phenomenon of path dependency, which describes how the reinforcement of a given set of arrangements over time raises the cost of changing them.[16] Most public

---

13 B.R. Schneider, *Hierarchical Capitalism in Latin America: Business, Labor, and the Challenges of Equitable Development* (New York, NY: Cambridge University Press 2013).

14 A. Nölke and A. Vliegenthart, "Enlarging the Varieties of Capitalism: The Emergence of Dependent Market Economies in East Central Europe" (2009) 61 *World Politics* 4, 670–702.

15 M. Olson, "Big Bills Left on the Sidewalk: Why some Nations are Rich and Others Poor" (1996) 10 *Journal of Economic Perspectives* 3.

16 For a helpful overview of path dependence theories, see P. Pierson, "Increasing Returns, Path Dependence, and the Study of Politics" (2000) 94 *American Political Science Review* 251; and

institutions exhibit increasing returns to scale and network effects, making it very difficult for rival institutions that demonstrate superior qualities to emerge. Existing institutions also generate biased feedback loops that tend to confirm prior institutional expectations about existing institutional arrangements rather than providing exposure to and information about institutional alternatives. In addition, vested interests both within and outside existing institutional regimes often derive substantial benefits from these regimes, hence creating concentrated sources of resistance to institutional change. All of these factors, according to North, tend to create strong forms of institutional path dependency that often render radical institutional reform infeasible. While occasionally revolutions occur or charismatic leaders emerge that may offer the prospects of a decisive break with the past, these contingencies are much more the exception rather than the rule.

3.6   What can countries with bad institutions do to acquire better institutions?

To a large extent, responses to this question are constrained by the reasons for the persistence of bad institutions. Much advice that has been offered on this question borders on the banal. For example, Olson concludes: "The best thing a society can do to increase its prosperity is to wise up".[17] The *Economist* in a survey article on Africa in 2000 concluded: "Africa's people need to regain their self-confidence".[18] These proposals do not offer much in the way of concrete, actionable reforms.

Recent experience with institutional reform in developing countries underscores how daunting this challenge is. A recent survey by Andrews, *The Limits of Institutional Reform in Development*,[19] reports that 40–60 per cent of recent attempts at institutional reform in developing countries appear to have had no effect on government effectiveness. A recent book on rule of law reform and development describes the mixed to weak results of many rule of law reform initiatives in

---

M. Prado and M. Trebilcock, "Path Dependence, Development and the Dynamics of Institutional Reform", (2009) 59 *University of Toronto Law Journal* 341.

17 Olson, *supra* note 15, at 21.

18 "Africa: The Heart of the Matter", *The Economist*, 13 May 2000, at 22–4.

19 M. Andrews, *The Limits of Institutional Reform in Development* (New York, NY: Cambridge University Press, 2013).

developing countries.[20] Current faltering initiatives to install democratic regimes in many developing countries, such as Iraq, Afghanistan, Egypt and Libya provide further illustrations of these challenges.

Serious thinking about how to grapple with these challenges needs to address the complexities of the path dependence dynamic described by North. After a detailed review of the economic and political scholarly literature on path dependence,[21] we draw the following tentative implications that follow from attention to path dependence in formulating institutional reform strategies, focusing especially on the key elements of self-reinforcing mechanisms; institutional interdependencies; switching costs; and critical junctures.

First, because of context-specific factors that explain the evolution of existing institutions (and networks of institutions), no one-size-fits-all blueprint for legal reform or broader institutional reform in developing countries is likely to be optimal. Other developing countries which share many of the same historical experiences and institutional characteristics as the country whose institutions are the focus of reform efforts are likely to be a more useful source of information, experience and ideas as to what is likely to work than countries which share few of these common characteristics.[22] Future research on reform options, to be effective, will often have to be led by scholars within the countries in question complemented by scholars with relevant comparative expertise pursued through collaborative research initiatives.

Second, as a result of switching costs and institutional interdependencies, ambitious or highly innovative across-the-board political, bureaucratic or legal reforms carry significantly greater risk of failure than more modest or incremental reforms. Disillusionment with progress with democratic and rule of law reforms in many developing countries may, in this respect, reflect unrealistic expectations.

Third, if more ambitious or innovative institutional reforms are to be pursued successfully, they should focus on institutions that can

---

20 M. Trebilcock and R. Daniels, *Rule of Law Reform and Development: Charting the Fragile Path of Progress* (Cheltenham, UK and Northampton, MA, USA: Edward Elgar, 2008).

21 Prado and Trebilcock, *supra* note 16.

22 See S. Mukand and D. Rodrik, "In Search of the Holy Grail: Policy Convergence, Experimentation and Economic Performance" (2005) 95 *American Economic Review* 374.

be more easily detached from mutually reinforcing mechanisms, and become relatively free-standing, although even in such cases complementary reinforcing institutional reforms over time are likely to be necessary.

Fourth, detached, free-standing institutions, pilot programmes, or decentralized initiatives enlisting enthusiastic participants are likely to be more successful than across-the-board centralized reforms of existing institutions that conscript unwilling participants by imposing significant switching costs on them. Demonstration effects from pilot projects may subsequently persuade sceptics on either the demand or supply sides of the institutional reform equation that switching costs are not as large as previously assumed or that the benefits of incurring these costs are larger than expected. Such pilot projects also have the virtue of reversibility in the event that they generate unintended consequences, and thus entail lower risks.

Fifth, in reforms that are sensitive to switching costs from the institutional status quo, it is important to identify the different kinds of switching costs that may be salient – whether they reflect political economy factors that have shaped and been reinforced by the initial choice of institutions; lack of financial or technical resources; learning effects; coordination or network effects; or deeply entrenched cultural or religious beliefs or practices. While these factors can be conceived of as exogenous constraints on institutional reforms, one can equally view them as endogenous factors that have shaped the evolution of the institutional status quo. On either view, they will also significantly shape feasible margins of reforms, but in different ways.

Sixth, political and economic crises or catharses ("critical junctures") may provide opportunities for more radical institutional change, but also present risks of denial, deferral or repression, or precipitous adoption of ill-conceived policy or institutional choices in response to public consternation or disaffection. To mitigate these risks, the reform process must broaden the pool of policy ideas by enlisting previously marginalized constituencies and incorporating them into more enduring institutional reforms so as to create a new alignment of ideas, interests, and institutions.

It will be clear from these tentative conclusions that institutional reform in developing countries, whether related to the ends or means of development, cannot be treated as a technocratic, apolitical exercise, as many aid agencies have conventionally tended to do.[23]

3.7 Conclusion

The scholarly community has reached a relatively broad consensus around the idea that institutions matter for development, but we still do not know how to reform dysfunctional institutions. Even if certain ends of development were thought to be universal (which is contestable), the different starting points or initial conditions of the large universe of developing countries may suggest that there will be very few universally effective blueprints with respect to substantive economic and social policies and the processes and institutions appropriate for implementing, administering and enforcing such policies. However, if one views these differences as overwhelming any commonalities, then, as Arndt puts it, we are simply resigning ourselves to the proposition that each country should "write its own history".[24] In this case, nothing is to be learned through successes and failures of policies, processes and institutions in addressing similar problems in other developing countries.

It may be argued that at least among developing countries that share much in common in terms of economic, social, political, geographic and historical experience, some problems are sufficiently common that at least limited generalization is possible. Without some potential for at least cautious or qualified generalizations of problem diagnoses and prescriptions, the whole field of development as a scholarly or analytical enterprise is called into serious question.

---

23 See T. Carothers and D. de Gramont, *Development Aid Confronts Politics: The Almost Revolution* (Washington, DC: Carnegie Endowment for International Peace, 2013).

24 H.W. Arndt, *Economic Development: The History of an Idea* (University of Chicago Press, 1989) at 105.

PART II

THE RULE OF LAW AND DEVELOPMENT

4 The rule of law and development: a legal perspective

4.1 Introduction

Modern efforts to promote legal reform as a development strategy date back to the late 1950s and 1960s. This is the period in which many former colonies became independent and developed country governments and multilateral agencies were widely committed to some version of modernization theory, which included modernizing a developing country's substantive laws and legal institutions. This period of law and development scholarship and policy activism is often referred to as the "first law and development movement".[1]

More recently, with the emergence and increasing influence of institutional theories of development in academic and policy circles, there has been a new or revived interest in the relationship between law and development. As we noted in Chapter 3, recent empirical studies of the impact of governance on development find dramatic impacts of the rule of law on development outcomes. Reflecting this view of the relationship between the rule of law and development, beginning in the 1990s there has been a massive surge in development assistance for law reform projects in developing and transition economies involving investments of many billions of dollars. This instrumentalist view of the relationship between law and development is what we call an economic perspective of law and development.

Alongside this economic perspective, there is also a wide array of principled justifications to promote rule of law reforms in developing countries. These justifications have gained a great deal of prominence recently, in what some would consider a "new law and development

---

1 For an extensive description and critique of this movement, see D. Trubek and M. Galanter, "Scholars in Self-Estrangement: Some Reflections on the Crisis in Law and Development Studies in the United States" (1974) *Wisconsin Law Review* 1062.

movement".[2] Unlike its predecessor, this most recent movement has been more attuned to the idea that law has a value in and of itself, and has adopted a stronger discourse of promoting rights for their own sake (not as an instrument to achieve some other goal). This chapter focuses on this non-instrumental or deontological perspective on the rule of law, while the next chapter will turn to an economic perspective on the rule of law.

4.2 The relationship between law and development

The relationship between law and its broader social context dates back to antiquity. For example, the systematization and codification of Roman law during the Roman Empire, and the general pre-eminence accorded to jurists involved in this undertaking, was seen as an important manifestation of the superior civilizational qualities of the Roman Empire. The subsequent rediscovery of Roman law and its diffusion and adaptation in many European countries during the Middle Ages points to its enduring influence. The law merchant that emerged in this period from the customs of merchants facilitated broader trading networks both within and across nations and was often drawn on in both common law and civil law jurisdictions as the basis for formalizing legal principles.

Adam Smith in his *Lectures on Jurisprudence* (1762–63), divided history into four stages: the age of hunters; the age of shepherds; the age of agriculture and the age of commerce, and considered that law would and should adapt to and serve the different functions implied by this process of transition. Other eighteenth, nineteenth and early twentieth century scholars such as Montesquieu, Main and Weber were also deeply interested in various aspects of the relationship between law and development in a European context.

Weber's views are of particular interest in a contemporary law and development context in that he argued that law was not only a reflection of the underlying structure of a country's economy, but could importantly shape it. According to him, the systematization and rationalization of European law imbued it with autonomy, conscious design and universality. These qualities preceded and indeed

---

2 D.M. Trubek and A. Santos (eds), *The New Law and Economic Development: A Critical Appraisal* (New York, NY: Cambridge University Press, 2006).

importantly facilitated the emergence of successful capitalist econo-mies, in contrast to what he regarded as less rational systems of law that prevailed in many other countries (including many countries that we would today regard as developing countries).[3] The transplantation by imperial powers of elements of their legal systems to their colonies has also been the subject of extensive scholarship.[4]

While building on these earlier academic works and practices, the law and development movement has taken one additional step by propos-ing that legal reforms could be used as a strategy to promote develop-ment. What are the causal mechanisms that translate improvements in the quality of the rule of law into enhanced development outcomes? From an economic perspective, protection of private property rights and enforcement of contracts are of central importance because they are thought to translate into enhanced incentives to engage in produc-tive investments and hence higher economic growth (as we explore in the next chapter). More generally, the stability and the predictabil-ity of a legal system are regarded as having similar effects. From a non-instrumental or deontological perspective, such as that adopted by Amartya Sen's concept of development as freedom, an enhanced commitment to the rule of law may be justified as an end in itself. The rule of law provides protection for basic individual freedoms. Thus, its existence does not need to be justified by reference to instrumental objectives.

4.3   Optimists versus sceptics

Proponents of an optimistic view of the relationship between the rule of law, or law more generally, and development have made extremely bold claims about the potentially beneficial impact of legal reforms. For example, in his influential book, *The Other Path*, Hernando de Soto makes statements such as: "The legal system may be the main

---

3 See D. Trubek, "Toward a Social Theory of Law: An Essay on the Study of Law and Development" (1972) 82:1 *Yale Law Journal* at 11–16; and more generally D. Kennedy, "Three Globalizations of Legal Thought: 1850–2000" in Trubek and Santos, *supra* note 2.

4 See J.H. Merryman, "Comparative Law and Social Change: On the Origins, Style, Decline, and Revival of the Law and Development Movement" (1977) 25 *American Journal of Comparative Law* 457; R. Daniels, M. Trebilcock and L. Carson, "The Legacy of Empire: The Common Law Inheritance and Commitments to Legality in Former British Colonies" (2011) 59 *American Journal of Comparative Law* 111; D. Berkowitz and K. Pistor, "The Transplant Effect" (2003) 51 *American Journal of Comparative Law* 163.

explanation in the difference in development that exists between industrialized countries and those that are not industrialized", and that "the law is the most useful and deliberate instrument of change available to people".[5]

On the other hand, various law sceptics doubt the ability of legal reformers to identify appropriate legal reforms; consider that legal reforms often face potentially insurmountable economic, political and cultural obstacles; or argue that legal reform is often irrelevant because informal alternatives to law are often of overriding importance as mechanisms of social control in many developing countries. In this respect, sceptics point to the failure of the first law and development movement in the late 1950s to early 1970s,[6] and argue that we may be condemning ourselves to repeating earlier mistakes by ignoring the lessons of history.[7]

Reflecting one strand of this sceptical view, the first law and development movement did not prove enduring and, shortly after its inauguration, was declared dead by two of its founders, David Trubek and Marc Galanter. In a widely cited article, they extensively critiqued what they call "the model of liberal legalism", which motivated the first law and development movement, arguing that this paradigm has little application or relevance to many, perhaps most, developing countries:[8]

> The ethnocentric quality of liberal legalism's model of law in society is apparent. Empirically, the model assumes social and political pluralism, while in most of the Third World we find social stratification and class cleavage juxtaposed with authoritarian or totalitarian political systems. The model assumes that state institutions are the primary locus of social control, while in much of the Third World the grip of tribe, clan, and local community is far stronger than that of the nation-state. The model assumes that rules both reflect the interests of the vast majority of citizens and are normally internalized by them, while in many developing countries rules are imposed on the many by the few and are frequently honoured more in the breach than in the observance. The model assumes that courts are central actors in social control, and that they are relatively autonomous from political, tribal,

---

5 H.H. de Soto, *The Other Path: The Invisible Revolution in the Third World* (New York, NY: Basic Books, 1989) at 185, 187.

6 See Trubek and Galanter, *supra* note 1.

7 See K. Davis and M. Trebilcock, "The Relationship Between Law and Development: Optimists versus Sceptics" (2008) 56 *American Journal of Comparative Law* 895.

8 Trubek and Galanter, *supra* note 1.

religious, or class interests. Yet in many nations courts are neither very independent nor very important.[9]

In a book entitled *The New Law and Economic Development*, David Trubek and Alvaro Santos argue that there are significant differences between the first law and development movement and its most recent instantiation.[10] However, it remains an open question whether this revival will be able to avoid the pitfalls that led to the demise of the movement in the 1970s.[11]

4.4   Defining the rule of law

Despite the now fashionable pre-eminence accorded to it in many development circles, there are widely divergent understandings of the concept of the rule of law. According to Tamanaha, in a recent intellectual history of the rule of law, "there are almost as many conceptions of the rule of law as there are people defending it".[12] Similarly, Professor Dani Rodrik of Harvard University has stated: "Am I the only economist guilty of using the term the rule of law without having a good fix on what it really means? Well, maybe the first one to confess to it".[13] Conceptions of the rule of law run the gamut from the deontological (for example, protection of basic human rights) to the instrumental (for example, protection of property rights and contracts), and from extremely "thick" conceptions (that largely equate the rule of law with a just legal system, which in turn is largely elided with a just society), to very "thin" or formalistic conceptions (that emphasize that laws should be publicly promulgated, be predictable in their application, apply to all citizens, including government officials, and be subject to some form of neutral adjudication in the event of disputes as to their interpretation or application).

Objections to "thick" conceptions of the rule of law point out that such conceptions largely deprive the rule of law of any independent

---

9 *Ibid.*, at 1080–81.

10 Trubek and Santos, *supra* note 2.

11 D. Trubek, *Law and Development: 40 Years after Scholars in Self-Estrangement – A Preliminary Review* (2013) [unpublished].

12 B. Tamanaha, *On the Rule of Law: History, Politics, Theory* (Cambridge, UK: Cambridge University Press, 2004) at 3.

13 Briefing, "Economics and the Rule of Law: Order in the Jungle" *The Economist*, 15 March 2008 at 83.

meaning by equating it with "justice" and hence with the ends of development rather than conceiving it as a means of vindicating those ends. Objections to "thin" conceptions of the rule of law point out that even grossly unjust or immoral societies, such as Nazi Germany or apartheid South Africa, might meet purely formalistic criteria, lacking any elements of basic civil and political rights. Intermediate conceptions of the rule of law are possible, which stress due process or natural justice values of the kind familiar to Western constitutional and administrative lawyers, as well as basic civil rights. Extending the conception to include political rights (as Sen would argue) elides the rule of law with democracy, and extending it further to include economic and social rights merges it with conceptions of justice and the ends of development.

4.5   A brief review of recent rule of law reform experience in developing countries

We now turn to a brief review (substantially elaborated on elsewhere[14]) of the efficacy of recent reforms to legal institutions in Latin America, Africa, Central and Eastern Europe, and Asia.

4.5.1   The courts

A prominent focus of rule of law reforms has been judicial reform such as reducing court backlogs. Reform efforts to this end have involved improving court record-keeping through enhanced information technology and more proactive case management techniques. Complementary reform initiatives have often involved externally supported judicial training programmes. In some cases, these initiatives seem to have had a positive impact on court backlogs, although various scholars have noted that enhancing judicial capacity by increasing the volume of cases processed says little or nothing about the quality of judicial decision-making.

Judicial corruption and incompetence is endemic in many developing countries, particularly at lower levels of the court system and outside major urban centres. Reform efforts have barely penetrated these courts and are thus largely ineffective, since most citizens only have contact (if any at all) with courts at the lowest level of the system.

---

14 M. Trebilcock and R. Daniels, *Rule of Law Reform and Development: Charting the Fragile Path of Progress* (Cheltenham, UK and Northampton, MA, USA: Edward Elgar, 2008).

Attempts to strengthen judicial independence through the creation of semi-autonomous Judicial Councils to vet appointments and promotions and to maintain a disciplinary regime for judicial misconduct have often been met with fierce resistance from the executive and legislative branches of government, as well as the judiciary itself.

4.5.2   Legal education

Individual belief systems or patterns of adaptive behaviour surrounding existing court systems and processes are often reinforced by legal education. Historically such education in many developing countries is an undergraduate, vocational degree and has focused heavily on rote learning and regurgitation in exams rather than critical or interdisciplinary analysis of legal problems. There is no associated premium on original research and writing.

In Latin America, many public law schools also suffer from overpopulation with many part-time students and instructors. While private law schools have recently proliferated in many countries in the region, they are of highly variable quality, ranging from internationally recognized law schools to part-time degree or diploma mills.

Legal education institutions in Central and Eastern Europe have historically been tightly controlled by the state, which has led to a standardized, inflexible and increasingly inappropriate legal curriculum. In some countries in this region, with the support of international nongovernmental organizations (NGOs) and other institutions, efforts have been made to reform the curriculum in ways that are relevant to the new economic, social and political environments in which these countries find themselves, and to reduce or eliminate the ideological connection between law and the state that prevailed in the communist era.

Legal education in Africa is extremely varied with respect to institutional support, funding and curriculum development. South Africa, a relatively rich nation on the continent, has considerable infrastructure, but continues to suffer from under-funding and low quality of historically black institutions. Many other African countries have much weaker legal education infrastructures that suffer from a serious lack of resources, including such basic resources as teaching and library materials. As in Latin American, many African law schools continue to emphasize rote, black-letter learning, although significant recent efforts have been made to incorporate both clinical legal education and human rights dimensions into some law school curricula. In many Asian countries there are a large number of legal education institutions of widely variable quality, with recent dramatic proliferation of these institutions in China.

Resistance to legal reforms in many developing countries seems attributable in part to the vested interests of professors, judges and existing practitioners. They seek to insulate themselves from changes in curriculum or reforms of substantive or procedural features of the existing legal system, in part because these changes entail a depreciation of their existing human capital and require investments in new human capital. Lawyers who were trained and practice, adjudicate or teach in a socially dysfunctional legal system and have made substantial investments in human capital in learning how to function in such a system are often not a progressive force for legal reform.

4.5.3   The police

Judicial reforms in developing countries rarely account for relevant macro processes in a legal system that connect what happens inside the courtroom with a series of events that precede or succeed the courtroom proceedings (for example, enforcement of judgments). In particular, recent rule of law reforms have paid limited attention to reforming the most relevant law enforcement agency, the police force, despite the fact that historically in many countries the police have been viewed as a form of paramilitary organization, primarily dedicated to regime maintenance in societies dominated by military or authoritarian governments. This has made policing of secondary importance in many developing and transitional economies and has led incumbent political regimes to support, or at least acquiesce in, extensive human rights abuses by police forces, including torture, coerced confessions, indefinite detention without trial and rampant corruption.[15]

In an attempt to deal with these forms of abuse, modest efforts have been made in some developing and transitional economies to

---

15 See M. Prado, M. Trebilcock and P. Hartford, "Police Reform in Violent Democracies in Latin America" (2012) 4 *Hague Journal on the Rule of Law* 252; violent forms of abuse of poor citizens in many developing countries and gross shortcomings in the criminal justice system are extensively documented in G. Haugen, *The Locust Effect* (New York, NY: Oxford University Press, 2014).

implement civilian police oversight mechanisms and reform of criminal procedure laws. These laws, at least in theory, enable courts to act as a check on these forms of abuse through, for example, rules that deem evidence to be inadmissible where obtained illegally. However, in practice, courts in many developing and transitional economies have not been assertive monitors of abuses of public office, in part because of their historical subservience to the executive branch of government in terms of appointments, promotions and resources.

4.5.4   Correctional systems

The problem of ignoring other elements of the legal system, like the police, in rule of law reforms is replicated in penal reforms. These reforms seek to improve correctional institutions in many developing countries and transitional economies, but often ignore their relationship with the criminal justice system. Reform efforts in this context have focused on developing correctional institutions as professional public institutions, often through training programmes for correctional personnel provided by international agencies and NGOs, and the provision of paralegal advisory services to inmates to advise them of their rights relating to abuses suffered within correctional institutions, and their related legal rights under the country's criminal justice system. Some countries, especially in Latin America, have appointed official ombudsmen to investigate prisoners' complaints and report thereon to government, while in other countries (such as a number of countries in sub-Saharan Africa), pursuant to regional treaty commitments, official rapporteurs make periodic visits to and report publicly on conditions in correctional institutions.

Severe prison overcrowding has been a chronic problem, leading to a very high incidence of infectious diseases such as HIV/AIDS and TB. However, reforms focused on correctional institutions often ignore the fact that a significant source of overcrowding in correctional institutions in many developing countries is the high percentage of inmates held on remand awaiting trial for often lengthy periods because of inefficiencies in the broader criminal justice system. Where reforms to the criminal justice system have been undertaken, providing judges with greater discretion to impose non-custodial forms of sentence, the judiciary has often shown a reluctance to invoke these powers, particularly in contexts of widespread public concern over high and rising violent crime rates. Thus, penal reform efforts need to deal with their relationship to the broader criminal justice system.

Correction, dealing as it does with a small and marginalized sub-set of the population, is (perhaps more than any other institution) inextricable from the broader successes and failures of rule of law reform. It depends, at least, on the efficiency of court processes, the effectiveness of law enforcement, the broader complex of social factors determining crime rates more generally, a vigorous legal bar willing to defend prisoners' rights, and a culture of human rights robust enough to conceptualize prisoners within its ambit.

4.5.5   Administrative agencies

Other institutional interconnections that are relevant to rule of law reforms involve the bureaucracy. In many developed and developing countries important aspects of the administration of justice are vested in specialized law enforcement or administrative agencies that deal with matters as diverse as tax administration, public utilities regulation, environmental regulation, competition law enforcement, election management bodies, and so on. One of the advantages of these agencies is that they are more easily detachable from the existing bureaucracy, entailing less complex or sweeping reforms that may be less likely to suffer from path dependence problems.

Tax administration is an example of a specialized law enforcement or regulatory function which all developing countries must perform, and hence provides an important example of the challenges that developing countries face with the performance of such agencies. Effective performance of this function is of critical importance to all developing countries because a constrained ability to collect revenues that are legally due also constrains governments in terms of expenditure on pressing development priorities. In many developing countries the gap between taxes nominally due and taxes actually collected is extremely large – often in the range of 40 per cent – which suggests the potential margins for improved performance in tax administration.

To improve the tax system, a number of developing countries have set up large taxpayer units (LTUs), with a view to developing specialized and integrated expertise in tax assessment, given that LTUs are where much of the effective taxable capacity in many developing countries resides. In addition, a number of developing countries have also set up semi-autonomous revenue agencies (SARAs), designed to ensure the fiscal autonomy of the organization and much greater freedom in personnel policies and IT development. Many of these reforms appear to have been successful in broadening the taxpayer base and increasing the percentage of taxes nominally due that are actually collected. However, the experience with SARAs over time has been mixed: typically, these agencies appear initially to have a significant impact on the percentage of taxes actually collected, but subsequently their performance tends to deteriorate, in some cases because of rampant corruption within the agency, and in some cases because of increasing political interference from the Ministry of Finance and other executive arms of the government in personnel and assessment processes. This suggests that the ability of these agencies to maintain themselves over time as islands of virtue in an otherwise corrupt or incompetent general public administration may be quite limited without complementary reforms, over time, of the surrounding institutional matrix.

Another similarly motivated example of reforms is the implementation of independent regulatory agencies (IRAs) for infrastructure sectors such as telecommunications, electricity and water. During the 1990s US-style IRAs were adopted in many Latin American countries, in the context of privatization of state-owned utility companies. IRAs were intended to provide a credible commitment by the government to existing rules and norms, supposedly protecting investors from arbitrary and unjustifiable modifications to the regulatory framework. However, the implementation of IRAs has met with a series of obstacles. In some cases, their creation was resisted by bureaucrats, who were also opposed to privatization and a competitive environment in infrastructure services. This resistance may exemplify high switching costs and the installed base problem. In other cases, the transfer of civil servants from the pre-existing bureaucracy to the IRAs brought deeply embedded practices that are difficult to change, impairing some of the institutional innovations adopted by IRAs, such as those designed to insulate these agencies from political and electoral interests. This illustrates the difficulty of mitigating self-reinforcing mechanisms, especially when they are embedded in the institutional culture. Finally, some of the institutional guarantees of independence in these agencies were not effective because they were operating in a different institutional matrix from the country of origin of the transplant. Thus, the creation of IRAs largely ignored the importance of institutional interconnections.

4.6   Explanations for the mixed-to-poor record

Rule of law deficiencies are persistent and serious in many developing countries despite the fact that over the past 20 years external donors have invested billions of dollars in rule of law reform initiatives in many developing countries. The World Bank's governance data on the status of the rule of law reported that only three out of 18 Latin American countries had positive rule of law ratings in 2008 (Chile, Costa Rica and Uruguay) and in sub-Saharan Africa, only six out of 47 countries had positive rule of law ratings in 2008 (Botswana, Cape Verde, Mauritius, Namibia, Seychelles and South Africa). In all 12 countries of the former Soviet Union, ratings were negative in 2008. On the other hand, the countries of Central Europe present a far more positive picture. The Asian region presents a mixed setting with its huge diversity of countries, varying enormously in size, colonial history, legal heritage, political ideology and religious complexion. Notable exceptions to generally low rule of law ratings are Singapore and Hong Kong. Over the course of the prior decades few countries with weak ratings significantly improved their ratings, and some deteriorated further. While rule of law measures used by the World Bank in its government database are susceptible to methodological criticisms, it is unlikely that the general conclusion about serious and persistent impediments to establishing a rule of law is unfounded. More recent and more detailed assessment by the World Justice Project (sponsored by a non-profit organization in Washington, DC) of now almost 100 countries generally corroborates many of the deficiencies noted above.[16]

Michael Trebilcock and Ron Daniels hypothesize that the potential impediments that countries may encounter in implementing even a limited, procedural conception of the rule of law fall into three crude (and often overlapping) categories.[17]

4.6.1   Resource constraints

Despite political will generally on the part of their leadership and citizens, some developing countries simply lack the financial, technical or specialized human capital resources to implement good institutions

---

16 The World Justice Project, *The Rule of Law Index 2012–2013* (Washington, DC: The World Justice Project, 2012–13), available at http://worldjusticeproject.org/sites/default/files/WJP_Index_Report_2012.pdf (accessed 28 April 2014).

17 Trebilcock and Daniels, *supra* note 14.

generally, including legal institutions. This lack of resources impairs a country's development prospects by making it poorer and, in turn, further diminishes its ability to implement good institutions, hence creating a vicious downward spiral.

In such cases, reform requires either more effective or efficient deployment of existing resources devoted to a country's legal system, a re-ordering of a country's domestic priorities and reallocation of resources from other areas of expenditure to the legal system, or the infusion of resources from external donors (in the form of financial assistance or technical advice and training, and so on). Indeed, on the narrowly instrumental economic rationale for rule of law reform, governments lacking the necessary resources should be prepared to borrow the money required to finance rule of law reforms and finance borrowing costs from future economic growth and increased tax revenues.

4.6.2   Social-cultural-historical constraints

Another category of explanation for impediments to reform relates to a variety of factors that might loosely be placed under the rubric of social-cultural-historical factors. These refer to a set of social or cultural values, norms, attitudes or practices that are inhospitable to even a limited procedural conception of the rule of law.[18] In a recent article, Licht, Goldshmidt and Schwartz argue that societies that accord higher weight to social embeddedness than individual autonomy, and social hierarchy rather than egalitarianism, exhibit lower commitments to the rule of law, democracy and non-corrupt governance, although there is significant unexplained variance around the mean.[19]

Whether culture is conceived of as a form of consciousness or as a form of law-like social norms, the policy prescriptions entailed in overcoming this class of impediment are not nearly as obvious as in the case of technical or resource-related impediments. No impact is likely to be immediate, dramatic or predictable. That is to say, changing culture, however conceived, may present at least as formidable a set of

---

18 See R. Ehrenreich Brooks, "The New Imperialism: Violence, Norm, and the Rule of Law" (2003) 101 *Michigan Law Review* 227; A. Cohen, "Thinking with Culture in Law and Development" (2009) *Buffalo Law Review* 11.

19 A.N. Licht, C. Goldshmidt and S.H. Schwartz, "Culture Rules: The Foundations of the Rule of Law and Other Norms of Governance" (2007) 35 *Journal of Comparative Economics* 659.

challenges as changing laws and legal institutions if the purpose is to change human behaviour.[20]

4.6.3   Political economy constraints

A third class of potential impediments to the effective implementation of even a limited conception of the rule of law is related to the lack of effective political demand for reforms, on the one hand, and vested supply-side interests, on the other. These render these reforms politically difficult to realize even if (by assumption) they would make most citizens better off in terms of their own values.

On the demand side, a procedurally oriented conception of the rule of law has many of the attributes of a public good – "everybody's business is nobody's business" – creating a major collective action problem. In other words, diffuse citizen commitment to the rule of law is unlikely to translate into effective political mobilization for reforms. Also, one should not naively assume that all external constituencies are likely to benefit from rule of law reform. Indeed, those who derive benefits from corruption, cronyism, favouritism and so on in existing institutional arrangements and legal processes are likely to resist such reforms.

On the supply side, vested or incumbent interests in institutions or processes that do not comport even with a minimalist, procedurally oriented conception of the rule of law – for example, a corrupt or incompetent judiciary, public prosecution, police, correctional system, tax administration or other specialized law enforcement, administrative or regulatory agency, members of the private bar and legal education institutions – are likely to resist reforms that threaten their interests.

4.7   Identifying feasible reform strategies

Approaches to rule of law reforms that do not take into account adaptive behaviour with respect to the particular institutional context in question, as well as mutually reinforcing effects among interdependent institutions, are unlikely to be successful. If one takes the obstacles described above (which amount to what we call the path depend-

---

20 See Cohen, *supra* note 18.

ence problem) seriously, future reform strategies will be significantly constrained and shaped by the legacies of history.

There are two potential (and complementary) strategies for dealing with this conundrum. First, reformers may be able to identify some institutions that can be more easily detached from a broader mutually reinforcing institutional matrix or be created *de novo* (such as SARAs, new constitutional or human rights courts or commissions, semi-IRAs, one-stop government agencies (like the Brazilian *Poupatempo*[21]) for issuing, for example, passports, driving licenses, ID cards and health cards, and alternative forms of dispute resolution).[22] This strategy may enable more ambitious stand-alone reforms that nevertheless have important showcase effects. They may demonstrate lower switching costs or greater benefits than sceptics had assumed, although even here the experience with SARAs and IRAs suggests that these institutions are likely to be fragile without complementary reforms over time to the surrounding institutional matrix.

The second strategy is to reform existing institutions that are interconnected and mutually reinforcing in a time-sensitive manner by prioritizing a sequence of reforms. While beginning with certain core reforms, reformers must recognize that further complementary reforms will be necessary in the future to reinforce the initial reforms. This implies that reforms should be incremental, which is quite different from many current reform practices that are either stand-alone without being incremental or are so encompassing as to be infeasible.

One of the lessons of path dependence is that we are not writing on a blank slate. It is true that in abnormal times – "critical junctures" (for example, the aftermath of economic collapse, civil war or military invasion) – the credibility and legitimacy of incumbent elites may be weakened by such crises, creating new political openings for marginalized constituencies.[23] At the same time, it is unlikely that all

---

21 See M. Prado and A.C. Chasin, "How Innovative was the Poupatempo Experience in Brazil? Institutional Bypass as a New Form of Institutional Change" (2011) 5:1 *Brazilian Political Science Review*.

22 See T. Heller, "An Immodest Postscript" in E. Jensen and T. Heller (eds), *Beyond Common Knowledge: Empirical Approaches to the Rule of Law* (Stanford: Stanford University Press, 2003).

23 See M. Trebilcock, "Journeys Across the Divides" in F. Parisi and C. Rowley (eds), *The Origins of Law and Economics: Essays by the Founding Fathers* (Cheltenham, UK and Northampton, MA, USA: Edward Elgar, 2005).

pre-existing economic, social and cultural factors that create costs for switching to new institutional regimes can be ignored entirely (as contemporary challenges to institutional reform in, for example, Iraq, Afghanistan, Egypt and Libya exemplify). Reformers should recognize not only the importance of switching costs, but also be sensitive to the different kinds of switching costs associated with reform.

First, in terms of political economy considerations, switching costs may be high for those who benefit from the institutional status quo.[24] These costs may be mitigated by reforms that create or strengthen a countervailing political constituency that benefits from the reforms. Alternatively, vested interests may need to be bought-off or grandfathered in some way to mute opposition to the reforms. Second, switching costs may also reflect individual learning costs in adapting to a new regime (the "installed base" problem). These can be mitigated by state-sponsored public education programmes and gradual processes of transition that avoid the need for abrupt adaptation to a new regime. Third, switching costs may reflect the scarcity of financial and human resources required to implement new institutional regimes, which can be mitigated by external financial and technical assistance. Finally, switching costs may reflect deeply embedded cultural beliefs or practices that are resistant to change. Here, reforms that adapt traditional institutions (such as traditional forms of alternative dispute settlement or communal property rights) may mitigate problems of cultural dissonance. Moreover, institutional reforms implemented over time may in turn lead to modifications in cultural belief systems.

In this respect, various forms of alternative dispute resolution (ADR) make up a class of reform that appears to have shown significant promise, largely through demonstration effects. ADR sometimes builds on traditional or community-based forms of dispute settlement, such as adaptations of the Lok Adalat system in India, the Shalish system in Bangladesh, the Gacaca Tribunals in Rwanda in the aftermath of years of civil war and genocide, the Casas de Justicia in Latin America and Alternative Law Groups in the Philippines. These have sought to marry indigenous methods of dispute settlement with broader rule of law norms, such as equality before the law, so as to minimize cultural

---

24 Resistance to reform can also be higher if there is uncertainty regarding the identity of potential beneficiaries. The uncertainty is higher in large-scale reforms: D. Rodrik and R. Fernandez, "Resistance to Reform: Status Quo Bias in the Presence of Individual-specific Uncertainty" (1990) 81 *American Economic Review* 1148.

switching costs. In these cases, reformers have struggled to navigate the difficult compromise between two, sometimes conflicting, models of dispute resolution and the respective roles of the formal court system and informal modes of dispute settlement. Despite these difficulties, these ADR reforms have a major benefit: they acknowledge and rely on context-specific forms of institutional vindication or instantiation of rule of law values, thus reducing cultural switching costs and nurturing an increasingly robust domestic constituency for rule of law reforms more generally over time. In this sense, these reforms enable a broadly representative range of social, economic and political interests to see their interests and values as aligned with the promotion and preservation of the rule of law.

4.8   Conclusion

Nurturing an increasingly robust domestic constituency for the rule of law over time that reflects a demand-side perspective requires that a broadly representative range of social, economic and political interests come to see their interests and values as aligned with the promotion and preservation of the rule of law. In this respect, we question (along with others) the aptness of the relatively high priority often accorded to formal judicial reform by the international community in the rule of law initiatives that it has promoted in developing countries in recent years, and the relative lack of attention to institutional reforms that are more likely to affect the day-to-day interactions of the citizenry with the legal system.[25]

Civil justice surveys of representative samples of the population that have been undertaken in recent years in a number of developed countries provide helpful examples of instruments for identifying the relative frequency and shortcomings of citizen interactions with state agencies.[26] These include police, prosecutors, specialized law

---

25 See T. Carothers, "The Rule of Law Revival" (1998) 77 *Foreign Affairs* 95; S. Golub, "A House Without Foundation" in T. Carothers (ed.), *Promoting the Rule of Law Abroad: In Search of Knowledge* (Washington, DC: Carnegie Endowment for International Peace, 2006); B. Garth, "Building Strong and Independent Judiciaries for the New Law and Development: Beyond the Paradox of Consensus Programmes and Perpetually Disappointing Results" (2003) 52 *DePaul Law Review* 383.

26 See, for example, P. Pleasence and N. Balmer, "Caught in the Middle: Justiciable Problems and the Use of Lawyers" in M. Trebilcock, T. Duggan and L. Sossin (eds), *Middle-Income Access to Justice* (Toronto: University of Toronto Press, 2012).

enforcement and administrative agencies, including agencies of government that issue, for example, passports, driving licences, ID cards, health cards, building permits and business licences,[27] and access to justice initiatives – such as informal community-based dispute resolution mechanisms (often reflecting adaptations to and elaborations of traditional dispute settlement mechanisms) – where more visible and immediate material benefits from successful institutional reform are likely to be experienced by a wide cross-section of the citizenry.

While we acknowledge that the success of institutional reforms in one context ultimately often depends, to an important extent, on complementary institutional reforms in other contexts,[28] this does not realistically mean that everything can be pursued at once. Judicial reforms (and, we should probably acknowledge, reforms to legal education) are likely to have longer-term and less visible social pay-offs to the citizenry at large and hence are less likely to engage their interest and support than other reforms noted above, given the many more pressing and immediate survival challenges citizens in developing countries often face. Thus, both domestic and international proponents of rule of law reform in developing countries face a hitherto under-acknowledged challenge of rendering rule of law reform politically salient to most citizens of these countries. Strategic choices on sequencing are important in addressing this challenge. However, for the time being, we have to confront Carothers' sobering observation that "the rapidly growing field of rule of law assistance is operating from a very thin base of knowledge at every level. . ."[29]

---

27 Famously described by C. Reich as "The New Property" (1964) 73 *Yale Law Journal* 733, lack of effective access to which in many developing countries is equally famously described by de Soto, *supra* note 5, and is increasingly well documented in various reports in the World Bank's "Doing Business" surveys.

28 See R. Kleinfeld, "Competing Definitions of the Rule of Law" (2005) Carnegie Paper No. 55, Carnegie Endowment, Washington, DC.

29 Carothers, *supra* note 25, at 27.

5 The rule of law: an economic perspective

It has become conventional wisdom amongst most economists that, whatever else the state does, it should provide effective institutions and processes to protect private property rights and enforce contracts, which are regarded as prerequisites to efficient and dynamic market economies.[1] On this view of the rule of law, law plays a critical instrumental role in promoting economic development and should be accorded the highest developmental priority. In this chapter, we address the property rights protection pillar of this conventional wisdom (section 5.1), then we turn to the contract rights pillar (section 5.2). Going beyond contracts and property rights, we briefly review a wide range of other determinants of the vitality of the private sector in developing countries (section 5.3). Finally, we discuss the importance of an instrumental perspective on the rule of law to promote other goals, such as environmental protection (section 5.4).

5.1 Property rights

5.1.1 The benefits of secure property arrangements

Perhaps most reflective of the importance of property rights in contemporary thinking on economic development has been the success and influence of Hernando de Soto's book, *The Mystery of Capital: Why Capitalism Triumphs in the West and Fails Everywhere Else.* He argues that strong protection for private property rights is the key factor in explaining the economic success of the developed world and the economic stagnation of many developing countries. On de Soto's account, the potential benefits of formalization of property rights are substantial. De Soto claims that "the total value of the real estate held but not legally owned by the poor of the Third World and former

---

1 K.W. Dam, *The Law-Growth Nexus: The Rule of Law and Economic Development* (Washington, DC: Brookings Institution Press, 2006) at 91.

communist nations is at least $9.3 trillion", which he characterizes as "dead capital".[2]

The theoretical and empirical literature that has emerged in support of this claim has been used to advocate titling and registration programmes as a general solution to the problem of property rights insecurity. The economic literature has identified a number of distinct economic benefits that effective protection of private property can bring:

1. Exclusive use leads to resources being used more efficiently.
2. Security of tenure and easy transferability of property increase access to credit.
3. Security of tenure increases incentives for investment.
4. Security of tenure decreases inefficient and wasteful competition for resources.

5.1.2   The debate over the necessity for a formal property rights regime

Many development scholars and policy-makers contend that the benefits of private property are best achieved by a formal state-run property system. When fully functional and accessible, such a system provides a clearer and more secure allocation of property rights than any informal measures could provide. Where there is a credible third-party enforcer of property rights – in particular the state – uncertainty is reduced or completely eliminated. Moreover, a formal property system can also reduce transaction costs in market interactions by providing increased information to third parties about the rights that an individual has over land. Similar arguments are also often made for formalizing title to personal property, in particular for facilitating the granting and taking of security interests in personal property to enhance access to credit.

These broad assertions, however, leave a great deal of indeterminacy regarding the actual policies to strengthen the protection of property rights. In some cases, stronger formal property rights may well be unwarranted and counter-productive. Thus, a more nuanced approach is required to craft successful development policies regarding property

---

2 H. de Soto, *The Mystery of Capital: Why Capitalism Triumphs in the West and Fails Everywhere Else* (New York, NY: Basic Books, 2000) at 35.

rights.[3] Moreover, a formal property rights regime may not be the only method of securing the benefits discussed above. Indeed, informal mechanisms may provide many of the same benefits as a private property rights regime.

Within the literature examining informal mechanisms as a substitute for formal mechanisms, there are two strands that explore how this can occur. First, the *game theoretic literature* explores how cooperation can emerge as a result of repeated interactions among individuals.[4] Second, the *law and social norms literature* examines the evolution of informal norms as a mechanism of social order and control.[5] Both of these perspectives have strong implications for the possiblity of efficient, informal property regimes, as they suggest that either spontaneous cooperation or informal norms can often substitute for a formal property regime maintained by the state.

The empirical evidence on formalization of private property rights tends to suggest that formal regimes may lead to more efficient use of property, but in many contexts informal regimes are often a reasonably close substitute, and mechanisms for limited forms of alienability often evolve without formal property rights. As to whether formalization of property rights increases access to credit, the evidence is mixed. Where informal credit markets are strong, there appears to be little benefit from formalization. Similarly, where credit markets are weak for other reasons, formalization is likely to have limited impact on access to credit. While formal property rights seem to lead to increased investment in productive assets, this increase depends on the security afforded by informal norms. Similarly, the evidence is fragmentary on formal property rights reducing inefficient forms of resource competition.[6]

While there may be benefits in the formalization of property rights regimes, such regimes may also entail various costs, related to:

---

3 See D. Kennedy, "Some Caution about Property Rights as a Recipe for Economic Development" (2011) 1 *Accounting, Economics and Law*, Article 3, at 42–8.

4 R. Axelrod, *The Evolution of Cooperation* (New York, NY: Basic Books, 1984).

5 See, for example, R. Ellickson, *Order Without Law: How Neighbors Settle Disputes* (Cambridge, MA: Harvard University Press, 1991); E. Ostrom, *Governing the Commons: The Evolution of Institutions for Collective Action* (Cambridge, UK: Cambridge University Press, 1990).

6 M. Trebilcock and P.-E. Veel, "Property Rights and Development: The Contingent Case for Formalization" (2008) 30 *University of Pennsylvania Journal of International Law* 397.

1. setting up a land registration or recordation system, including initial surveys and the cost of updating the system;
2. undermining the possibility of communal tenure, resulting in the emergence of a landless class with few, if any, other economic opportunities, sources of insurance or social safety nets;
3. undermining effective informal institutions by creating dysfunctional conflicts between the formal and informal regimes;[7]
4. increased social conflict, which occurs when a badly designed system exposes latent divisions between or among claimant groups that had previously lain dormant;
5. flaws in the titling process, which are likely to be exploited by politically or economically powerful groups at the expense of women and other marginalized groups who face various barriers to accessing a formal property rights system;
6. unsuccessful implementation of a well-designed formal property rights regime because it is sharply antithetical to deeply entrenched informal norms;
7. lack of effective complementary institutions, including the judiciary, the legal profession and the police; complementary reforms to these other institutions may be necessary to guarantee that the system will be effective.

In sum, the creation of a formal property rights regime is not without cost, and it will not necessarily be the case that the benefits of such a regime will clearly outweigh the costs. Given, however, that formal property regimes are ubiquitous in the developed world, there are reasons to believe that, at a certain stage in a country's economic development, a formal property rights regime is necessary to secure further economic development. China, for example, has experienced rapid, market-driven economic growth over the past three decades without a well-defined or enforced formal property rights regime,[8] but has recently been devoting increasing attention to formalizing property rights.[9]

---

7 See D. Fitzpatrick, "Evolution and Chaos in Property Rights Systems: The Third World Tragedy of Contested Access" (2006) 15 *Yale Law Journal* 996.

8 See F. Upham, "From Demsetz to Deng: Speculations on the Implications of Chinese Growth for Law and Development Theory" (2009) 41 *NYU Journal of Inernational Law and Politics* 551.

9 Trebilcock and Veel, *supra* note 6, at 397.

5.1.3   Informal mechanisms for securing the benefits of private property

At relatively low levels of development, an informal regime may be adequate to realize many of the benefits of private property. Where economic life is largely organized around small units (for example, villages), the mobility of the population is low and resources such as land are not overly scarce, informal mechanisms are likely to be sufficient to provide the benefits of private property. Put differently, if individuals expect to be living in the same location, the expectation of repeated interactions will create the conditions necessary for cooperation. At this point, informal mechanisms are likely to suffice, so a formal property regime would entail significant social and economic costs without significant benefits.

As countries undergo economic changes, however, the relative benefits of a formal private property regime are likely to increase. There are three broad reasons for this consequence. First, as the economy grows, communities are likely to become less close-knit, and informal norms may become less effective in maintaining order. Second, at higher levels of economic development, the value of land, goods and investments may increase substantially, leading to more substantial benefits from more secure property rights.[10] While informal mechanisms may be sufficient to provide an individual with the incentives to make minor investments, more capital-intensive, asset-specific investments are likely to require greater certainty and security. Moreover, as the capital-intensiveness of activities increases, formal credit is likely to play a greater role in economic development, thereby increasing the benefits of clear and secure title. Third, at higher levels of economic development, the relative costs of creating a formal property regime may be lower. As a country's tax base increases, it will be relatively easier for the state to make the expenditures required for creating a formal property regime. Similarly, where the state takes an increasingly larger role in providing social benefits to its population, the equity concerns of potential landlessness are likely to be mitigated. Finally, the very forces that undermine informal tenure can also mitigate the effects of increased landlessness and social unrest. As mobility and migration opportunities increase, individuals will be more able to seek alternative economic opportunities elsewhere, thus lowering the cost to individuals of changes to property arrangements.

---

10 See H. Demsetz, "Toward a Theory of Property Rights" (1967) 57 *American Economic Review* 347.

The above considerations suggest that the focus of certain previous titling programmes may have been misguided. First, while many titling programmes have focused on providing formal title to agricultural landowners, the above discussion suggests that, with the exception of newly settled frontier land, established social norms in rural areas may be sufficient to provide an adequate degree of informal property rights protection. Urban titling programmes, especially those aimed at newly developing squatter settlements, may yield a greater social return. The greatest return from titling programmes may come, however, from providing formal ownership to firms' land and assets, as informal norms may be lacking in such circumstances or inadequate to provide the certainty required for large investments or transactions entailing significant sunk costs and long pay-off periods. Second, to the extent that there are substantial benefits to providing stronger land rights to agricultural landowners in a given case, those benefits may be largely realized through the recognition and formalization of customary land tenure.[11] This model of formalization in the agricultural sector may bring about the benefits of security of tenure at a lower social cost than would the *de novo* creation of an individual-centred system of alienable land rights. Both of these conclusions, however, should be taken only as general propositions, as any analysis of the relative costs and benefits of formalization is a highly context-dependent exercise.

Finally, it should be noted that, while the above discussion has largely focused on titling, in some cases the primary source of insecure property rights is not the threat of expropriation by other households or landowners, but rather expropriation by the state. Where this is the main source of insecurity, formal title per se may not be necessary or sufficient to increase individuals' perceptions of tenure security. Rather, what is required in such cases to create the perception of strong property rights is a credible commitment by the state not to expropriate land or other assets. This can be a significantly less costly and more effective mechanism for gaining the benefits of private property rights than formal titling programmes.

---

11 For an insightful exploration of many of these issues of institutional design, see D. Fitzpatrick, "Best Practice Options for the Legal Recognition of Customary Tenure" (2005) 36 *Development and Change* 449.

5.1.4   Reform strategies

Because of the complex interactions between a property rights regime and the social, economic, political, and legal framework within which such a regime operates, it is not fruitful simply to argue for or against the formalization of a property rights regime or for "strong and clear" property rights. Rather, the relationship between property rights and development is much more complex, and a more nuanced approach to these issues is required.

The context dependence of successful property regimes leads to three important considerations for reformers. First, property formalization programmes cannot be considered as isolated economic development projects as one might consider certain physical infrastructure projects. Rather, such programmes must be considered as a part of a general framework for economic development, typically including a wider set of reforms aimed at the promotion of the rule of law.[12] Second, in determining what role outsiders can play in helping to promote a state's formal property regime, it is essential to ask a broader question about the similarities among optimal property regimes. In practice, local or regional models of property regimes may be more success-ful than Western blueprints.[13] Finally, contrary to conventional eco-nomic thinking, the formalization of property rights is not necessarily desirable at all states of development or for all property owners.

Because of these considerations, unless there is clear and compelling evidence pointing to the need for a systematic state-led formaliza-tion programme, the optimal response may be an optional or sporadic system of title registration. Although a sporadic programme of title representation is not without its own costs, such a programme brings substantial benefits relative to a systematic formalization programme. In the face of limited resources and state capacity, a sporadic system of land registration has the benefit of providing the additional secu-rity and clarity of formal property rights to those desiring it most. By simply providing an additional vehicle or option for owning property, a sporadic registration programme does not require disturbing the arrangements of those groups that are content with the status quo. Moreover, a voluntary system overcomes the collective action problem of providing the machinery for the enforcement of property rights by

---

12 Dam, *supra* note 1.

13 See S. Mukand and D. Rodrik, "In Search of the Holy Grail: Policy Convergence, Experimentation, and Economic Performance" (2005) 95 *American Economic Review* 374.

having the state provide it and allowing people to opt into it. Perhaps the strongest benefit, however, of a sporadic and voluntary formalization system is that it avoids the myriad unforeseeable and potentially negative consequences that can result from the top down imposition of a uniform system of property arrangements. A gradual and reversible process of voluntary change at the individual level can mitigate such potentially harmful consequences.[14]

Even in situations where a systematic programme is clearly superior to a voluntary or sporadic programme, drastic and irreversible changes should be avoided. Rather, changes should be incremental in nature. For example, where communal property is prevalent, rather than registering individual, fully alienable freehold titles to specified plots of land to the exclusion of all others, a rudimentary titling programme could be undertaken utilizing simple compass and chain surveys where only the base group title would be registered and without prejudice to existing usufructuary rights of non-group members. Landowning groups might also be given a more formal legal structure and clearer decision or governance rules (akin to private corporations with restrictions on share transferability), while maintaining some limits on outright alienability of group land.[15] Such programmes lessen the potential for serious social conflict or disruption from abrupt legal change and facilitate an evolutionary process for the emergence of strong private property rights.[16]

5.2 Contract rights

5.2.1 The controversial case for formal contract rights

Nobel Laureate Douglass North advances the strong claim that "the inability of societies to develop effective, low-cost enforcement of contracts is the most important source of both historical stagnation and contemporary underdevelopment in the Third World".[17] Nobel Laureate Oliver Williamson argues that neither spot-market

---

14 See M. Trebilcock, "Communal Property Rights: The Papua New Guinea Experience" (1984) 34 *University of Toronto Law Journal* 377.

15 See generally, D. Fitzpatrick, "Best Practice Options for the Legal Recognition of Customary Tenure" (2005) 36 *Development and Change* 449.

16 See Ostrom, *supra* note 5.

17 D.C. North, *Institutions, Institutional Change and Economic Performance* (Cambridge, UK: Cambridge University Press, 1990) at 54.

transactions nor transactions within vertically integrated firms require formal enforcement mechanisms, because both entail minimal transaction costs. Conversely, the vulnerability experienced by at least one party to long-term, non-simultaneous transactions creates a significant need for a credible third-party enforcement mechanism. Credible third-party enforcement addresses the reluctance of private sector agents to participate in non-simultaneous economic transactions, which often entail significant sunk costs, because of a lack of assured protection of the parties' economic interests.[18]

According to both authors, a formal mechanism for contract enforcement is not always necessary. Williamson contemplates a continuum of microeconomic activity: at either end of this continuum are types of activity that do not require a formal mechanism, while in the middle lie economic activities that require some degree of external enforcement. Similarly, North first identifies self-enforcement as the primary feature of contracts used in tribes, primitive societies and close-knit small communities – settings in which personal knowledge of transacting parties about one another is extensive, and repeat dealings are pervasive. North then points out the limits of self-enforcing (relational) contracts in a world of increasingly impersonal exchange. In such a world, simultaneous exchange and repeat dealings are no longer the prevailing norm; thus self-enforcing contracts become insufficient because there no longer exists a dense social network of interactions to enable transacting to take place at low cost. Instead, individual specialization and exchange expansion in both time and space require additional contract enforcement mechanisms to assure compliance.

While the contract-formalist approach to development taken by North regards formal contract enforcement as fundamentally important for a nation's economic development, an alternative school of thought has emerged that downplays the need for a formal third-party mechanism for contract enforcement. Relying on empirical evidence that emphasizes the fundamental role played by social norms and relational networks in rendering private transactions self-enforcing, scholars have argued that many economic activities that foster economic development do not need a means of formal third-party enforcement. According to Avner Greif, for example, "many exchange relations in historical and contemporary markets and developing economies are

---

18 O.E. Williamson, *The Mechanisms of Governance* (New York, NY: Oxford University Press, 1996). See also Dam, *supra* note 1 at 124–8.

not governed – directly or indirectly – by the legal system".[19] Greif argues that, in fact, much of the world's economic development has occurred in the absence of a legal system to govern private economic transactions.[20]

5.2.2   Empirical evidence on formal and informal contracts

A provisional reading of the empirical evidence (extensively reviewed elsewhere[21]) is that the proponents of contract formalism and the proponents of contract informalism can both point to supporting bodies of theory and empirical evidence, but both risk over-stating, or at least over-simplifying their cases.

To take first the case made by the contract formalists, it is clear that in both developed and developing countries, many contracts are self-enforcing. Often because of ethnic, religious or cultural ties, informal transacting norms arise and are enforced through informal, extra-legal sanctions. Even in the absence of such contracting networks, long-term, incomplete contingent claims contracts are commonplace between arm's length business parties in both developed and developing economies. Where these contracts include substantial investments in relationship-specific assets, there are strong incentives to maintain the relationship. Of course, even long-term relational contracts eventually come to an end and, depending on the nature of the dependencies or interdependencies that they create, these contracts are vulnerable to problems of hold up and opportunism ("end-game" problems). These problems can sometimes only be solved by complete vertical integration, although this may not otherwise be efficient.

As noted above, Williamson argues that both spot-market and hierarchical (corporate integration) transactions require little support from the formal legal system; in contrast, middle range transactions (long-term contracting) are particularly vulnerable in the absence of credible third-party enforcement mechanisms.[22] Even with respect

---

19 A. Greif, "Contracting, Enforcement, and Efficiency: Economics beyond the Law" in M. Bruno and B. Pleskovic (eds), *Annual World Bank Conference on Development Economics 1996* (1997) at 239 (challenging the neoclassical theory that only legal contract enforcement facilitates exchange).

20 *Ibid.*, at 241–2.

21 M. Trebilcock and J. Leng, "The Role of Formal Contract Law and Enforcement in Economic Development" (2006) 92 *University of Virginia Law Review* 1517.

22 Williamson, *supra* note 18, at 332.

to Williamson's two polar cases, however, it is not true that vertical integration can completely avoid the problems of a weak formal legal system. As a number of commentators have argued, and corroborated empirically, countries with poorer investor protection, measured by both the character of legal rules and the quality of legal enforcement, have smaller and narrower capital markets; this is particularly evident when minority shareholders are subject to serious agency costs (opportunism) by managers or controlling shareholders.[23] Moreover, employment contracts and collective agreements often require a formal enforcement mechanism. At the other pole, even spot transactions (for example, commodity contracts) may raise quality or product defect problems that require resort to the formal legal system, at least in the absence of industry or trade associations with their own codes of conduct, norms and alternative dispute settlement mechanisms.[24]

Between these two poles, Williamson exaggerates the importance of formal contract enforcement by giving insufficient weight to the role of relational contracting[25] and contract enforcement by private sector third parties – such as credit bureau, bourses, exchanges, arbitrators and industry associations – in both personal and impersonal relationships. The contract informalists, in turn, risk over-stating their case to the extent that they imply that most contracts are self-enforcing, rendering formal third-party enforcement unnecessary or unimportant for economic development. As noted above, long-term relational contracts may lead to end-game problems that require resort to the courts for resolution. Moreover, in many contracts for large investments in non-salvageable assets (sunk costs) – such as infrastructure or complex technology – parties will seek a fully specified, formal contingent claims contract.

Often the investors will not share a common ethnic, cultural or religious network with counterparties to these transactions; nor will investors wish to leave subsequent negotiation of contract details or enforcement to the vagaries of arbitrary domestic political, regulatory or legal processes. For example, circumstances that arguably

---

23 See, for example, T. Beck and R. Levine, "Legal Institutions and Financial Development" in C. Menard and M.M. Shirley (eds), *Handbook of New Institutional Economics* (Dordrecht, the Netherlands: Springer, 2005) 251, at 253–4.

24 See L. Bernstein, "Opting Out of the Legal System: Extralegal Contractual Relations in the Diamond Industry" (1992) 21 *Journal of Legal Studies* 115, at 130–35.

25 See G. Baker, R. Gibbons and K. Murphy, "Relational Contracts and the Theory of the Firm" (2002) 117 *Quarterly Journal of Economics* 39.

have facilitated Japan's economic success in the post-war years and more recently, China's, do not readily generalize to most other developing countries. Japan is a remarkably culturally homogeneous society where reliance on informal social norms and sanctions may be particularly effective. In addition, Japan has been strikingly non-dependent on large-scale FDI for its economic success. While China has recently relied on large infusions of FDI, much of this investment has come from ethnic Chinese business networks (*guanxi*) outside of China or has relied on rather unique kinds of corporatist ties to local governments.[26] China's success in attracting foreign investment cannot easily be replicated in other developing economies that do not have a huge diaspora, members of which are not only capital-rich but also willing to invest in their home countries. Unlike Japan and China, for many developing countries, long-term economic growth is significantly dependent on expanding international trade and on attracting large-scale FDI from parties who do not share common ethnic, cultural or social characteristics. Here, the absence of effective formal contract enforcement mechanisms is likely to entail a number of adverse implications for investment and international trade.[27]

Moreover, relational contracting has the potential to create significant adverse, external effects.[28] Private ordering "sometimes harms efficiency by excluding new entrants from trading or by achieving price collusion".[29] Indeed, ethnicity-based business networks can render it nearly impossible for an outsider to enter the circle on a business level.[30] This "shortage of new firms and new people" and "inability to enter into long-term contracts can inhibit the adoption and development of complex technologies".[31] In the African context, "whenever business communities are built along ethnic, religious, or gender lines,

26 H. Shaoqin, "A Study of Contract Enforcement Mechanisms in China during Transition (zhongguo zhuangui shiqi hetong zhixing jizhi yanjiu)" (2006) 3 *Journal of Legal and Economic Studies* (Hong Fan Ping Lun) 184, at 192.

27 See D. Berkowitz, K. Pistor and J. Moenius, "Legal Institutions and International Trade Flows" (2004) 26 *Michigan Journal of International Law* 163, at 166–8.

28 A. Dixit, *Lawlessness and Economics: Alternative Modes of Governance* (Princeton, NJ: Princeton University Press, 2004) at 79.

29 J. McMillan and C. Woodruff, "Private Order under Dysfunctional Public Order" (2000) 98 *Michigan Law Review* 2421, at 2423.

30 C.W. Gray, "Reforming Legal Systems in Developing and Transition Countries" (September 1997) *Finance & Development* at 14.

31 *Ibid.*

network effects result in apparent discrimination".[32] Not surprisingly, an ethnic bias in assigning trade credit has been "detrimental to entrepreneurs of African descent and favorable to entrepreneurs originating outside of Africa".[33] Thus, while ethnicity-based business networks may provide the predictability that helps facilitate certain economic transactions, such transactions may come at the cost of both discrimination against individuals outside that network and inefficiency from potentially mutually beneficial exchanges forgone.

McMillan and Woodruff usefully distinguish between formal contract law in dysfunctional and functional legal systems. They note that in a functional legal system, relational contracting tends to complement the formal state-enforced contract framework, while in a dysfunctional legal system, relational contracting may be an imperfect substitute for a system of formal contract enforcement.[34]

5.2.3   Reform strategies

The mix of mechanisms that are likely to ensure both a fair and efficient domain of contracting in developing countries is a function of highly context-specific factors that defy easy generalizations. This caution has also been strongly voiced in recent development literature that stresses the need to adopt highly context-specific analysis in studying institutions. Two considerations may be of particular relevance to this exercise.

First, as noted above, growth modes and income levels matter to the extent that catch-up economies starting from low-level economic equilibria have different demands for institutions from those of middle-income economies. Moreover, new evidence from patterns of international trade also generates support for this discriminating treatment: the nature of traded goods (of varying levels of complexity) can influence the relative importance of formal, as compared to informal, contracting.[35] This conclusion corroborates the view that the requirements of formal institutional quality become more demanding as economies move up the development curve. This view is also corroborated

---

32 M. Fafchamps, *Market Institutions in Sub-Saharan Africa: Theory and Evidence* (Cambridge, MA: MIT Press, 2004).

33 *Ibid.*, at 368.

34 McMillan and Woodruff, *supra* note 29, at 2425.

35 See Berkowitz et al., *supra* note 27.

by recent evidence from China that the quality of contract adjudication and enforcement has dramatically improved in rapidly growing urban centres but continues to languish in more economically backward rural areas.[36]

Second, prevailing societal structures for organizing the behaviour of individuals in the early stages of market development – such as the different modes of social interaction in communalist and individualist societies – also matter. Communalist societies tend to rely more on relation-based contract enforcement institutions that emphasize informal intra-group sanctions. Individualist societies, by contrast, tend to support more transactions across different groups with formal contract enforcement institutions.[37]

In addition to being mindful of different contexts, reformers also need to consider transitional strategies, as building contract enforcement institutions takes time.[38] In this process, informal solutions, although transitional at particular stages of development, can serve value-adding and welfare-improving functions before formal institutional reform has taken hold and become effective. This is especially true for countries at early stages of industrialization, as East Asian economies have demonstrated. As Dixit has observed: "it is not always necessary to create replicas of Western-style state legal institutions from scratch; it may be possible to work with such alternative institutions as are available, and build on them".[39] Thus, there is a legitimate justification for incorporating efficient indigenous institutions of contract enforcement into contemporary legal regimes, rendering formal and informal enforcement institutions as complements rather than substitutes, and making the law more legitimate in the perceptions of the general population, thereby facilitating its implementation on the ground.

A more controversial transitional strategy that has already become widespread practice in international business transactions is to outsource contract interpretation and enforcement. Many major international transactions are now negotiated in English, contracts are

---

36 See X. He, "Formal Contract Enforcement and Economic Development in Urban and Rural China" Working Paper, School of Law, City University of Hong Kong, 2008.

37 See A. Greif, "Commitment, Coercion, and Markets: The Nature and Dynamics of Institutions Supporting Exchange" in Menard and Shirley (eds), *supra* note 23, at 727, 762.

38 J. McMillan and C. Woodruff, "Dispute Prevention without Courts in Vietnam" (1999) 15 *Journal of Law Economics and Organization* 637, at 637–8.

39 Dixit, *supra* note 28.

written in English, and choice of law and/or choice of forum clauses in such contracts stipulate that they are governed by the law of New York or England, and that disputes will be resolved by international commercial arbitration (with arbitral awards enforceable in domestic courts where countries are signatories to the New York Convention on the Recognition and Enforcement of Foreign Arbitral Awards).[40] This strategy, reflected in the rise of global law firms, largely bypasses domestic legal institutions (except for residual risks associated with the enforcement of foreign arbitral awards) and has raised caveats on that account: it largely removes foreign investors as a political constituency for domestic legal reforms while leaving many domestic parties captive to the frailties of domestic legal institutions, including abuses of human rights beyond the domain of commercial transactions, and risks rendering a transitional strategy as the permanent status quo (a low-level equilibrium trap).[41]

5.3   Beyond contract and property rights (i): the prerequisites for a thriving private sector

While an instrumental perspective on the rule of law has traditionally focused on the formal protection of private property rights and the enforcement of contracts as necessary conditions for private sector investment and growth, they are by no means sufficient conditions (and at low levels of development perhaps not even necessary conditions).

In a recent analysis of the potential role of law in promoting private sector investment and growth, Cooter and Schaefer[42] argue that economic growth is achieved through innovation,[43] but funding innovation creates a conundrum. Investors are unlikely to fund innovators without knowing in advance what they are funding, while innovators will resist disclosing their innovations before receiving the funds, as both will be afraid of being exploited by the other ("the double-trust

---

40 See J. Dammann and H. Hansmann, "Globalizing Commercial Litigation" (2008) 94:1 *Cornell Law Review* at 1.

41 See T. Ginsburg, "International Substitutes for Domestic Institutions: Bilateral Investment Treaties and Governance" (2005) 25 *International Review of Law and Economics* 107.

42 R. Cooter and H.-B. Schaefer, *Solomon's Knot: How Law Can End the Poverty of Nations* (Princeton, NJ: Princeton University Press, 2012), chapter 3.

43 For a more detailed elaboration of this argument, known as endogenous theory of growth, see Chapter 2.

dilemma"). To deal with this conundrum, institutional solutions are necessary. For very small businesses, most sources of finance are relational (family and friends). Although not discussed in this book, for many small informal enterprises, micro-credit has now become a substantial source of arms'-length financing in many developing countries, with enforcement of obligations ensured through informal mechanisms, such as group responsibility for individual group members' debts.[44] As businesses grow, and enter the small and medium-sized enterprise (SME) sector, Cooter and Shaefer argue that not only are secure property rights a necessary condition for growth, but also access to arms'-length debt finance, typically in many developing countries through commercial banks. Such finance is unlikely to be forthcoming in the absence of effective formal contract enforcement mechanisms, and the business models adopted by most micro-credit institutions are not well-adapted to the larger and longer-term financing requirements of SMEs.[45] As businesses grow larger still, they will often require access to public finance in the form of equity. Here Cooter and Shaefer argue that legal prerequisites are not only effective protection of private property rights and effective enforcement of contracts, but also corporate law, securities law and bankruptcy law.

However, even this specification of the role of law in promoting private sector investment and growth is probably too parsimonious. In a series of annual "Doing Business" Reports published by the World Bank, beginning in 2004, and now embracing 185 different countries, surveys conducted by the bank attempt to describe and rank countries in terms of the costs, complexity, and delays in performing a range of business functions in particular countries, including starting a business; obtaining construction permits; securing electricity; registering property; obtaining credit; protecting investors; paying taxes; trading across borders; enforcing contracts; resolving insolvency; and hiring and firing workers. In many countries, a wide range of burdensome legal and bureaucratic requirements constrains business formation and expansion.

---

44 The number of very poor families with a microloan has grown more than 18-fold from 7.6 million in 1997 to 137.5 million in 2010 (Microcredit Summit Campaign (2012)) cited in A. Banerjee, E. Duflo, R. Glennerster and C. Kinnan, "The Miracle of Microfinance? Evidence From a Randomized Evaluation" J-PAL, Working Paper (updated April 2013).

45 For a searching evaluation of the strengths and limitations of microfinance as a development tool, see D. Roodman, *Due Diligence: An Impertinent Inquiry into Microfinance* (Washington, DC: Brooking Institution Press, 2012).

Even beyond this fuller specification of a congenial business environment, other surveys point to an additional range of factors that affect business operations in many developing countries, including: macroeconomic instability (for example, hyper-inflation, high interest rates, extreme exchange rate volatility); policy instability often associated with changes in political regimes; lack of access to adequate physical infrastructure; lack of skilled workers; endemic organized, violent, or street crime; and pervasive corruption.[46] One might also add to this list policies that are conducive to export-led growth, such as avoidance of over-valued currencies; the creation of export processing zones; public investment in technological innovations; and policies conducive to FDI.[47] This is by no means a comprehensive list.

In sum, many of these determinants of the vitality of private sectors in developing countries can only tenuously be related, if at all, to the core concepts of the protection of private property rights and the enforcement of contracts. But to expand the instrumental conception of the rule of law to include all of these prerequisites to private sector vitality is largely to drain it of any tractable or discrete content, raising serious questions as to the independent value of instrumental conceptions of the rule of law.

The question about the determinants of a thriving private sector brings to the fore yet another set of concerns: Is the generic nature of a legal system an important determinant of economic growth? A rapidly proliferating body of literature, principally in the financial development field, investigates whether legal origins have influenced the financial development of countries, which in turn is often asserted to be a major determinant of their rates of economic growth.[48] This literature asserts a causal linkage between legal origins and financial development and, indirectly, economic growth. This claim is largely based on cross-country studies that purport to show that common law jurisdictions have, in general, developed more sophisticated financial institutions

---

46 See S. Hafeez, "The Efficacy of Regulation in Developing Countries" DESA Discussion Paper 31 (New York, NY: United Nations, Department of Economic and Social Affairs, January 2003).

47 See J. Lin, *The Quest for Prosperity: How Developing Economies Can Take Off* (Princeton, NJ: Princeton University Press, 2012).

48 R. La Porta, F. Lopez-de-Silanes, A. Shleifer and R.W. Vishny, "Legal Determinants of External Finance" (1997) 52 *The Journal of Finance* 1131–50. R. La Porta, F. Lopez-de-Silanes and A. Shleifer, "The Economic Consequences of Legal Origins" (207) National Bureau of Economic Research Working Paper 13608.

and financial markets than civil law jurisdictions. Amongst civil law jurisdictions, the French civil law system has lagged behind other civil law systems such as the Germanic and Scandinavian systems. These studies find that countries with more sophisticated financial markets generally recognize more extensive rights of shareholders and creditors, and that common law jurisdictions are superior in these respects to civil law jurisdictions – in particular, the French civil law system.

The legal origins literature relies on two inter-related mechanisms through which legal systems influence finance. The political mechanism holds that legal traditions differ in terms of the priority they attach to private property through common law precedents developed by judges, vis-à-vis the rights of the state reflected in statutory codifications that constrain judicial discretion. The adaptability mechanism stresses that legal traditions differ in their formalism and ability to evolve with changing conditions.

This literature has been persuasively critiqued in a recent book by Kenneth Dam, in which he points out that the regulation of shareholders' and creditors' rights in most jurisdictions (civil and common law) is a matter mostly of relatively recent statutes and not of the common law or private law civil codes, so that drawing sharp differences between civil and common law systems on this account is unwarranted.[49] Dam also points out that France generally enjoyed more rapid per capita economic growth than Britain from 1820 to 1998; that recent governance studies by the World Bank find legal origins to have a small to non-existent impact on the quality of the rule of law or economic growth records, especially among poorer countries, and that the much broader governance measures employed by the World Bank provide a much more helpful framework of analysis for an institutional reform agenda.[50]

We should also add that, drawing on recent comparative legal research with which Michael Trebilcock has been associated,[51] the contemporary performance of legal systems in former British colo-

---

49 Dam, *supra* note 1, chapter 2.

50 See D. Kaufmann, "Governance Redux: The Empirical Challenge" in X. Sala-i-Martin (ed.), *The Global Competitiveness Report 2003–2004* (New York, NY: Oxford University Press, 2004).

51 R. Daniels, M. Trebilcock and L. Carson, "The Legacy of Empire: The Common Law Inheritance and Commitments to Legality in Former British Colonies" (2011) 59 *American Journal of Comparative Law* 111.

nies that inherited the common law from their imperial overseers varies markedly from one another, including measures of the rule of law. Thus, variations in performance within legal families are often much greater than variations between legal families. This suggests that many variables other than legal origins alone explain subsequent legal performance – in particular, it is argued, the degree to which the British colonial authorities afforded representation to the indigenous population in legislative bodies, and the extent to which indigenous and British common law courts and animating values were integrated, fostering the development of a localized common law jurisprudence.

5.4   Beyond contract and property rights (ii): environmental protection

Once instrumental conceptions of the rule of law are invoked, it is by no means clear why they should be confined to promoting the vitality of the private sector. Instead these conceptions could reasonably be expanded to include a wide range of other ends of development (for example, wealth redistribution; environmental protection) where legal mechanisms such as taxes, transfers and subsidies might be enlisted in furtherance of these goals.

As discussed in Chapter 2, environmental protection has recently gained prominence as an important goal of development policies. Interestingly, if we were to invoke the rule of law for the protection of the environment, the most widely cited article in the law and economics literature, "The Problem of Social Cost", written by Nobel Laureate Ronald Coase in 1960, brings contracts and property rights back to centre stage.[52] According to Coase, the problem of externalities – in other words, the fact that the benefits that one party may generate by engaging in a particular activity may impose costs on another party – may be efficiently solved through bargaining between the parties involved as long as property rights are well defined, and transaction costs are low.

For example, a manufacturing plant may pollute a river generating negative externalities for families who live downstream and want to

---

52 R.H. Coase, "The Problem of Social Cost" (October 1960) III *The Journal of Law and Economics* 1.

use the water for fishing, bathing, swimming, cooking, and so on. According to Coase, regardless of the initial allocation of the rights (either the plant has a right to pollute, or the home-owners have a right to a clean river), the parties will be able to bargain out of the initial allocation if it is efficient for them to do so. For instance, the plant may pay the households to buy filters, if this is cheaper than changing its production process to eliminate pollution. Alternatively, the households may pay for the plant to stop polluting the river, if this is cheaper than dealing with the costs of pollution themselves. Thus, regardless of the initial allocation of rights, Coase claims that well-defined property rights and low transaction costs would allow parties to adopt the most efficient solution for the problem.

Coase's article has been very influential as a theoretical model, but it has limited practical implications due to the fact that many environmental problems do not entail low transaction costs in their resolution. Reaching agreements can be costly, for instance, if there is a diffuse or dispersed group of people affected by the externalities who are likely to face major collective action problems in organizing a bargaining coalition (and resolving attendant free-rider and hold-out problems). In addition, distributional concerns arise if one class of affected parties lacks the resources to adopt abatement precautions themselves or to pay another party to do so (even if efficiency considerations dictate one or the other of these solutions). Finally, Coase's model also assumes that the parties have perfect information regarding the costs and benefits of pollution, which is rarely the case.

The problem of climate change is perhaps the most dramatic illustration of these obstacles to achieving efficient private ordering solutions to environmental problems.[53] Public ordering solutions to the risks of climate change require formidable institutional capacity both in domestic policy formulation and implementation, and in negotiating and implementing effective international commitments (which have proven elusive to date) to resolve what, by its nature, is a global challenge that yields major collective action problems both within and among countries. Many developing countries are likely to find their institutional capacity severely taxed by these problems.

---

53 See W. Norhause, *The Climate Casino: Risk, Uncertainty and Economics for a Warming World* (New Haven, CT: Yale University Press, 2013). M. Trebilcock, *Dealing with Losers: The Political Economy of Policy Transitions* (New York, NY: Oxford University Press, 2014), chapter 8.

Finally, it is important to note that conceiving of the rule of law as an instrument to advance diverse policy goals, such as promoting private markets, environmental protection or redistribution of wealth, largely elides the rule of law with the ends of development. In doing so, similar to "thick" conceptions of the rule of law reviewed in the previous chapter, such capacious instrumental conceptions of the rule of law deprive it of much independent content.

PART III

POLITICS, IDENTITY AND DEVELOPMENT

6   Political regimes and development

What role can political institutions play in promoting development? Does democracy promote economic development (growth), or vice versa? Do democracies tend to do better than autocracies on other social indicators such as life expectancy, infant and maternal mortality rates, access to basic education and literacy rates?

Most of the rich countries in the world are democracies and most of the poorest countries are not, or have not been for most of their histories.[1] Recently, however, this reality seems to be changing. The last quarter century has seen a wave of democratization.[2] In 2013, 118 countries were classified as electoral democracies, compared to only 39 in 1974.[3] Many of these countries have also adopted new constitutions, entrenched bills of rights and made provisions for constitutional judicial review (the so-called "new constitutionalism").[4] Does this wave of democratization provide a basis for optimism that these countries are now on a much stronger development trajectory?

6.1   Defining democracy

To examine the relationship between democracy and development, it is necessary to clarify what is meant by "democracy". Democracy is often understood as a political regime that protects the freedom of individuals

---

1 For the African experience, see M. Meredith, *The Fate of Africa – A History of Fifty Years of Independence* (New York, NY: Public Affairs, 2005); for the Latin American experience, see M. Reid, *Forgotten Continent* (New Haven, CT: Yale University Press, 2007); and for the Asian experience, see M. Pei, "The Puzzle of East Asian Exceptionalism" (1994) 5:4 *Journal of Democracy* 90.

2 L. Diamond, *The Spirit of Democracy: The Struggle to Build Free Societies Throughout the World* (New York, NY: Henry Holt, 2008).

3 Freedom House, *Freedom in the World 2013: Democratic Breakthroughs in the Balance* (Washington, DC: Freedom House, 2013).

4 K. Davis and M. Trebilcock, "The Relationship Between Law and Development: Optimists Versus Skeptics" (2008) 56 *American Journal of Comparative Law* 895.

and expresses the will of the majority through free and fair elections, protection of minority rights and respect for basic human rights.[5] However, notwithstanding this general conception of democracy, there is no consensus on precisely how to define or measure democracy.

There are "thin" or "thick" definitions of democracy (as with the rule of law).[6] Thin definitions focus on very basic features, while thick definitions graft a wide range of substantive and procedural elements onto the concept. An example of a thin concept is Joseph Schumpeter's definition of democracy, which is a system "for arriving at political decisions in which individuals acquire the power to decide by means of a competitive struggle for the people's vote".[7] In contrast, Larry Diamond's definition of democracy is a thick concept; Diamond suggests that a system is only a democracy if it exhibits the following attributes:

• substantial individual freedom of belief, opinion, discussion, speech, publication, broadcast, assembly, demonstration, petition, and even the Internet;
• freedom of ethnic, religious, racial, and other minority groups (as well as historically excluded majorities) to practice their religion and culture and to participate equally in political and social life;
• the right of all adult citizens to vote and to run for office (if they meet certain minimum age and competency requirements);
• genuine openness and competition in the electoral arena, enabling any group that adheres to constitutional principles to form a party and contest for office;
• legal equality of all citizens under a rule of law, in which the laws are "clear, publicly known, universal, stable, and non-retroactive";
• an independent judiciary to apply the law neutrally and consistently and to protect individual and group rights;
• due process of law and freedom of individuals from torture, terror, and unjustified detention, exile, or interference in their personal lives – by the state or non-state actors;

---

5 Economist Intelligence Unit, "The Economist Intelligence Unit's Index of Democracy 2008" *The Economist* (29 October 2008), available at https://graphics.eiu.com/PDF/Democracy%20Index%20 2008.pdf (accessed 28 April 2014); and M. Coppedge, "Defining and Measuring Democracy" (April 2005) IPSA/APSA Committee on Concepts and Methods Electronic Working Paper Series, available at http://ebookbrowsee.net/1-defining-and-measuring-democracy-michael-coppedge-pdf-d39217726 (accessed 28 April 1014).

6 Coppedge, *supra* note 5, and Diamond, *supra* note 2, at 21.

7 J. Schumpeter, *Capitalism, Socialism, and Democracy* (New York, NY: Harper, 1947, 2nd edn) at 269.

- institutional checks on the power of elected officials, by an independent legislature, court system, and other autonomous agencies;
- real pluralism in sources of information and forms of organizations independent of the state, and thus, a vibrant "civil society"; and
- control over the military and state security apparatus by civilians who are ultimately accountable to the people through elections.[8]

While earlier scholars categorized countries as either democratic or non-democratic, scholars and development agencies have more recently abandoned this dichotomy and replaced it with the idea that there are degrees of democracy (as with degrees of autocracy) and have adopted graduated scales that measure these differences.[9]

6.2   The case for democracy

Adopting the modernization theory of the 1950s and 1960s, where "all good things go together",[10] proponents of democracy make four basic contentions. First, democracy exhibits an enhanced capacity for mediating intergroup and distributional conflicts. Second, democracy generates better information and more reliable feedback on the effects of present or proposed policies when dissent or criticism is an avenue of recourse available to ordinary citizens and is not dependent on extraordinary, self-sacrificial heroes. Third, democracy provides greater protection of property rights than non-democratic or authoritarian regimes. Finally, democratic regimes are more likely than totalitarian or authoritarian regimes to act in the general interest, or at least to reduce predatory tendencies that will often be exhibited by autocratic rulers.[11]

Some theorists focus on the connection between democracy and orthodox measures of development, such as economic growth. However, others claim that there is a positive relationship between democracy and broader definitions of human development that include improved

---

8 Diamond, *supra* note 2, at 22.

9 See, for example, Freedom House ratings of state of democracy in many countries, available at http://www.freedomhouse.org (accessed 28 April 2014).

10 L.L. Frischtak, "Governance Capacity and Economic Reform in Developing Countries" (1994) World Bank Technical Paper No. 254, Washington, DC: The World Bank.

11 M. Olson, *Power and Prosperity: Outgrowing Communist and Capitalist Dictatorships* (New York, NY: Basic Books, 2000).

quality of life and enhanced social welfare, including health and educational status, and individual freedoms. For example, Sen has famously argued that it is not a coincidence that there has never been a famine in a functioning multi-party democracy.[12] He argues that in a democratic country, like India, political activism and the condemnation of governments, in cases of open starvation, have been effective in preventing famine. Similarly, beginning with Immanuel Kant, a number of political scientists and philosophers have claimed that democracies are highly unlikely to go to war with one another.[13] Many of these thinkers claim that democracies generate relatively stronger incentives for political leaders to promote broader goals of development than autocratic regimes because competition among elites for voters' favour should produce a situation in which elites are accountable to the citizenry at large, including a society's most impoverished citizens, and because the institutions of democracy tend to foster a well-developed civil society which can play important roles in providing services to the poor and as advocates and mobilizing agents for less powerful political constituencies.[14]

Other arguments in favour of democracy do not centre on claims about incentive effects. For instance, Rodrik has argued that participatory political institutions are the most reliable "meta-institutions" from a developmental perspective because they are best suited to elicit and aggregate the local knowledge required to develop other norms and institutions. Following thinkers such as John Stuart Mill, Rodrik has also argued that the deliberative processes typically associated with democracy tend to make people more public-spirited and willing to compromise. He argues that democracies exhibit superior qualities to autocracies in managing social conflict and in fashioning social compromises to deal with adjustments to macro-economic shocks.[15]

For his part, Sen argues that democracy is a value in and of itself. While democracy can be a means to better development outcomes, it also has intrinsic value.[16] Sen, in his recent book *The Idea of Justice*, also argues that the relationship between public reason and justice demands some

---

12 A. Sen and J. Dreze, *Hunger and Public Action* (New York, NY: Oxford University Press, 1989).

13 M. Doyle, "Kant, Liberal Legacies and Foreign Affairs, Part I" (1983) 12 *Philosophy and Public Affairs* 323.

14 J. Gerring, S. Thacker and R. Alfaro, "Democracy and Human Development" (2012) 74 *Journal of Politics* 1.

15 D. Rodrik, *One Economics, Many Recipes: Globalization, Institutions and Economic Growth* (Princeton, NJ: Princeton University Press, 2008), chapter 5.

16 A. Sen, *Development as Freedom* (New York, NY: Knopf, 1999) at 148.

form of participatory governance, or "government by discussion", since government decisions must be publicly justified.[17] He rejects the idea that democracy has a uniquely Western heritage and points to many historical examples of "government by discussion" in widely different societies, which often take very different forms from modern Western multi-party democracies.

6.3   The case against democracy

Democracy is not always viewed as being conducive to promoting development. Several arguments are commonly made against democracy and in favour of more authoritarian regimes, at least in the early stages of a country's development. There are at least four major arguments against democracy.[18]

First, democracy is likely to unleash pressures for immediate consumption, which occurs at the cost of savings and investment, and hence of economic growth. Second, authoritarian regimes often insulate the state from particularistic, special-interest group pressures, and are able to take a more comprehensive, single-minded and decisive approach to pro-development policies that may entail short-run pain in order to secure long-term gain. Third, democracy may threaten the security of private property rights in cases where median voters (given a typically skewed income distribution) and special interests strongly favour redistributive policies. Finally, democracies may exacerbate ethnic and other intergroup conflicts if parties organize themselves along ethnic, religious or regional lines and electoral competition yields dominant parties or political bodies that practice "winner-takes-all" politics (as we discuss more fully in the next chapter). On this view, citizens of countries in the early stages of economic development face "a cruel choice" between democracy and development. Proponents of the view "economic development first, democracy later" often point to the post-war economic successes of East Asian autocracies, including most recently China, as evidence that democracy need not precede development.

---

17 A. Sen, *The Idea of Justice* (Cambridge, MA: Harvard University Press, 2009), chapters 15 and 16.

18 M. Halperin, J. Siegle and M. Weinstein, *The Democracy Advantage: How Democracies Promote Prosperity and Peace* (New York, NY: Routledge, 2010, rev. edn), chapter 1.

6.4   The empirical evidence

The empirical evidence concerning the relationship between democracy and development is as contentious as the theorizing. Eighteen studies, containing 21 observations about the relationship between democracy and growth, contain eight observations favouring democracy, eight favouring authoritarianism, and five finding no difference.[19] A sample of about 100 countries from 1960 to 1985 shows that the effects of democracy on *subsequent* economic growth appear to be minimal.[20] A subsequent statistical study of 137 countries between 1950 and 1990 finds that the net effect of democracy or autocracy on economic growth is zero.[21] However, a more recent study for the period between 1960 and 2001 finds that democracies (at least full liberal democracies) generally outperform autocracies in terms of economic growth by a significant margin, as well as experiencing less economic volatility and far fewer "economic disasters".[22]

Some studies also find that democracies perform better on other social indicators such as literacy rates, life expectancy rates and infant mortality rates.[23] However, these findings have been recently challenged as these effects (using infant mortality rates as a proxy) are only pronounced if democracy becomes institutionalized over many decades.[24] Such effects are insignificant in the short term (for example, in the immediate aftermath of a change in political regimes). Even with long-established democracies, there are some important anomalies: India, a vibrant democracy since independence in 1947, has appalling basic health and education indicators today, compared to many other countries in the region (including China).[25]

Proponents of democracy also argue that the economic success of East Asian autocracies has little to do with the political regime but

---

19 A. Przeworski and F. Limongi, "Political Regimes and Economic Growth" (1993) 7 *Journal of Economic Perspectives* 51.

20 J.F. Helliwell, "Empirical Linkages Between Democracy and Economic Growth" (1994) 24 *British Journal of Political Science* 225.

21 A. Przeworski, M. Alvarez, J.A. Cheibub and F. Limongi, *Democracy and Development: Political Institutions and Well-Being in the World 1950 – 1990* (New York, NY: Cambridge University Press, 2000).

22 Halperin et. al., *supra* note 18.

23 *Ibid.*, chapter 2.

24 Gerring, Thacker and Alfaro, *supra* note 14.

25 See J. Dreze and A. Sen, *An Uncertain Glory: India and Its Contradictions* (Princeton, NJ: Princeton University Press, 2013).

rather is related to the adoption of outward-oriented growth policies and the insulation of the bureaucracy from day-to-day political pressures. In addition, economies such as Burma, Cambodia and Laos have performed poorly under authoritarian regimes. Furthermore, the tendency in the region is toward the evolution of authoritarian-pluralist regimes with increasingly democratic features (for example, Japan, Taiwan, South Korea and Singapore), although China does not seem to clearly fit this pattern.[26]

Based on this mixed body of evidence, some commentators conclude that democracy may not be conducive to the emergence of capitalism and its early growth, but that it is the regime most likely to develop and be sustainable once market economies reach a certain level of economic development. Other commentators contest the proposition that authoritarian governments have been better than democratic governments, at least in recent years, at pursuing major economic reforms.[27] As *The Economist* points out, if authoritarian governments eventually make countries rich, especially in the early stages of economic development, Africa would be or should soon become an economic colossus. Instead, some of the more pessimistic prognoses for the future of many countries in Africa depict a mafia-like world of social and political disintegration characterized by war, tribute, predation and criminalization of economic activity.[28]

Focusing on the poorest billion people in the world, living in 60 countries, Collier finds that democracy is actually damaging to the reform process if it means little more than elections.[29] At very low levels of per capita income, moving from despotism to a nominally democratic regime may actually increase political violence and do nothing to enhance accountability or legitimacy. In the absence of effective checks and balances, despots will engage in various forms of intimidation, repression and bribery of voters, fraud and other electoral irregularities, and then claim the façade of democracy to further entrench themselves in power, and mute international criticism or opposition.

---

26 Pei, *supra* note 1.

27 For a review of the literature, see Halperin et al., *supra* note 18, at chapter 1.

28 "Why Voting is Good for You" *The Economist* 332:7878 (27 August 1994), 15–17.

29 P. Collier, *Wars, Guns, and Votes: Democracy in Dangerous Places* (New York, NY: HarperCollins, 2009) at 45.

6.5   Challenges to reforming political institutions

Despite the euphoria in many development circles over the recent wave of democratization, Carothers offers a sobering assessment: of the nearly 100 countries considered as being in transition to democracy, fewer than 20 are clearly on their way to becoming successful, well-functioning democracies.[30] The 1999 Pakistani coup initiated the reversal of the wave of democratization from its peak, and there has been democratic recession ever since.[31] Diamond argues that this reversal was symptomatic of "deep-seated problems of governance with which many other new and fragile democracies were also struggling".[32] The troubled attempts to install democratic political regimes in Iraq, Afghanistan, Egypt and Libya are some of the more prominent contemporary examples of the challenging task of democratic reform. In a 2013 report, Freedom House found that civil liberties and political rights had been declining for seven consecutive years, while the number of democracies in the world increased by three in 2012.[33]

Carothers argues that five questionable assumptions define the conventional transition paradigm. First, any country moving away from dictatorial rule can be considered to be a country in transition toward democracy. Second, democratization tends to unfold in a set pattern of stages: the opening, the breakthrough and the consolidation. Third, elections are of determinative importance. Fourth, the underlying conditions in transitional countries – their economic level, political history, institutional legacies, ethnic make-up, socio-cultural traditions or other "structural" features – will not be major factors in either the onset or the outcome of the transition process. Fifth, democratic transitions making up the recent wave of democratization are being built on coherent, functioning states.

Contrary to these assumptions, Carothers argues that many countries in transition from authoritarianism to democracy reflect two persistent syndromes: "feckless pluralism" and "dominant power politics". "Feckless pluralism" refers to situations in which small, deeply

---

30 T. Carothers, "The End of the Transition Paradigm" (2002) 13:1 *Journal of Democracy* 5, at 5. See also T. Carothers, *Aiding Democracy Abroad* (Carnegie Endowment for International Peace, 1999).

31 Diamond, *supra* note 2, at chapter 4.

32 *Ibid.*, at 60.

33 Freedom House, *supra* note 3.

entrenched political elites periodically alternate power and enrich themselves at the expense of the general population. "Dominant power politics" refers to situations where one party, despite periodic elections, dominates government over long periods of time and often governs with little heed for the general interests of the population.

Some scholars caution that the deliberation, cooperation and compromise ideally associated with democracy must occur from the bottom- up, through thick prior networks of associational activity – civil society or "social capital" – that have already cultivated these norms. Only then can they be scaled up to regional or national democratic governments.[34] However, other scholars point out that many forms of social capital are parochial, exclusionary, discriminatory or repressive, such as the social capital that resided within the Klu Klux Klan and the Mafia. These scholars argue that desirable forms of social capital cultivate a wider radius of trust and that these forms of social capital evolve organically and are not readily constructible by deliberate public policies.[35]

6.6   Conclusion

In designing reforms of political institutions, it is important to be sensitive to the specific characteristics of each country. Democratic political regimes even in the developed world vary vastly in their formal institutional features: some are presidential, others parliamentary; some are unicameral, some bicameral; some are unitary states, others federal states; some have tight political party structures, while others have much looser structures; some employ majority or first-past-the-post voting, some a form of proportional representation, while others have adopted an entrenched bill of rights and constitutional judicial review as constraints on legislative and executive action, and so on.[36] The political arrangements that are feasible in a country will, to an important extent, be a function of each country's history, culture and institutional legacies. As with the rule of law and other institutional reforms, path

---

34 See, for example, R. Putnam, *Making Democracy Work: Civic Traditions in Modern Italy* (Princeton, NJ: Princeton University Press, 1994); P.B. Evans, "Government Action, Social Capital and Development: Reviewing the Evidence on Synergy" (1996) 24 *World Development* 1119.

35 F. Fukuyama, "Social Capital, Civil Society, and Development" (2001) 22 *Third World Quarterly* 7.

36 F. Fukuyama, "Development and the Limits of Institutional Design" in *Political Institutions and Development: Failed Expectations and Renewed Hopes* (Global Development Network, 2007).

dependence may significantly constrain the reform options that are feasible for a country's political regime.

Perhaps more disconcerting for proponents of democracy on intrinsic grounds, such as Amartya Sen, are claims that some cultures, especially those that emphasize social embeddedness and hierarchy, are inherently less hospitable to democracy and the individual freedoms that it presupposes.[37] For example, it is sometimes claimed that the Arab/Islamic world, with its deference to religious authority and theocratic leadership, is not congenial to democracy. Yet Islamic (albeit not Arabic) countries, such as Turkey, Malaysia and Indonesia, defy this claim.[38] It is also often claimed that in many African societies politics is inherently patrimonial where "Big Men" emerge as political leaders by cultivating patronage networks based on kinship ties ("all politics are tribal").[39] Yet again an increasing number of African countries defy this generalization. It is often claimed that "Asian values" that reflect deference to established authorities and to family and communal traditions and obligations are inhospitable to conceptions of individual freedom and equality. However, a number of Asian countries that are vibrant democracies defy this generalization.[40] It is also often claimed that Latin American cultures reflect an historical predilection for "strong men" (*caudillo*) political regimes in the tradition of Simon Bolivar. Yet the wave of democracy that has swept through Latin America over the past three decades challenges this generalization.[41]

Thus, "culture" does not seem to be political destiny, although it is difficult to gainsay the likelihood that cultural values and traditions will play some role in shaping political transition processes and the ultimate political arrangements that evolve. External agencies seeking to influence these transitions cannot ignore the profoundly political, particularistic and non-technocratic nature of the reform enterprise.[42]

---

37 See A. Licht, C. Goldschmidt and S. Schwartz, "Culture Rules: The Foundations of the Rule of Law and Other Norms of Governance" (2007) 35 *Journal of Comparative Economics* 659.

38 See M. Trebilcock, "Between Institutions and Culture: The UNDPS Arab Human Development Reports 2002–2005" (209) *Middle East Law and Governance* 210.

39 See P. Chabal and J.-P. Doloz, *Africa Works: Disorder as Political Instrument* (International African Institute and Indiana University Press, 1999); and Meredith, *supra* note 1.

40 See Pei, *supra* note 1.

41 See Reid, *supra* note 1.

42 T. Carothers and D. de Gramont, *Development Aid Confronts Politics: The Almost Revolution* (Washington, DC: Carnegie Foundation for International Peace, 2013).

7 Ethnic conflict and development

Ethnic conflicts represent the majority of armed conflicts around the world; in 2009, of 30 ongoing conflicts, 19 were ethnic in nature.[1] These conflicts are largely concentrated in developing countries. They occur when there is intense rivalry, disputes or clashes of interests between groups that are organized along racial, religious, linguistic or communal lines. Ethnic conflict includes (but is not limited to) political competition between ethnically based political actors, various forms of discrimination, and violence between ethnic groups. Examples include Israel's conflicts with Hamas and Hezbollah; the Kabul Government in Afghanistan's conflict with al-Qaeda and the Taliban and India's conflict with Kashmiri militants. Ethnic conflict is also listed as one of the contributing causes for conflict in the DRC; Nigeria, Somalia, Sudan and Syria.[2]

These conflicts not only subvert peace and stability, resulting in enormous human suffering and losses, but also destroy vital infrastructure and impose significant economic costs. As a consequence, ethnic conflict threatens human security and well-being, undermines economic growth and detrimentally affects many other development indicators. As Collier puts it, ethnic conflict is "development in reverse".[3] Thus, the question of whether and how these conflicts can be avoided or mitigated is extremely important from a development perspective.

---

1 Center for Systemic Peace, "Major Episodes of Political Violence 1946–2008" (May 2009), available at http://www.systemicpeace.org/warlist.htm (accessed 28 April 2014).

2 "World at War, Ongoing Significant Conflicts as of January 2010" (January/February/March 2010) XXXIX:1 *The Defense Monitor* at 3–4.

3 P. Collier, *The Bottom Billion: Why the Poorest Countries are Failing and What Can Be Done About It* (Oxford: Oxford University Press, 2007) at 27.

7.1   Why do people organize along ethnic lines?

Determining whether and how ethnic conflict can be resolved or managed, and assessing the potential role of institutions in responding to such conflict requires an understanding of the root causes of ethnic conflict. This is no easy task, however. Beyond a general agreement that ethnic conflict has devastating consequences, virtually every aspect of ethnic conflict is contested in the academic literature. Scholars from fields as diverse as anthropology, history, economics, law, political science, psychology and sociology have weighed in on matters ranging from the nature of ethnicity and ethnic affiliation, to ethnic mobilization, the sources of ethnic conflict, and to the role of institutions and other social structures in triggering or mitigating ethnic conflict.

Despite the lack of consensus in the literature on definitions, methodologies, causalities or conclusions, drawing on the work of Horowitz,[4] Bardhan divides the field as follows:

> existing theories of ethnic conflict are often characterized by two sharply distinguished views of ethnicity – the "hard view", which sees ethnicity as a primordial condition that evokes intense passions and takes ethnic groups as exogenously defined, and the "soft" view, which takes a more strategic constructivist approach where ethnicity is subject to interests and calculations and group boundaries are somewhat malleable.[5]

For those who take the strategic constructivist approach to ethnicity, with its emphasis on interests and calculations, the salience of ethnic affiliation is a function of its instrumentality. Ethnicity emerges in response to societal needs and/or the interests of certain groups, often as a mechanism to solve collective action problems. Collier, for example, suggests that in rural societies where people live at subsistence levels, strong ethnic affiliations act as a form of insurance; in the case of a catastrophe or personal difficulties, the ethnic group provides for the needs of its members.[6] In this context, ethnic affiliations generate a strong and lasting expectation of loyalty, which in turn reduces the problem of free-riding; one cannot enjoy the benefits of being a

---

4   D.L. Horowitz, *Ethnic Groups in Conflict* (Berkeley and Los Angeles, CA: University of California Press, 2000, 2nd edn).

5   P. Bardhan, *Scarcity, Conflicts, and Cooperation: Essays in the Political and Institutional Economics of Development* (Cambridge, MA: MIT Press, 2005) at 169–70.

6   P. Collier, *Wars, Guns, and Votes: Democracy in Dangerous Places* (New York, NY: HarperCollins, 2009) at 53.

member of an ethnic group during difficult times but then abandon the group as one's personal fortunes improve.

While ethnic affiliation is a useful mechanism for organizing collective action, many of the goods and utilities provided by the ethnic group can in principle be delivered by a functioning state.[7] The problem is that in countries where there are no well-functioning states, the importance of ethnic groups is heightened. For instance, the bonds of ethnic affiliation ("ethnic capital") "ensures to most African people the provision of many services that a modern state has taken over in rich countries, including security, social insurance, education, norms of behaviour, contract enforcement, justice and so on".[8] There are therefore strong incentives to organize most facets of life along ethnic lines in countries with weak state structures.

Scholars point to two types of socio-economic factors that make ethnicity the preferred vehicle for pursuing social, political and economic opportunities: historical and emergent factors. Historical factors include the cultural division of labour and a split labour market, while emergent factors include labour migration and immigration. The coincidence of ethnic divisions with economic divisions brings ethnicity to the fore as an efficient means of collective organization in the pursuit of jobs and other opportunities. Political opportunities also serve as a basis for ethnic mobilization. The factors that act as an incentive to mobilize along lines of ethnic affiliation include: (1) common language and culture, and the existence of ethnic organizational structures that can allow contenders for political office to minimize transaction costs; (2) possession of large deposits of exploitable natural resources (for example, petroleum, natural gas, diamonds and other minerals, and so on.) by an ethno- regional group; and (3) historical domination of some groups by others.[9]

7.2   Why do ethnic groups become rivals?

While there are many reasons why groups may decide to organize along ethnic lines, this does not necessarily mean that there will be conflict

---

7 *Ibid.*, at 56.

8 J.-P. Azam, "The Redistributive State and Conflicts in Africa" (2001) 38 *Journal of Peace Research* 429, at 430.

9 J.M. Mbaku, P.O. Agbese and M.S. Kimenyi (eds), *Ethnicity and Governance in the Third World* (Aldershot: Ashgate, 2001) at 63–5.

among these groups. The factors that lead to rivalry and tension – which often precede periods of conflict – are different from those that lead groups to organize according to ethnic lines. According to the literature, there is a set of three broad inter-related factors that influence the intensity of ethnic rivalry and tension in the polity: (1) contact and ethnic difference; (2) the degree of diversity; and (3) institutional structures.

7.2.1   Contact and ethnic difference

When groups that were formerly isolated from each other come into contact (as a result of processes such as modernization, urbanization, centralized education and economic specialization), they must find a means of effectively communicating and coordinating their actions. Major decisions also have to be made about how ethnic groups will order their coexistence within the polity. Coexistence and coordinated action ultimately require some degree of homogenization of the ethnic groups' different norms, institutions, social structures, language and cultural practices. The groups that are unable to impose their language, social structures and institutions on the others must bear the transaction costs associated with learning a new language and set of institutional practices. Moreover, conceding/assimilating groups are less likely to be able to dominate social, political and economic institutions and structures of the shared polity and, consequently, have restricted access to the scarce resources available through these institutions. The process of homogenization thus engenders conflict because each group has strong incentives to resist making concessions in the determination of the common language, norms and institutions.

7.2.2   Degree of diversity

Ethnic diversity per se does not increase the risk of conflict. In a truly diverse society, where there is a high degree of ethnic fragmentation, no ethnic group is large enough to secure a monopoly on power. Cross-ethnic alliances are necessary to secure access to political power and influence. In this context, ethnic elites have strong incentives to adopt moderate, non-ethnic positions and strategies. By contrast, in polarized polities, elections tend to divide the polity along ethnic lines, having a negative impact on electoral competition.[10] Collier suggests

---

10 W. Cho, "Ethnic Fractionalization, Electoral Institutions, and Africans' Political Attitudes" (January 2007) Afrobarometer Working Paper No. 66, available at http://www.afrobarometer.

that electoral competition in polarized societies can take political agendas to extremes since a candidate will draw larger support the more he or she promises to favour one group over another. Elites attempt to solidify support from their respective ethnic groups by "rallying the faithful" through the use of ethno-centric rhetoric. In this regard, elites from the same ethnic group often attempt to "outbid" each other for the support of their group by adopting increasingly radical platforms to demonstrate that they are the best protector of the group's interests. Once elected, the ethnic elites in power must safeguard their own group's interests by providing access to influence and the scarce resources of the state while excluding elites from other ethnic groups from the political process. Elites must avoid the perception that they have made concessions to other ethnic groups or adopted moderate or conciliatory policies. This turns competition for political power into a zero-sum competition for resources and public goods.[11] Moreover, this competition is framed in terms of ethnic identity. In sum, elites in fragmented societies have incentives to be bridge-builders between ethnic groups while elites in polarized societies have incentives to adopt ethno-centric and divisive platforms that increase the risk of conflict between ethnic groups.

7.2.3   Institutional structures

The negative impact that higher degrees of ethnic polarization have on the political system may be influenced by the political structures that govern ethnically diverse societies. Rational choice theorists and public choice theorists argue that inter-ethnic violence arises or intensifies in response to a particular set of incentive structures. On this view, some socio-economic and political structures are more likely to give rise to tension than others because of the incentive structures they create. Institutions that establish or perpetuate the domination of one group over another, or provide a group with a monopoly over wealth and/or power within a certain polity, tend to generate more conflict than institutions that force ethnic groups to share power.[12] For instance, incentives to organize electoral competition along ethnic lines are higher in

---

org/publications/working-papers/item/113-ethnic-fractionalization-electoral-institutions-and-africans-political-attitudes (accessed 28 April 2014).

11 Collier, *supra* note 3, at 44–6.

12 D. Horowitz, "Structure and Strategy in Ethnic Conflict: A Few Steps Toward Synthesis" in B. Pleskovic and J.E. Stiglitz (eds), *Annual World Bank Conference on Development Economics 1998* (Washington, DC: World Bank, 1999) 345.

democratic regimes that permit ethnically-based party systems and have electoral rules such as winner-takes-all.[13]

Thus, the risk of heightened ethnic tension that is associated with ethnic polarization and dominance may be managed by institutional arrangements (for example, electoral rules, constitutional provisions and property rights) that provide fair, predictable and efficient rules to govern the competition for scarce political and economic resources. In addition to political institutions, some socio-economic structures contribute to inter-ethnic rivalry. Socio-economic structures that either establish the dominance of one ethnic group over another (ethno-classes) or establish a monopoly of one ethnic group over limited resources to the detriment of others (middlemen minorities) can contribute to an increase in ethnic tension.[14]

7.3   What can trigger and sustain ethnic conflict?

Why does violent conflict erupt between communities that have coexisted relatively peacefully for significant periods of time despite historical animosities? While institutional arrangements may increase tension and aggravate rivalries in ethnically diverse societies, they will not necessarily trigger conflict. In many cases, there are factors that suddenly emerge, creating a shock to the social structure and triggering violent conflict. Many of these factors are not the sole cause of conflict, but when combined with political, social and economic structures that have generated tensions and rivalry for years, they may be the tipping point that triggers violence. In sum, these factors help to explain what triggers and sustains violent conflicts.

Scholars who draw on rational choice theory argue that violence may be used strategically as a modality of political action. Breakdowns in existing institutional arrangements create uncertainty and undermine the security of ethnic groups; in these circumstances, ethnic groups may resort to violence as a pre-emptive measure to safeguard their vital interests. Here, "violence can be analyzed in terms of cost–benefit analysis, theories of bargaining, game theory and rational choice".[15]

---

13 Bardhan, *supra* note 5, at 183–4.

14 *Ibid.* at 171–6.

15 B. Mehta, "Ethnicity, Nationalism and Violence in South Asia" (1998) 71 *Pacific Affairs* 377.

Institutions that place some ethnic groups at a competitive disadvantage in the pursuit of political and economic resources are also likely to trigger violence.[16] Proponents of public choice theory (a sub-set of rational choice theory) argue that institutional structures that do not create fair, stable and efficient rules to govern competition by ethnic groups for political and economic power generate incentives to resort to violence.[17] Alternatively, moments of institutional instability may create a window of opportunity for a bad dynamic to be set in motion, being reinforced and institutionalized over time. The cumulative effects of this dynamic may lead to conflict down the road, as exemplified by some of the former communist countries such as Kosovo and Macedonia.[18]

Economic decline and stagnation can also intensify inter-ethnic competition. During such periods, groups tend to compete more aggressively for a shrinking pool of resources.[19] In countries where ethnic divisions coincide with class divisions, adverse consequences of international economic policies can exacerbate pre-existing ethnic tensions.[20] As with international economic policies, the consequences of economic decline can be unevenly distributed, impacting on some groups more than others. Uneven distributive effects may occur if certain sectors of the economy are more affected than others, or if a specific geographic area where one group is concentrated is especially affected by the downturn. In either case, groups that have borne the brunt of economic decline will press for policies to mitigate these effects and to redistribute resources. The risks of conflict can become especially high if the ethnic group benefiting from existing arrangements strongly resists redistributive policies. Institutional arrangements thus may play an important role in mediating the competing interests of ethnic groups during periods of economic upheaval.

---

16 Mbaku et al., *supra* note 9, at 75.

17 *Ibid.*, at 77–9.

18 M. Koinova, *Ethnonationalist Conflict in Postcommunist States: Varieties of Governance in Bulgaria, Macedonia, and Kosovo* (Philadelphia PA: University of Pennsylvania Press, 2013).

19 M.Z. Bookman, *Ethnic Groups in Motion: Economic Competition and Migration in Multi-Ethnic States* (Portland, OR: Frank Cass, 2002) at 31.

20 A. Chua, "Markets, Democracy, and Ethnicity: Toward A New Paradigm for Law and Development" (1998)108 *Yale Law Journal* 1.

7.4   Institutional solutions to prevent ethnic conflict

Thus far, we have examined the factors that motivate people to affiliate along ethnic lines, the circumstances that can increase tension and rivalry among existing ethnic groups, and the proximate causes that can actually trigger conflict in peaceful societies. In the discussion of all these issues, we suggested that institutions may play an important role in managing the dynamics of inter-ethnic relations. We turn now to a discussion of how specific institutional arrangements may reduce the risk of conflict.

The rules that govern the political system are important institutional factors that influence a country's political dynamics through the incentives they generate. These rules include, for example, the design of democratic regimes and power-sharing mechanisms, such as federalism and concurrent majorities. Depending on their design, democratic governance structures may be more suitable political regimes for ethnically diverse societies than authoritarian regimes.[21] Although diversity makes democratic politics more challenging, according to some authors ethnic diversity "is likely to make dictatorship lethal".[22] However, not all democratic regimes will be effective in mitigating conflict. Electoral systems, for instance, may help mitigate tensions or may polarize societies even further, depending on their design.[23] The Westminster "first-past-the-post" (or "winner-takes-all") system tends to heighten tension while proportional representation is generally regarded as having a moderating effect on ethnic tension.[24]

Regarding the design of democratic systems, some authors support the idea that constraints on political elites, such as those imposed by systems of checks and balances, are one of the most important features of a democratic system in avoiding rent-seeking behaviour, especially when large amounts of natural resources are discovered.[25] The

---

21 P. Collier, "The Political Economy of Ethnicity", (1998) paper prepared for the Annual World Bank Conference on Development Economics, Washington, DC, 20–1 April 1998.

22 Collier, *supra* note 6, at 63–6.

23 J. McGarry and B. O'Leary, "The Political Regulation of National and Ethnic Conflict" (1994) 47 *Parliamentary Affairs* 94, at 106.

24 Bardhan, *supra* note 5 at 183.

25 D. Acemoğlu, S. Johnson and J. Robinson, "An African Success Story: Botswana" in D. Rodrik (ed.), *In Search of Prosperity: Analytic Narratives on Economic Growth* (Princeton, NJ: Princeton University Press, 2003).

challenge, then, is to create effective mechanisms for the separation of powers. One of the major obstacles to this endeavour is institutional interconnections. Creating an effective system of checks and balances and separation of powers will largely depend on:

1. electoral rules that guarantee proportional representation or otherwise ensure a fair distribution of seats in the legislature among the different ethnic groups;
2. a party system that is representative of the diverse composition of the nation, such as one that features a power-sharing executive; and
3. the rules of standing for judicial review, which should grant ethnic minorities access to the constitutional or highest appellate court to challenge unconstitutional measures.

In other words, institutional interdependencies will affect whether separation of powers mechanisms will reduce the risk of conflict and possibly mitigate negative effects of ethnic diversity. Each of these features also has independent value as a means of creating incentives for cooperation and for increasing the security of ethnic groups in the polity.

An interesting development in the study of the design of democratic systems to manage conflicts is consociational democracy.[26] The concept was pioneered by Lijphart, who argued that it is not impossible to achieve and maintain a stable democratic government in a plural society if the appropriate institutional conditions exist. Lijphart proposed that elite cooperation could counteract the centrifugal tendencies inherent in a plural society. He identifies four essential features of a consociational democracy, each of which plays a role in promoting cooperative attitudes and behaviour among the elite:

1. a grand coalition government which incorporates all of the political parties representing the main segments within the society;
2. a policy of proportionality with respect to political representation, employment, and expenditures in the public sector;
3. norms of self-governance and community autonomy over matters which are of the greatest concern to groups; and
4. constitutional vetoes for minorities.

---

26 A. Lijphart, "Consociational Democracy" (1969) 21 *World Politics* 207, at 216; and A. Lijphart, *Democracy in Plural Societies* (New Haven, CT: Yale University Press, 1977).

Lijphart originally presented consociational democracy as an empirical model, drawing on the experiences of a few deeply divided European democracies.[27] However, his arguments have acquired a more normative tone over time, and consociational engineering (which incorporates the features described above in the design of political institutions) is today regarded by many as a way to achieve stable democracy in highly factionalized societies.[28]

Federalism is a prominent example of a power-sharing mechanism that has been adopted in a wide range of fragmented societies. The strength of federalism as a means of mitigating conflict, however, is highly contested in the academic literature.[29] Federalism seems to have potential as an institutional arrangement for governance structures in countries that feature geographically concentrated ethnic communities within a country. A number of authors have claimed that decentralization and federalism are a potential antidote to identity-based tensions in these cases, because they devolve power to sub-national governments, granting higher levels of political, economic and social autonomy to ethnic groups concentrated in certain geographic areas.[30] But this claim has been disputed, given that decentralization and federalism also have the potential to reinforce ethnic identities and to increase ethnic tensions.[31] Devolving power to certain regions may ultimately lead to demands for more power, culminating in claims for secession.[32] Proponents of federalism respond to this argument by pointing out that ethnic communities

---

27 A. Lijphart, "Typologies of Democratic Systems" (1968) 1 *Comparative Political Studies* 3.

28 R. Premdas, "Ethno-racial Divisions and Governance: The Problem of Institutional Reform and Adaptation" Research Project on Racism and Public Policy, United Nations Research Institute for Social Development (2001).

29 S. Choudhry and N. Hume, "Federalism, Secession and Devolution: From Classical to Post-Conflict Federalism" in T. Ginsburg and R. Dixon (eds), *Research Handbook on Comparative Constitutional Law* (Cheltenham, UK and Northampton, MA, USA: Edward Elgar, 2010).

30 See for example, J. McGarry, "Federal Political Systems and the Accommodation of National Minorities" in A.L. Griffiths (ed.), *Handbook of Federal Countries, 2002* (Montreal: McGill-Queen's University Press, 2002); A. Lijphart, R. Rogowski and R.K. Weaver, "Separation of Power and Cleavage Management" in R.K. Weaver and B.A. Rockman (eds), *Do Institutions Matter? Government Capabilities in the United States and Abroad* (Washington, DC: Brookings Institution Press, 1993) 302–44; and C. Hartzell and M. Hoodie, "Institutionalizing Peace: Power Sharing and Post-civil War Conflict Management" (2003) 47 *American Journal of Political Science* 318.

31 E.M. Penn, "Citizenship versus Ethnicity: The Role of Institutions in Shaping Identity Choice" (2008) 70 *Journal of Politics* 956 and W. Kymlicka, "Is Federalism a Viable Alternative to Secessionism?" in P.B. Lehning (ed.), *Theories of Secession* (New York, NY: Routledge Press, 1998).

32 E. Nordlinger, *Conflict Regulation in Divided Societies*, Occasional Paper No. 29 (Cambridge, MA: Harvard University Center for International Affairs, 1972) at 32.

are already escalating their claims for autonomy. Federalism responds to these claims by devolving a degree of power to these communities, thereby moderating demands for full secession.

Federalism can also apply to non-geographically specific matters: decision-making power over certain issues (for example, culture and social services) can be devolved to ethnic groups regardless of where the members of the group live. This unique federalist system was implemented in Belgium in the 1970s.[33] Another power-sharing mechanism is concurrent majorities, also called "mutual vetoes". This mechanism grants veto powers on certain issues to minority groups that constitute a significant portion of the population. As a consequence, even if one ethnic group dominates one branch of government (or more than one), other ethnic groups have a means of exerting influence over the development and implementation of policies and of securing their interests.

Practically speaking, the mutual veto creates incentives for moderation and accommodation since decisions that are not acceptable to other major ethnic groups risk being vetoed.[34] The list of protected items can range from a pre-defined set of basic issues (for example, basic individual rights specified in the constitution) to broader economic and political reforms. There are also different forms of veto – for example, a delaying veto, a direct veto and an indirect veto.[35] The first allows groups to delay a decision by using parliamentary procedures or by referring it to the constitutional court; the second is exemplified by the principle of double majority, where the majority of each group need to approve a provision for it to pass ("community majority law"); the third allows groups to stop political action indirectly, as exemplified by presidential vetoes. In all these cases, mutual vetoes reduce the risk of subjugation and dominance.[36] Their efficacy, however, depends on the government's ability to secure a credible commitment, providing certainty that it will adhere to these legal (often constitutional) arrangements.[37] Such commitment largely depends on

---

33 A. Lecours, "Belgium" in Griffiths, *supra* note 30, at 58.

34 Nordlinger, *supra* note 32, at 24–5.

35 U. Schneckener, "Models of Ethnic Conflict Regulation: The Politics of Recognition" in U. Schneckener and S. Wolff (eds), *Managing and Settling Ethnic Conflicts: Perspectives on Successes and Failure in Europe, Africa and Asia* (New York, NY: Palgrave Macmillan, 2004) at 28–9.

36 Bardhan, *supra* note 5 at 191.

37 B.F. Walter, "Bargaining Failures and Civil War" (2009) 12 *Annual Review of Political Science* 243, at 251.

strong political and legal institutions, especially an independent and impartial judiciary.[38]

In sum, institutions can play an important role in managing ethnic tension and rivalry. Some aspects of the constitution-making process by which these institutions are selected and designed in post-conflict low-trust societies – such as inclusiveness and transparency – are likely to influence the final outcomes and legitimacy of the process.[39] As stated at the outset of this chapter, ethnic conflicts are complex phenomena, and it is unlikely that institutional design alone can avoid the problem; often institutional reforms that were expected to reduce the risk of conflict have not proved effective. However, this should not preclude a potentially fruitful debate about which institutions in particular contexts may mitigate ethnic conflict and its potentially devastating consequences for a country's development prospects.

7.5   Non-institutional solutions to prevent ethnic conflict

In his book *Identity and Violence*, Sen suggests that inter-ethnic tensions only exist because people often place excessive emphasis on one-dimensional notions of identity, be it ethnicity or nationality.[40] The objective reality, however, is that each person's identity is multi-faceted rather than one-dimensional. Moreover, each person has the capacity and the freedom to determine which group loyalties and affiliations to prioritize.[41] On this view, the reduction of a person's identity to the single dimension of ethnicity or nationality should be avoided as it has the potential to generate conflict. In line with this, Sen's proposals for institutional reforms both at the national and international levels are not related to notions of identity, but instead address exclusion from the global economy and aim at reducing levels of inequality between poor and rich countries. They deal with grievances generated by exclusion and inequality that might contribute to a rise in conflict.

---

38 S. Choudhry, "After the Rights Revolution: Bill of Rights in the Post Conflict State" (2010) 6 *Annual Review of Political Science* 301 at 309.

39 T. Ginsburg, Z. Elkins and J. Blount, "Does the Process of Constitution-Making Matter?" (2009) 5 *Annual Review of Law and Social Science* 201.

40 A. Sen, *Identity and Violence: The Illusion of Destiny* (New York, NY: W.W. Norton, 2006).

41 *Ibid.*, at 4–5. See also K.A. Appiah, *Cosmopolitanism: Ethics in a World of Strangers* (New York, NY: W.W. Norton, 2006).

Other authors appear to advocate the deliberate choice of policies that can help to downplay ethnicity by superimposing a constructed national identity or assimilating ethnic groups into a shared, civic identity.[42] Collier cites Tanzania and Indonesia as successful examples in this regard: by using, creating or imposing a national language, Tanzanian President Julius Nyerere and Indonesian President Suharto managed to mitigate ethnic divisions. In Tanzania, language policy was coupled with the creation of symbols of national identity, political reforms and education policies to reshape cultural identity. For example, Nyerere eschewed a multi-party system by creating village committees and prohibiting campaigns based on ethnic platforms.[43] Collier argues that, as both ethnic and national identities are constructed, these policies could be successfully replicated in other countries. Other authors, however, are more cautious about the prospects of transferability.[44] Moreover, Kymlicka argues that such policies may be sources of conflict in and of themselves since the process of forming a national or civic identity requires at least one group to assimilate to the characteristics of whatever is deemed to be the "national" or "civic" identity.[45]

Another set of proposals is to use the constitution to construct a country's national identity. More specifically, Jurgen Habermas, a prominent German scholar, argues that a bill of rights could alter the self-understanding of citizens, by creating a political community of individuals with equal status.[46] While Germany may be a successful example of this idea, Canada arguably provides a counter-example and raises questions about its limitations. The Canadian Charter of Rights and Freedoms of 1982 was designed to create a pan-Canadian patriotism to counter Quebec's nationalism, but has been seen as an imposition by many Quebec citizens. As Choudhry explains:

---

42 See H.D. Forbes, *Ethnic Conflict: Commerce, Culture and the Contact Hypothesis* (New Haven, CT: Yale University Press, 1997) and J. Orman, *Language Policy and Nation-Building in Post-Apartheid South Africa* (Dordrecht, Netherlands: Springer 2009), particularly the chapter entitled "Language Policy, Language Planning and National Identity: Theoretical Perspectives".

43 Collier, *supra* note 6 at 67.

44 See W. Kymlicka and A. Patten (eds), *Language Rights and Political Theory* (Oxford: Oxford University Press, 2003).

45 See W. Kymlicka, "Misunderstanding Nationalism" in R. Beiner (ed.), *Theorizing Nationalism* (Albany, NY: State University of New York Press, 1999).

46 J. Habermas, *Between Facts and Norms: Contribution to a Discourse Theory of Law and Democracy*, (Cambridge, MA: MIT Press, 1996).

it is very difficult for bills of rights, on their own, to serve a constituting role in defining a new political identity. The German example suggests that for a bill of rights to serve as the basis of a common political identity, it must be situated in a contingent historical and political context. . .The difficulties may be greater still for countries emerging from violent conflict.[47]

7.6 Conclusion

The analysis provided in this chapter suggests that institutions can be used as important tools in reducing the risk of conflict, or decreasing the likelihood of another onset in post-conflict societies. However, there is no one particular design that can be touted as a panacea for ethnic conflict. As Yash Ghai puts it, "there is no one type of 'multi-ethnic constitution'".[48] Each constitutional arrangement will perform a different function. Some will have a regulative role, preventing the abuse of public power; others will secure a credible commitment to an established settlement in a post-conflict scenario; and a third type may have a constitutive role, serving as the pillar on which a new national identity will be constructed.[49] In some cases these roles may overlap, while in others they will be clearly separated. In some cases a bill of individual rights may perform some of these functions, while in others group rights (for example, indigenous rights) will be preferable. In sum, designing an appropriate institutional arrangement will be highly context specific and likely to vary on a case-by-case basis, as with most of the issues discussed in this book.

---

47 Choudhry, *supra* note 38, at 318.

48 Y. Ghai, "Constitutionalism and the Challenge of Ethnic Diversity" in J.K Heckman, R.L. Nelson and L. Cabatingan (eds) *Global Perspectives on the Rule of Law* (New York, NY: Glasshouse, 2010).

49 For a map, see Choudhry, *supra* note 38.

8   Gender and development

Included among the eight Millennium Development Goals (MDGs) announced by the United Nations in 2000,[1] gender equality and women's empowerment are both constitutive of and instrumental to development. As we show in this chapter, there are multiple reasons to promote gender equality and women's empowerment, and much progress has been achieved over the last two decades, particularly in girls' education and female literacy rates.[2] However, many challenges remain. Formal legislation,[3] as well as informal rules and norms continue to present obstacles to gender equality and women's empowerment. Acknowledging that institutional frameworks can be important instruments to achieve these goals, but can also hinder well-intentioned efforts to promote change, we conclude the chapter with an assessment of institutional reform strategies.

8.1   Why promote gender equality?

One of the arguments for promoting gender equality is that it is an end in itself. In *Development as Freedom*, Amartya Sen argues that the objective of development is to enhance individual capabilities in various arenas (family, social, political, economic).[4] Women make up about half of the world's population, a substantial majority of the

---

1 United Nations General Assembly Resolution 55/2, 18 September 2000. This Declaration includes the goal: "To promote gender equality and the empowerment of women as effective ways to combat poverty, hunger and disease and to stimulate development that is truly sustainable".

2 United Nations, *The Millennium Development Report 2013* (New York, NY: United Nations, 2013) at 16, 18.

3 "Almost 90% of the 143 economies covered by Women, Business and the Law 2014 have at least one legal difference restricting women's economic opportunities", The World Bank and IFC, *Women, Business and the Law* (2014).

4 A. Sen, *Development as Freedom* (New York, NY: Knopf, 1999) discussed in Chapter 1. See also M. Nussbaum, *Women and Human Development: The Capabilities Approach* (Cambridge, UK: Cambridge University Press, 2000) at 5–6.

world's poor, and are also more likely to be malnourished and more deprived in health and education than men.[5] Reducing these disparities is likely to promote individual capabilities and provide women with the possibility of living lives they have a reason to value (Sen's hallmark for evaluating freedom).

Noting that "development is a process of expanding freedoms equally for all people"[6] and asserting that women and men have "an innate and equal right to achieve a life of material and moral dignity, the ultimate goal of human development",[7] many international organizations have embraced this idea of gender equality as an end in itself. Indeed, over the past decade a number of indices have started to measure women's capabilities. The United Nations' Gender Development Index (GDI) compares how males and females score on health (life expectancy at birth), education (adult literacy and enrollment rates) and wealth (GDP per capita). The UN's Gender Empowerment Indices (GEM) measures women's participation and decision-making power in political, economic and social spheres. The World Economic Forum's Gender Gap Index (GAP) calculates the gap between women's and men's achievements in economics, education, health and politics. Finally, the OECD's Gender Institutions and Development Index (GID) assesses institutions that affect gender equality (for example, family law, women' s civil liberties and ownership rights).

Gender equality is also instrumental to development. There is growing evidence that greater gender equality can enhance economic growth and improve other development outcomes.[8] By increasing labour force participation, gender equality may have a large impact on productivity. Increasing women's economic empowerment and control over resources is also seen as leading to increased investments in children's health, education and nutrition (and therefore contributing to eco-

---

5 M.P. Todaro and S.C. Smith, *Economic Development* (Toronto: Pearson, 2012, 11th edn) at 22 and 239–40.

6 The World Bank, *World Development Report 2012: Gender Equality and Development* (Washington, DC: World Bank, 2012) at 47.

7 *Arab Human Development Report 2005: Towards the Rise of Women in the Arab World* (New York, NY: UNDP and the Arab Fund for Economic and Social Development, 2005), available at http://www.arab-hdr.org/contents/index.aspx?rid=4 (accessed 28 April 2014), at 5; see M. Trebilcock, "Between Institutions and Culture: The UNDP's Arab Human Development Reports" (2009) 1 *Journal of Middle East Law and Governance* 210.

8 *World Development Report 2012, supra* note 6, at 47; Sen, *supra* note 4; I. Coleman, "The Payoff from Women's Rights" (June 2004) 83:3 *Foreign Affairs* 80.

nomic growth and human well-being). Further, improving women's political and social agency is also seen to produce better policy choices, institutions and outcomes.[9] Because of these benefits, international organizations and private foundations, such as the Bill and Melinda Gates' Foundation, have prioritized female empowerment and family health by investing in family planning and maternal, new-born and child health.[10]

The United Nations General Assembly recognized both the principled and instrumental rationales for promoting gender equality in the global action plan adopted at the 2010 Summit on the MDGs, confirming that "achieving gender equality and empowerment of women is both a key development goal and an important means for achieving all of the Millennium Development Goals".[11]

While both rationales are strong, in a 2012 article entitled "Women Empowerment and Economic Development", economist Esther Duflo cautions that promoting gender equality is not the "free lunch" it is sometimes touted to be. Reviewing the evidence on the impact of women's empowerment on efficient allocation of resources, economic development and other measures of social well-being, she finds that targeted policies may have costs both for short-term and long-term development outcomes.[12] For example, women's empowerment in the household may lead to improvements in children's health and nutrition but not education.[13] Similarly, other studies have found that politically empowered women invest more in drinking water, but less in schools or roads.[14] While acknowledging that women's empowerment is a laudable goal in and of itself, Duflo calls for a greater recognition of the implicit trade-offs in such policies and for a greater measure of realism among policy-makers.

---

9 *World Development Report 2012, supra* note 6, at 47–8.

10 Bill and Melinda Gates Foundation, "What we do: Family Planning Strategy Overview" available at http://www.gatesfoundation.org/What-We-Do/Global-Development/Family-Planning (accessed 21 October 2013).

11 UNGA Resolution 65/1, "Keeping the Promise: United to Achieve the Millennium Development Goals", adopted on 22 September 2010 (at paragraph 12).

12 E. Duflo, "Women Empowerment and Economic Development" (2012) 50 *Journal of Economic Literature* 1051, at 1074–6.

13 See *ibid.,* at 1074 and 1076.

14 See *ibid.,* at 1074.

8.2   Recent progress

There has been significant recent progress in promoting gender equality and women's empowerment in several key areas: education, life expectancy, fertility rates and participation in the labour force.

8.2.1   Educational attainment

There have been significant improvements in closing the gaps between the education of girls and boys in developing countries. By 2008, primary school enrolment around the world had become nearly universal for both girls and boys.[15] Even the regions with the largest gender gaps, South Asia, North Africa, and sub-Saharan Africa, have made considerable progress: between 1990 and 2011, the ratio of girls to boys in primary school in South Asia rose from 74 girls per 100 boys to 98 girls; over the same period, the ratio in North Africa increased from 82 to 94 while in sub-Saharan Africa, there are now 93 girls per 100 boys, up from 83 in 1990.[16] In addition to enrolling at higher rates, girls now tend to make better progress in primary school with lower repetition and lower dropout rates than boys in all developing regions.[17]

The progress at the secondary level has also been significant: enrolment rates for girls in low- and medium-income countries increased from 22 per cent in 1990 to 34 per cent in 2010. In the same period, there was an increase from 30 to 40 per cent for boys.[18] As a result of the higher increase in the number of girls, in one-third of developing countries girls outnumbered boys in secondary education in 2008.[19] Tertiary enrolment growth is also stronger for women than for men, with tertiary enrolment rates for women only lagging behind men in 36 out of 96 developing countries.[20]

---

15 Coleman, *supra* note 8, at 1051.

16 *The Millennium Development Report 2013, supra* note 2, at 18.

17 M.J. Grant and R.J. Behrman, "Gender Gaps in Educational Attainment in Less Developed Countries" (2010) 36:1 *Population and Development Review* 71, cited in *World Development Report 2012, supra* note 6, at 61.

18 Coleman, *supra* note 8, at 1051.

19 *World Development Report 2012, supra* note 6, at 61.

20 *Ibid.*

8.2.2   Life expectancy

Life expectancy in developing countries is increasing for both men and women: between 1960 and 2008, life expectancy rose from 54 to 71 for women and from 51 to 67 for men. This increase is particularly notable in low-income countries, where life expectancy rose from 48 to 69 for women and from 46 to 65 for men during the same period. Except for sub-Saharan Africa, every region added between 20 and 25 years of life between 1960 and 2008.[21] These figures reflect in part declining maternal mortality rates:[22] from 1990 to 2008, 147 countries experienced declines in maternal deaths. Out of these 147 countries, 90 had a decline of 40 per cent or more during this period. From 1990 to 2010, the highest reductions in maternal mortality were in Eastern Asia (69 per cent); Northern Africa (66 per cent) and Southern Asia (64 per cent).[23]

8.2.3   Falling fertility rates

Contributing to the reductions in maternal mortality rates have been the dramatic declines in fertility rates in most developing countries over the last two decades: today few countries have a total fertility rate of six or higher.[24] Compared to earlier declines in industrialized nations, the pace of the decline has been very fast. For example, it took 100 years for fertility to decline from 6 births to 2.3 in the United States, whereas India observed this decline over a span of 30 years (from 1960 to 1990).[25] Concurrent with falling fertility rates has been increased access to and utilization of contraception. Between 1990 and 2011, the percentage of women between the ages of 15–49, married or in union, who wish to delay or avoid pregnancy but do not use any form of contraception dropped from 15 per cent to 12 per cent. However, the unmet need for contraception remains high in parts of the developing world, especially in Oceania and sub-Saharan Africa, where it is still at 25 per cent.[26]

---

21 *Ibid.*, at 62.
22 *Ibid.*, at 62–3.
23 *The Millennium Development Report 2013, supra* note 2, at 29.
24 World Bank, World Development Indicators (2013), available at http://databank. worldbank.org/data/views/variableSelection/selectvariables.aspx?source=world-development-indicators (accessed 28 April 2014).
25 *World Development Report 2012, supra* note 6, at 63.
26 *The Millennium Development Report 2013, supra* note 2, at 32.

Beyond increased access to family planning services, the declines in fertility rates may also reflect stronger educational outcomes among women; a 2014 study focused on Rwanda (one of the fastest growing African economies) finds that improved female education levels account for the largest part of the fertility decline in that country, with improving household living standards and the move toward non-agricultural employment being important secondary drivers.[27]

8.2.4   Major increases in female labour force participation

Between 1980 and 2008, the gender gap in labour force participation narrowed from 32 to 26 per cent, due to an increase in female labour force (as well as a slight decrease in labour force participation by males).[28] Increases were particularly large in regions where participation rates had been very low (Latin America, the Caribbean, the Middle East and North Africa) and were higher for women with more education.[29] Interestingly, the relationship between a country's development and its female labour force participation rate is U-shaped; while participation rates are high in very poor countries, they drop as per capita incomes (and male wages) increase, then rise again as further development continues and higher rates of education and wage increases draw women back into the workforce.[30] Thus, the smallest labour participation disparities are found in sub-Saharan African countries (which are typically less developed) as well as East Asian and developed economies (which are generally richer), while gaps in the low-to-middle-income countries of South Asia, the Middle East and North Africa hover around 50 per cent.[31]

8.3   Major outstanding challenges

Notwithstanding significant progresses in the past decades, major challenges remain. There are still excess deaths of girls and women (due to unequal access to health care, selective abortions and investment); significant disparities regarding access to and quality of girls'

---

27 T. Bundervoet, "What Explains Rwanda's Drop in Fertility between 2005 and 2010?" Policy Research Working Paper 6741, World Bank (2014).

28 International Labour Organization (ILO), *Key Indicators of the Labour Market* (Geneva: ILO, 2010), cited in *World Development Report 2012, supra* note 6, at 65.

29 *World Development Report 2012, supra* note 6, at 65.

30 *Ibid.*, at 65–6.

31 ILO, *Key Indicators of the Labour Market* (Geneva: ILO, 2013, 8th edn).

schooling; unequal access to economic opportunities (such as formal employment opportunities, access to credit, equal payment for equal work, equal share of childcare and housework and husband-centred land titling); and inequality in women's voice in the household and society (including in the political sphere), among other highly gendered issues not discussed here, such as sexual and domestic violence, sexual harassment, access to safe abortions, honour killings, forced marriage, unequal or non-existent parental leave legislation, and so on.

8.3.1   Excess deaths of girls and women

In the late 1980s, Amartya Sen estimated that there were up to 100 million "missing women" in the world, in other words, females that would be alive today if it were not for unequal treatment of the sexes.[32] The World Bank estimates a total of 3.9 million women were "missing" in 2008, due to missing girls at birth and excess female mortality under age 60.[33] The most significant cause of female mortality relates to unequal access to healthcare, with less evidence of unequal access to food.[34] Self-selective abortions also appear to have contributed significantly in recent years in China, Taiwan, South Korea and India.[35] Maternal mortality is another factor. While overall rates of maternal mortality have fallen by 34 per cent since 1990, they remain high in many parts of the world, specifically sub-Saharan Africa, South Asia, Oceania and Southeast Asia.[36]

The missing women problem exists throughout the developing world: in 1990, 2000 and 2008, sex ratios at birth and mortality across countries reveal persistent disadvantages for women in many low- and middle-income countries.[37] However, the phenomenon is particularly acute in China, India and the countries of sub-Saharan Africa, which collectively account for 85 per cent of the missing women. Out of

---

32 A. Sen, "Women's Survival as a Development Problem" (1989) 43:2 *Bulletin of the American Academy of Arts and Sciences* 14 and A. Sen, "More than 100 Million Women are Missing" (December 1990) *The New York Review of Books*, cited in S. Klasen, "Missing Women" in D.A. Clark (ed.), *The Elgar Companion to Development Studies* (Cheltenham, UK and Northampton, MA, USA: Edward Elgar, 2006) 389, at 389.

33 *World Development Report 2012, supra* note 6, at 77.

34 Klasen, "Missing Women", *supra* note 32, at 392.

35 *Ibid.*

36 *World Development Report 2012, supra* note 6, at 78.

37 *Ibid.* at 77.

the total of 101.3 million missing women in the world from the mid-1990s to early 2000s, 40.9 million are from China and 39.1 million from India.[38] In these countries, "investment" decisions also appear to play a role, with parents choosing to invest in sons, who are able to provide old-age support, continue the family name or carry out other symbolic functions.[39] In some countries, such as India, daughters are also costly because of substantial dowry payments in the event of marriage.

8.3.2   Disparities in girls' schooling

Despite the significant progress in education noted above, girls continue to lag behind boys with regards to both access to and quality of education in a number of developing countries. There has been little progress in girls' enrolment in primary and secondary school in many countries in South Asia and sub-Saharan Africa. In Eritrea, for instance, female net enrolment increased from 16 per cent in 1990 to only 36 per cent in 2008. Similarly, in Afghanistan, Chad and the Central African Republic there are fewer than 70 girls per 100 boys in primary school.[40] There are also disparities in tertiary education: in sub-Saharan Africa there were only 66 female tertiary students for every 100 male students in 2008, and only 76 in South Asia.[41] Further, in Southern Asia, the Middle East and sub-Saharan Africa illiteracy rates among adult females are 55 per cent, 51 per cent and 45 per cent respectively.

Within developing countries, these inequalities are more pronounced in low-income groups. For example, in the Democratic Republic of Congo a girl in the poorest fifth of the population studies three fewer years than a boy.[42] Moreover, even in countries in which girls have equal access to schooling, educational equality also requires equality in the learning process, equality of educational outcomes and equality of external opportunities, which are far more challenging to achieve than mere parity in enrolment rates.[43]

---

38 S. Klasen and C. Wink, "'Missing Women': Revisiting the Debate" (2003) 9:2–3 *Feminist Economics* 263, cited in Klasen, "Missing Women", *supra* note 32, at 390.

39 Klasen, "Missing Women" *supra* note 32, at 392.

40 *World Development Report 2012, supra* note 6, at 73.

41 *Ibid.,* at 74.

42 Coleman, *supra* note 8, at 84.

43 N. Kabeer, *Social Exclusion and the MDGs: The Challenge of "Durable Inequalities" in the Asian Context* (Asia 2015 Conference, March 2006) at 20, available at http://www.eldis.org/vfile/upload/1/document/0708/DOC21178.pdf (accessed 28 April 2014).

8.3.3   Unequal access to economic opportunities

Women are less likely to work, earn less than men for similar work, and are more likely to be in poverty even when they do work.[44] Some of these disparities can be explained by the fact that women (in both developed and developing countries) work in different industries and occupations than men. Indeed, women tend to work in low productivity activities and in the informal sector; they also tend to operate small informal businesses (often out of their homes) and work for smaller firms. This segregation in employment has contributed to earning gaps ranging from 20 per cent to 80 per cent in some developing countries.[45] Discriminatory labour laws can also contribute to these disparities. For instance, until recently the Brazilian labour laws offered lower levels of protection for domestic workers, a sector in which women represent 93 per cent of the total workers (6.7 out of 7.2 million).[46]

There are at least three reasons for this employment segregation. First, the cultural tradition of women having primary responsibility for care-giving within the family cannot always be combined with other types of economic activity, such as work outside the home. Second, the resources women bring to the labour market often reflect lower levels of health, nutrition, education, skills and fewer productive assets. Third, there is "active discrimination and unconscious biases" concerning women's skills, dispositions and resources.[47] Land, for instance, has the potential to provide women with income and a source of subsistence if they are able to commercialize their produce.[48] However, discriminatory property and inheritance laws often mean women do not have access to land. In most African countries and about half of Asian countries, land ownership laws disadvantage women.[49] In Kenya, 5 per cent of registered landholders are women; likewise in Brazil women own

---

44 US Agency for International Development, *Education from a Gender Equality Perspective* (Washington, DC, 2008), available at http://www.ungei.org/resources/files/Education_from_a_Gender_Equality_Perspective.pdf (accessed 28 April 2014).

45 *World Development Report 2012, supra* note 6, at 79.

46 *Domestic Workers across the world: Global and regional statistics and the extent of legal protection* (Geneva: ILO, 2013) at 26, available at http://www.ilo.org/wcmsp5/groups/public/---dgreports/---dcomm/---publ/documents/publication/wcms_173363.pdf (accessed 28 April 2014).

47 N. Kabeer, "Gender Labour Markets and Poverty: An overview" (January 2008) 13 *Poverty in Focus* 3–4.

48 See M. Trebilcock and M.M. Prado, *What Makes Poor Countries Poor? Institutional Determinants of Development* (Cheltenham, UK and Northampton, MA, USA: Edward Elgar, 2011) at 98.

49 *World Development Report 2012, supra* note 6, at 82–3.

only 11 per cent of land.[50] In many countries, women also lack access to non-land resources such as credit, fertilizers, equipment and labour, undermining their ability to use their land productively.[51]

8.3.4   Lack of political voice

In 2013, the Global Gender Gap Index reported that "the gap between women and men on economic participation and political empowerment remains wide". While 136 countries (90 per cent of the world's population) have closed almost 96 per cent of the gender gap in health outcomes and almost 93 per cent of the gender gap in educational attainment, only 60 per cent of the gender gap in economic outcomes and 21 per cent of the gender gap in political outcomes have been closed.[52] Globally, as of November 2013, only 21.3 per cent of national parliamentarians were women, with the lowest female participation rates found in the Middle East and the Pacific; however, optimistically, half of the countries in which women hold a third or more of parliamentary seats are in the developing world, with Rwanda topping the global list with 63.8 per cent.[53]

8.4   Principal impediments to gender equality

Significant disparities remain in women's control over resources, political voice, and domestic violence rates; and only limited progress has occurred with regards to female mortality and access to economic opportunities.[54] Why has progress been so limited?

Resistance to gender equality and women's empowerment is often deeply entrenched in social values, cultural norms and religious beliefs. Gender disparities are often a result of conservative, patriarchal practices, which are in many cases reinforced by religious values.[55] Thus, "[gender empowerment] often collides with the twin powers of culture and religion".[56] This creates a significant chal-

---

50 *Ibid.*, at 82.

51 *Ibid.*, at 98–103.

52 *The Global Gender Gap Report 2013* (Geneva: World Economic Forum, 2013) at 7–8.

53 Inter-Parliamentary Union, *Women in National Parliaments*, available at http://www.ipu.org/wmn-e/classif.htm (accessed 28 April 2014).

54 *World Development Report 2012, supra* note 6, at 76.

55 *Ibid.*, at 81.

56 Coleman, *supra* note 8, at 86.

lenge for those promoting institutional reforms to further this goal. Female empowerment has often been associated with secularism and Western values, which has sometimes prompted resistance from both men and women in non-Western nations.[57] Indeed, human rights are a cause of tension in countries like Saudi Arabia, Iraq and Afghanistan between religious extremists and those with more moderate, progressive views.[58] For instance, Arab leaders have traditionally given religious conservatives oversight over issues that have significance for women's rights including family law and personal status codes.[59]

8.5   Reform strategies

The development literature often presents women's empowerment and economic development as two self-reinforcing goals, suggesting that policies promoting one will necessarily advance the other, and vice versa. As mentioned earlier, Duflo argues for caution regarding these arguments. On one hand, she argues that gender-targeted policies may in some cases undermine growth. On the other hand, she also shows that promoting economic development is not enough to promote gender equality. The argument that policies to promote economic growth benefit women in general is supported empirically by evidence showing that decreasing poverty levels through economic growth is likely to reduce: (1) unequal allocation of resources among male and female children within the household; (2) gaps in educational attainment between boys and girls; (3) female infant mortality rates; and (4) fertility and maternal mortality rates. Economic growth is also strongly correlated with greater recognition of women's legal rights. However, Duflo argues that such economic policies can only do so much. Deeply entrenched discrimination, embedded in social practices and institutional arrangements, imposes obstacles that cannot be overcome by simply promoting economic development. Thus, targeted policies are still necessary, as long as we acknowledge that these may not always be conducive to growth.[60]

---

57 *Ibid.*, at 88 and see Nussbaum, *supra* note 4 (Introduction).

58 Coleman, *supra* note 8, at 81.

59 *Ibid.*, at 88. Coleman does note that young, Western educated leaders in Morocco, Jordan and Qatar recognise the importance of women to development and are pushing ahead with women's rights; and that the Arab Human Development Report 2002 assisted in these efforts.

60 Duflo, *supra* note 12.

Potential targeted policies range from targeted financial resources for women (for example, microcredit) to legal reforms that eliminate unequal treatment (for example, equal property rights) and political reforms that try to reduce representation gaps (for example, gender quotas in political institutions). A recent overview of the impact of women's economic rights over development outcomes in 100 countries across a span of 50 years found that reforms are associated with "greater participation of women in the labour force, greater movement out of agricultural employment, higher rates of women in wage employment, lower adolescent fertility, lower maternal and infant mortality, and higher female educational enrollment".[61] In sum, there is substantial consensus on the relevance and desirability of targeted reforms to promote gender equality and women empowerment. There is, however, less agreement on the appropriate strategies to implement them.

8.5.1   Top down approaches to reform

The philosopher Martha Nussbaum, among others, argues that nations should formulate a set of universal commitments to equality that can form the basis of international treaties and ultimately be enshrined in national constitutions.[62] According to Nussbaum, individual nation states (instead of NGOs) should play a fundamental role in this process, since governments are in general elected and therefore accountable to the public.

There are many examples of this "top down" approach. The Convention on the Elimination of All Forms of Discrimination against Women (CEDAW), adopted by the United Nations General Assembly in 1979 (and now with 187 state parties), is one example. Under the Convention, states commit to undertaking a series of anti-discrimination measures including abolishing all discriminatory laws and establishing institutions that will protect women against discrimination.[63] Other United Nations Conventions that specifically protect the rights of women include the 2003 Protocol to Prevent, Suppress and Punish Trafficking in Persons, especially Women and Children;[64] the Convention on

---

61 M. Hallward-Driemeier, T. Hasan and A.B. Rusu, "Women's Legal Rights over 50 Years: What Is the Impact of Reform?" Policy Research Working Paper 6617, World Bank (2013).

62 Nussbaum, *supra* note 4, at 101–5.

63 Article 2 CEDAW, noted by K. Pistor, A. Haldar and A. Amirapu, "Social Norms, Rule of Law, and Gender Reality" in J. Heckman, R. Nelson and L. Cabatongian (eds), *Global Perspectives on the Rule of Law* (London: Routledge, 2010) at 22.

64 This supplements the United Nations Convention against Transnational Organized Crime.

Consent to Marriage, Minimum Age for Marriage and Registration of Marriages (1962) and the Convention against Discrimination in Education 1960. Women's rights are clearly also covered by more general human rights treaties such as the Universal Declaration of Human Rights and the International Covenant on Civil and Political Rights and its two protocols.

The United Nations also held four world conferences on women's issues between 1975 and 1995, which "united the international community behind a set of common objectives with an effective plan of action for the advancement of women everywhere".[65] In 1995, the Beijing Declaration and Platform for Action was adopted, aimed at "removing all the obstacles to women's active participation in all spheres of public and private life through a full and equal share in economic, social, cultural and political decision-making".[66] The International Labour Organization also promotes gender equality[67] through labour standards established in relevant conventions and recommendations, as well as measuring whether progress has been made.[68] The UNDP's Arab Human Development Reports are also intended to "identify disadvantaged groups within the region, and suggest policies, strategies and opportunities for their empowerment".[69]

8.5.2   Incrementalism and decentralized initiatives

Some authors and policy-makers criticize the "top down" approach as being based on at least two misguided assumptions. First, the potency

---

65 United Nations Women, "World Conferences on Women", available at http://www.unwomen.org/ en/how-we-work/intergovernmental-support/world-conferences-on-women (accessed 28 April 2014).

66 United Nations System, Chief Executives Board for Coordination "Beijing Declaration and Platform for Action" (September 1995), available at http://www.unsceb.org/content/beijing-declaration-and-platform-action-0 (accessed 28 April 2014).

67 The ILO's Policy on Gender Equality and Mainstreaming, operationalized through the ILO Gender Equality Action Plan 2010–15 supports "systematically analysing and addressing in all initiatives the specific needs of both women and men, and targeted interventions to enable women and men to participate in – and benefit equally from – development efforts". ILO, "Gender Equality", available at http://www.ilo.org/global/topics/equality-and-discrimination/ gender-equality/lang--en/index.htm (accessed 21 October 2013).

68 See for example, *Women in Labour Markets: Measuring Progress and Identifying Challenges* (Geneva: ILO, 2010), available at http://www.ilo.org/wcmsp5/groups/public/---ed_emp/---emp_ elm/---trends/documents/publication/wcms_123835.pdf (accessed 28 April 2014).

69 UNDP, "Arab Human Development Reports", available at http://www.arab-hdr.org/ (accessed 28 April 2014).

of law, that is, that changing laws actually creates societal or political change. Second, the assumption that significant obstacles (such as political resistance, culture and religion) are easily surmountable. Contrary to such assumptions, these critics suggest that changes in formal institutions (for example, statutes and constitutional provisions) should be preceded by changes in informal institutions (culture, religion and societal practices).

An important study along these lines is a quantitative analysis by Katharina Pistor, Amtara Haldar and Amrit Amirapu that finds no correlation between the rule of law and gender equality in low-income countries. Turning to qualitative data, they found some evidence that "the status of women in society is determined primarily by social norms about gender equality and that these norms are only weakly affected by legal institutions".[70] India is used as a case study to show the contrast between "law on the books" and "law in action". The country is a signatory to most major international human rights conventions and has enacted a full spectrum of laws that promote equal treatment of women (from prohibitions on violence to ensuring positive socio-economic rights such as property and labour laws). Furthermore, institutions such as the National Commission for Women and the Human Rights Commission exist alongside the general court system to ensure that these laws are implemented. The reality of discrimination in India is, however, "fundamental and pervasive", with approximately 30 million "missing women" resulting from health and nutritional neglect of girls during childhood.[71] High rates of sexual violence,[72] marriages below the legal age and substantial dowry payments take place in spite of legal prohibitions, as does a 250 per cent pay differential. The authors conclude that having "neutral" institutions or laws in place does not necessarily result in changed social norms necessary for improvement in gender equity.[73]

Another example of failed top down reforms can be seen in attempts to give women more access to economic opportunities by guaranteeing equal property rights. Shahra Razavi provides a map of tensions and ambiguities in these reform efforts, highlighting three main areas of concern. First, formalization of title and liberalization policies do not con-

---

70 Pistor, Haldar and Amirapu, *supra* note 63.

71 *Ibid.*, at 20–21.

72 According to a study done by the World Health Organization, a woman is raped in India every 54 minutes (*ibid.*, at 21).

73 Pistor, Haldar and Amirapu, *supra* note 63, at 25.

sider the difficulties faced by women in accessing land through markets. Second, context-specific reforms can be troublesome if they endorse customary systems and land management structures that are not compatible with, or conducive to, gender equality. Third, as discussed above once granted access to land, women still need equal access to non-land resources (such as credit) to benefit equally from land tenure.[74] These difficulties are connected to informal rules and norms. While women may be legally entitled to acquire property, markets also embody gender structures and hierarchies grounded in the larger social context and may create severe obstacles to women having access to land. Thus, many reforms do not overcome the fact that opportunities for women to acquire land through markets are far more limited than they are for men. Such informal rules and norms may also influence governmental institutions in their interpretation and application of the law.

In addition to these obstacles, property rights and land reforms to promote gender equality might not be effective for other reasons. For instance, reforms promoted in Latin America have established co-ownership of land for men and women. This provides a guarantee for women that they will also have the title to the land if they become divorced or widowed. Women's movements have pressed for the adoption of such provisions in Africa, mostly to no avail.[75] In contrast, Brazil and Colombia were pioneers in implementing co-ownership provisions for land reform titling in 1988. These countries have implemented largely successful land titling reforms because they relied on innovative, community-driven approaches in which communities are given grants and access to credit and "the beneficiaries identify the land, negotiate the price, and purchase it, rather than relying on the government to hand them land acquired through expropriation".[76] However, by the mid-1990s there was a significant discrepancy between these two countries: while in Colombia 45 per cent of the beneficiaries of land reform were women, in Brazil they were only 12.6 per cent.[77] According to Carmen Diana Deere, this discrepancy

---

74 S. Razavi, "Liberalization and the Debates on Women's Access to Land" (2007) 28 *Third World Quarterly* at 1479–500; see also *World Development Report 2012*, *supra* note 6, at chapter 5.

75 A. Manji, *The Politics of Land Reform in Africa* (London: Zed Books, 2006) at 105–9 (analysing the case of Uganda).

76 N. Birdsall and A. de la Torre, *Washington Contentious: Economic Policies for Social Equality in Latin America*, Commission on Economic Reform in Unequal Latin American Societies (2001) at 57.

77 C.D. Deere, "Women's land rights and rural movements in the Brazilian agrarian reform" (2003) 3:1 and 2 *Journal of Agrarian Change* at 257–88.

was caused by three factors: (1) co-ownership was mandatory in Colombia and optional in Brazil; (2) the bureaucracy in charge of implementing land reform in Brazil adopted very discriminatory practices against women; and (3) it was not until recently that the land reform movements started to promote an agenda to foster gender equality. As a result of popular pressure from social movements, in 2001 the Brazilian government adopted a series of regulations aimed at promoting the inclusion of women in land reform, but while these changes make co-ownership clauses more effective in protecting married women there is still a lack of effort to promote inclusion of female-headed households.[78] Other Latin American countries have promoted affirmative action in this context to overcome the barriers imposed by past discrimination.[79] In sum, the details of institutional design matter because they will affect the incentives created by the formal law (a mandatory or optional provision can make a significant difference). Moreover, governmental authorities might adopt discriminatory practices in implementing or enforcing laws, and unless there are institutional guarantees of public participation in the reform process and its implementation phase, there might not be effective pressure from non-governmental groups for legal changes that better reflect social values.

While formalization of property and land markets may not always empower women, these reforms can sometimes provide a productive way for women to circumvent traditional authorities, customary rights and local land management systems. Similarly, dispute resolution systems outside customary practices may also provide a beneficial option for these women. In such circumstances, a combination of formal systems and customary practices allow women to "forum shop", combining different claims and using dispute mechanisms that will be most favourable to them on a case-by-case basis. Obstacles to the effective use of these options, however, include lack of information and low levels of education. In this regard, again, gender equality reforms need to be combined with initiatives that are conducive to granting women equal access to other resources beyond land.

Another concern is that the ability of women to create and accumulate wealth through land depends on their access to a series of non-

---

78 *Ibid.*

79 C.D. Deere and M. Leon, *Empowering Women: Land and Property Rights in Latin America* (Pittsburgh, PA: University of Pittsburgh Press, 2001), chapter 4.

land resources, such as fertilizer, equipment and labour, which itself depends on access to credit. Microcredit initiatives in Bangladesh (and other countries), such as the Grameen Bank, were created to overcome the credit obstacles presented by conventional discrimination.[80] Such initiatives are also seen to raise women's status and improve gender equity, particularly when designed to do so.[81] Unfortunately, this option is not available in all countries and the existing initiatives are often not self-sustainable (financial intermediaries are often dependent on donors).[82] Moreover, the impact of microfinance on women's status and gender equity is limited, given that women borrowers often only partially control the proceeds of loans.[83] A further related problem is that in many countries land is a complementary source of income, being combined with employment outside the household. In these cases, barriers for women in obtaining jobs can hinder their ability to benefit from land tenure. In sum, accounting for the complex economic, social and cultural environment in which formal institutional reforms (such as land tenure) are immersed can potentially increase their effectiveness.

While accounting for institutional interconnections is important, some interventions can produce a significant impact. An example of this kind of reform is conditional cash transfers, where cash is provided to female adults in return for children's attendance and performance at school and preventative health treatment.[84] While such measures are not specifically targeted at improving the welfare of women, such programmes have tended to enhance women's status in society. Gustavo Bobonis has researched the unintended effects of such schemes in Mexico on divorce and marriage rates and spousal abuse.[85] He finds, for example, that such schemes improve the marriage prospects of young, single women and have a "small but significant" effect

80 The World Bank, "Using Microcredit to Advance Women" (1998) PREMnotes 8.

81 L. Mayoux, "Microfinance and the Empowerment of Women: Review of Key Issues" Social Finance Programme Working Paper No. 23, ILO, Geneva (2000).

82 *Ibid.*

83 N. MacIsaac, "The role of microcredit in poverty reduction and promoting gender equity" (June 1997) South Asia Partnership Canada, Strategic Policy and Planning Division, Asia Branch Canada International Development Agency, available at http://www.spanish.microfinancegateway.org/files/3247_3247.pdf (accessed 28 April 2014) at 5.

84 See G.J. Bobonis, "The Impact of Conditional Cash Transfers on Marriage and Divorce" (January 2011) 59:2 *Economic Development and Cultural Change* 281, at 282.

85 See Bobonis *supra* note 84, and G.J. Bobonis, M. Gonzalez-Brenes and R. Castro, "Public Transfers and Domestic Violence: The Roles of Private Information and Spousal Control" 5:1 *American Economic Journal: Economic Policy* (2013), 179–205.

on increased marital dissolution rates.[86] Moreover, while conditional cash transfers are associated with increases in emotional abuse in the short term, they have resulted in reduced physical domestic violence.[87]

8.5.3   Translating universal values into the local context

While some have proposed a "top down approach" that relies heavily on international human rights and constitutional reforms (formal institutions), others have claimed that any successful strategy needs to account for cultural norms, religious beliefs and social practices (informal institutions) to change individual and collective behaviour effectively. Perhaps one way of reconciling these two views is to reject the dichotomy between rights (formal institutions) and culture (informal institutions). Sally Engle Merry argues that "[t]o regard violence against women as an opposition between culture and rights is to fail to acknowledge the contested and variable cultural support that these acts receive in different social groups".[88] According to her, international organizations should "focus attention on the strengths of local social arrangements in promoting human rights ideals and the importance of framing universalistic reforms in local cultural terms".[89] Thus, according to Merry, rights-based reformers should listen to the local population and engage in a "process of translation" that secures the conditions for protection of rights from within.[90]

8.6   Conclusion

Much progress has been made on gender equity and women's empowerment, but significant challenges remain. While broad-based economic growth policies are likely to increase economic opportunities for women and returns on investments in their education, other

---

86   Bobonis, *supra* note 84, at 3 and 19.

87   Bobonis et al., *supra* note 85. However, a previous study indicates that in the long term such schemes have little effect on spousal abuse rates: G.J. Bobonis and R. Castro, "The Role of Conditional Cash Transfers in Reducing Spousal Abuse in Mexico: Short-Term vs. Long-Term Effects" (March 2010) (unpublished manuscript), available at: http://homes.chass.utoronto.ca/~bobonis/BC_dviolence2_mar10.pdf (accessed 28 April 2014).

88   S.E. Merry, *Gender and Violence: A Cultural Perspective* (Malden, MA: Wiley and Sons, 2009) at 89.

89   *Ibid.*, at 92.

90   S.E. Merry, *Human Rights & Gender Violence: Translating International Law into Local Justice* (Chicago, IL: University of Chicago Press, 2009) at 132.

sources of gender inequality are likely to require gender-specific policy interventions. With respect to the latter, as Esther Duflo shows, policy-makers need to do a better job of accounting for the existing empirical evidence on the effects of such policies, and acknowledging the trade-offs involved in gender empowerment policies. In this context, institutions can also play an important role in addressing the challenges of women's empowerment, but they may also serve as obstacles to change. Thus, those proposing institutional reforms need to be aware of their risks and limitations. This includes not only paying attention to the particular design of institutional reforms, but also strategies for their implementation.

PART IV

THE STATE, THE MARKET AND DEVELOPMENT

9 Public administration and development

9.1 Introduction

The emergence of an institutional perspective on development over the past decade or so has entailed not only a sharper focus on the nature and quality of a country's political and legal institutions, but also on the organization of its bureaucracy or civil service. According to Salvatore Schiavo-Campo, formerly of the Public Sector Management Team at the World Bank, "the slide of today's 'failed states' can be traced back to, in part, the degradation of their public administrations".[1]

Public administrations embrace not only central and line agencies of government, but specialized administrative arms of government (such as SARAs and quasi-IRAs, discussed in Chapter 4). They also include a highly heterogeneous range of quasi-autonomous, non-governmental organizations (QUANGOs), such as public hospitals, universities, colleges, housing, transit and health authorities, conservation, planning and land-use agencies, and so on, each with their own governance structures. They also embrace state-owned enterprises (SOEs), which are a prominent feature of many developing countries' economies, and hybrid arrangements such as public-private partnerships (PPPs), discussed in Chapter 11. This institutional complexity is often replicated at sub-national levels of government, especially in federal states.

The frailties and failures of public administration in many developing countries have long been documented or remarked upon in the development literature. According to these accounts of bad government in developing countries, to quote Judith Tendler:

---

1 S. Schiavo-Campo, "Reforming the Civil Service" (1996) 33:3 *Finance and Development* 10–13.

Public officials and their workers pursue their own private interests rather than those of the public good. Governments over-extend themselves in hiring and spending. Clientelism runs rampant, with workers being hired and fired on the basis of kinship and political loyalty rather than merit. Workers are poorly trained and receive little on-the-job training. Badly conceived programs and policies create myriad opportunities for bribery, influence peddling, and other forms of malfeasance. All this adds up to the disappointing inability of many governments to deliver good public services and to cope with persistent problems of corruption, poverty, and macro-economic mismanagement.[2]

This view of government is exemplified in Hernando de Soto's widely cited book, *The Other Path*,[3] in which he documents the delays, costs, bureaucratic complexities and corruption entailed in registering title to residential land or obtaining approvals to open a small business in Peru. De Soto suggests that the existence of large informal economies in many developing counties is partly explained by the immense difficulties of doing business legally in these countries. These impediments to doing business in many countries have been more systematically documented in the World Bank's annual "Doing Business" Reports.

According to Tendler, a negative view of the performance of public administrations in many developing countries has tended to lead to advice, from donor institutions and others, directed at limiting the "damage" that the public sector can do in developing countries. The advice falls into three categories: (1) reducing the size of government by getting rid of "excess" workers, contracting out for services, privatizing and decentralizing; (2) terminating many of the policies and programmes that provide opportunities for bureaucrats to exert undue influence on the policy process and for citizens to bribe them; and (3) subjecting public agencies and their managers and workers to market-like pressures and incentives to perform.[4] However, as Tendler and others have pointed out, this view of the quality of public administrations in developing countries and prescriptions and antidotes for their deficiencies ignores the fact that, even on a limited view of the appropriate functions of government, a well-functioning public

---

2 J. Tendler, *Good Government in the Tropics* (Baltimore, MD: Johns Hopkins University Press, 1997) at 1.

3 H. de Soto, *The Other Path* (New York, NY: HarperCollins, 1989).

4 Tendler, *supra* note 2.

administration is indispensable to the effective performance of these tasks. Moreover, the focus on the deficiencies of public administration in many developing countries ignores many examples of good performance within and among developing countries, from which valuable and perhaps transferable reform lessons may be learned.

9.2   Measuring bureaucratic performance

Beginning in the mid-1990s, systematic quantitative efforts have been undertaken to measure bureaucratic quality using ratings generated by various organizations. Some studies, in addition to measuring bureaucratic performance, have tried to measure the impact of bureaucratic performance on economic growth.[5] By focusing on outcomes, these early quantitative studies are limited by their lack of specificity regarding the particular characteristics of a public administration that predisposed it to either good or bad performance, at least in terms of impacts on economic measures of development. There are also various case studies of the high-performing East Asian economies, which emphasize the positive role played by certain dimensions of East Asian bureaucracies in the region's spectacular industrialization.[6] These studies, however, tend to suffer from the limitations of most case studies – that is, their limited generalizability.

In two more recent companion papers, Peter Evans and James Rauch examine the characteristics of core state economic agencies and the growth records of a sample of 35 developing countries for the period from 1970 to 1990, based on country experts' assessment of key institutional characteristics.[7] They draw on the theorizing of Max Weber, where Weber argued that public administrative organizations characterized by meritocratic recruitment and predictable long-term career paths will be

---

5 P. Mauro, "Corruption, Country Risk and Growth" (1995) 7 *Economics and Politics* 207; see also J. Rauch and P. Evans, "Bureaucratic Structure and Bureaucratic Performance in Less Developed Countries" (2000) 75 *Journal of Public Economics* 49.

6 See, for example, R. Wade, *Governing the Market: Economic Theory and the Role of Government in Taiwan's Industrialization* (Princeton, NJ: Princeton University Press, 1990); J. Campos and H. Root, *The Key to the Asian Miracle: Making Shared Growth Credible* (Washington, DC: Brookings Institution, 1996); World Bank, *The East Asian Miracle: Economic Growth and Public Policy* (New York, NY: Oxford University Press, 1993).

7 See P. Evans and J. Rauch, "Bureaucracy and Growth: A Cross-national Analysis of the Effects of 'Weberian' State Structures on Economic Growth" (1999) 64 *American Sociological Review* 748; Rauch and Evans (2000), *supra* note 5.

more effective at facilitating capitalist growth.[8] In their studies, Evans and Rauch focus on meritocratic recruitment, internal promotion and career stability, and competitive salaries, and find that the institutionalization of meritocratic recruitment (public service exams or higher educational credentials) is crucial for ensuring high levels of bureaucratic performance. In contrast, internal promotion and career stability – which may facilitate institutional coherence, long-term policy goals and counter temptations to short-term gain (including corruption) – seem to be of secondary importance. Whether or not competitive salaries have any effect on bureaucratic performance remains unclear. There are notable regional variations in the relationship between bureaucratic performance and economic growth, with sub-Saharan Africa ranking lowest, then Latin America, and the East Asian high-performing economies ranking substantially higher (thus confirming, from a comparative perspective, the earlier findings of the East Asian case studies).

As noted in Chapter 3, the World Bank's governance studies now regularly measure the impact of countries' governance performance (including "government effectiveness", "regulatory quality" and "corruption") on various development outcomes, and find similar impacts to Evans and Rauch. Similarly, as noted above, the World Bank's more recent "Doing Business" Reports catalogue and compare time, costs and complexities in performing many routine bureaucratic and legal activities in many countries (developed and developing). However, both groups of studies (like some earlier studies) evaluate bureaucratic outputs, rather than bureaucratic inputs or particular characteristics of a public administration.

9.3 The reform experience

9.3.1 Lessons from the disappointing record of public administration reform

Schiavo-Campo, formerly of the World Bank, in a review in 1996 of the Bank's experience with civil service reforms in developing countries at that time, reports the following lessons:[9]

---

8 M. Weber, *Economy and Society*, edited by G. Roth and C. Wittich, with a new foreword by G. Roth, translated by E. Fischoff, H. Gerth, A.M. Henderson, F. Kolegar, C. Wright Mills, T. Parsons, M. Rheinstein, G. Roth, E. Shils and C. Wittich (Berkeley, CA: University of California Press [1904 –1911] 2013 (reprint)).

9 Schiavo-Campo, *supra* note 1.

1. A two-tier arrangement may make it possible to recruit, at a higher salary scale, new staff who meet more demanding standards of qualification.
2. Even at low salaries, young, better trained people can be induced to take up government employment for short periods if they are given challenging responsibilities and training.
3. In practice, centralized personnel management systems are generally more cost-effective than decentralized systems.
4. Individual salary negotiations between new staff and ministries should be avoided, because they result in distortions and inequities and compromise prospects for sustainable reform.
5. The temptation to "fence off" reform projects in order to insulate them from an inefficient system should be avoided; creating enclaves does not work, and civil service reform should be directed at the overall system.
6. For external assistance to be effective there must be genuine ownership of reform by the government as a whole if systemic reforms are attempted, or by a major government player if reforms are limited to a specific sector or function, and government must formulate – with appropriate participation by the public as well as government employees themselves – a clear, long-term vision of public sector reform in concrete detail.

Schiavo-Campo also notes that downsizing or retrenchment for fiscal reasons can often have unintended consequences if such programmes encourage the best people to leave (for example, through voluntary severance and early retirement programmes) and that short-term fiscal savings from compressing wages may also lead to the departure of better or more senior employees and increased difficulty in recruiting qualified outsiders. Finally, he argues that without improvements in accountability, downsizing and more adequate compensation may result in a small and well-paid, but no less inefficient or corrupt civil service. Hence, external accountability is essential for the civil service to become more responsive to the public (for example, through user surveys, wearing of nametags, whistle-blower protection and public opinion polls).

More recent reviews by the World Bank and other development agencies of the effectiveness of donor-assisted civil service reforms in developing countries report mixed to disappointing results, with between 40 and 60 per cent of such reforms yielding no measurable increase in government effectiveness. After reviewing this evidence, Matt Andrews in a recent book, *The Limits of Institutional Reform in*

Development,[10] argues that a root failing in many of these reform initiatives is that they are external donor-driven, often entail promoting best practice solutions from abroad, often require short-term signals by host governments to placate external donors rather than reflecting a genuine commitment to reform, and often enlist relatively isolated "heroes" in central agencies of government in host countries in promoting these reforms with limited engagement by or participation in the formulation of reform strategies by line civil servants charged with implementing them in the field. Drawing on prior writing by Richard Scott,[11] Andrews argues that institutional performance entails an interaction of formal regulative, informal normative, and cultural-cognitive elements that shape what is feasible by way of civil service reforms in particular societal contexts. These contexts, by their nature, are likely to be highly particularistic, and not to be especially receptive to "best practices" imported from abroad. Andrews argues for a new approach to public sector reforms in development that he calls problem-driven iterative adaptation (PDIA), and calls for interventions to focus on solving problems through purposive muddling that includes active, ongoing and experiential learning, with engagement by broad sets of agents who together ensure that reforms are viable and relevant.

In a somewhat similar vein, critiquing conventional technocratic approaches to civil service reform, Thomas Carothers and Diane de Gramont, in a recent book, *Development Aid Confronts Politics: The Almost Revolution*, argue for politically informed methods of institutional reform that would entail an analytic framework consisting of the following main elements:[12]

• *Structural or foundational factors*: What historical, geographic, social, economic and political conditions have shaped the country's development? What are the sources of state authority (or lack thereof), and how autonomous is the country in relation to international actors? What are the primary areas of economic activity? Which groups hold political and economic power, and how did they acquire it? What are the most important social and ideological cleavages?

---

10 M. Andrews, *The Limits of Institutional Reform in Development: Changing Rules for Realistic Solutions* (Cambridge, UK: Cambridge University Press, 2013), chapters 1 and 2.

11 W.R. Scott, *Institutions and Organizations* (Thousand Oaks, CA: Sage Publications, 2008, 3rd edn).

12 T. Carothers and D. de Gramont, *Development Aid Confronts Politics: The Almost Revolution* (Washington, DC: Carnegie Endowment for International Peace, 2013).

- *Formal and informal institutions*: What rules and institutional arrangements – formal and informal – bear most significantly on the country's development? What institutions (state or non-state) hold the most power? Are these institutions considered legitimate? What type of engagement exists between state and society? Where does political contestation primarily occur? How transparent are formal and informal institutions, and how do they interact with each other? How do patronage systems operate?
- *Actors*: Who are the key government, societal and external players influencing development processes? What are their interests and incentives? How do they make decisions? Who holds power? How do they use it? Who are the likely winners and losers of reform? Who has the ability to block reform? How do these actors relate to each other?
- *Processes*: How has developmental change occurred in the past? How do the structural, institutional and stakeholder variables interact and constrain each other? What relevant changes are in progress? Are any major socio-economic trends or pressures likely to change the rules of the game in the future? What are the most salient political issues today?
- *Implications for donors*: What are the primary constraints on development? What are the entry points for change? What are the likely risks? Who are potential supporters of reform, and what capacity do they have to contribute to change? Is it possible to accommodate the interests of powerful players within a programme for pro-poor change? Where is reform not feasible? Where is it desirable to work within the current political context and power holders and where is it necessary to try to expand the existing space for reform?[13]

We now briefly review more specific public administration reform strategies that have been proposed or implemented (at least in part) in recent years in developing countries.

9.3.2   The new public management

Beginning in the early 1980s and continuing through into the 1990s, many developed countries (originating with the United Kingdom) adopted a set of public administration reforms that later became known as the New Public Management (NPM). These reforms found echoes in

---

13 *Ibid.*, at 146–7.

a number of developing countries, in many cases at the behest of its external donor agencies. According to Pollitt and Bouckaert, in their recent book, *Public Management Reform: A Comparative Analysis – New Public Management, Governance and the Neo-Weberian State*, the NPM favoured adopting a more business-like or entrepreneurial approach to the delivery of government services, which involved developing performance management measures, introducing more competition to the public sector, offering quality and choice to citizens, and strengthening the strategic, as opposed to the operational, role of major ministries of government.[14] According to Pollitt and Bouckaert, NPM is a bundle of specific concepts and practices, including:

- greater emphasis on performance, especially through the measurement of outputs ("bottom-line bureaucracies");
- a preference for lean, flat, small, specialized (disaggregated) organizational forms over large, multi-functional forms (less centralized command-and-control);
- a widespread substitution of contracts for hierarchical relations as the principal coordinating device ("steering, rather than rowing");
- a widespread injection of market-type mechanisms including competitive tendering, internal markets where, for example, public hospitals and schools would compete for patients and students with public money following the patient or student, public sector comparative league tables, and performance-related pay;
- an emphasis on treating service users as "customers" and on the application of generic quality improvement techniques such as Total Quality Management.

These elements have often been summarized as "disaggregation + competition + incentivization".

Richard Batley's five year review of the effects of NPM on the economies of developing countries finds that results have been ambiguous.[15] Often performance outcomes are difficult to define and measure, and contracting out through often flawed and sometimes corrupt processes to an often thin and uncompetitive private sector is not always more

---

14 C. Pollitt and G. Bouckaert, *Public Management Reform: A Comparative Analysis – New Public Management, Governance, and the Neo-Weberian State* (Oxford, UK: Oxford University Press, 2001), chapter 1.

15 R. Batley, "The Role of Government in Adjusting Economies" (1999) in N. Manning, "The Legacy of the New Public Management in Developing Countries" (2001) 67:2 *International Review of Administrative Sciences* 297–312.

efficient. Nick Manning observes that NPM was "no more able than old public administration to provide governments with the incentives and the capacity to address poverty and provide better services".[16] Since the late 1990s there has been scepticism about generalized application of NPM, even amongst developed countries,[17] and even more so in the case of developing countries. However, strains of NPM thinking have remained influential in the privatization of SOEs and the growth in PPPs, discussed in Chapter 11.

9.3.3   Civil servants as communitarians

Tendler, in her widely cited book, *Good Government in the Tropics*, explores, through detailed case studies, four programmes in the state of Ceará, in Brazil's poor northeast region:[18]

- programmes in preventive health;
- public procurement from informal sector producers;
- a large emergency employment-creating public works programme; and
- agricultural extension services to small farmers.

She draws several lessons from her studies of "good government".

First, government workers in all these cases demonstrated unusual dedication to their jobs and reported feeling more appreciated and recognized, not necessarily by superiors but by their clients and the communities in which they worked. Second, the state government contributed in an unusual and sometimes inadvertent way to the new sense of recognition by creating a strong sense of "calling" and mission around these particular programmes and their workers through public information campaigns, prizes for good performance, public screening methods for new recruits, orientation programmes, and sheer boasting through the media about its successes. Third, workers carried out a larger variety of tasks than usual and often voluntarily, in part in response to their perception of what their clients needed and out of a vision of the public good. Workers were able to provide this more customized service because they had greater autonomy and discretion

---

16 *Ibid.*, at 303.

17 See M. Trebilcock, *The Prospects for Reinventing Government*, (Toronto: C.D. Howe Institute, 1994).

18 Tendler, *supra* note 2.

than usual. Fourth, the greater discretion and responsibility inherent in the self-enlarged jobs and their fuzzier job definitions would seem to make supervision more difficult than it already is in large public bureaucracies; however, workers wanted to perform better in order to live up to the new trust placed in them by their clients and citizens in general. The trust was a result of the more customized arrangements of their work and the public messages of respect from the state. The communities where these public servants worked watched over them more closely and the state's publicity campaigns and similar messages had armed citizens with new information about their rights to better government and how public services were supposed to work. All these features suggest that instead of approaching public servants as rational self-interested agents, as many public management proposals tend to do, reformers should think of these servants as members of a community.

9.3.4 Institutional bypasses

As discussed in Chapter 3, path dependence is a crucial factor that policy-makers should consider in developing institutional reform strategies. Such strategies may often depart from Schiavo-Campo's recommendations, especially his argument that one should never "fence off" bureaucratic reform projects, and are often more consistent with the thrust of Tendler's analysis. In recent papers, Mariana Mota Prado argues that many successful reforms have one common feature: instead of trying to fix an entire set of dysfunctional institutions, as most failed reforms do, they simply bypass them.[19] These "institutional bypasses" can be an effective way of overcoming the three traditional obstacles to institutional reform proposed by Trebilcock and Daniels: (1) lack of financial, human or technological resources; (2) social-cultural-historical factors; and (3) political economy-based impediments.[20] Moreover, it may help reformers to deal with the high levels

---

19 M.M. Prado and A.C. Chasin, "How Innovative Was the Poupatempo Experience in Brazil? Institutional Bypass as a New Form of Institutional Change" (2011) 5:1 *Brazilian Political Science Review* 11; M.M. Prado, "Institutional Bypass: An Alternative for Development Reform", available at http://papers.ssrn.com/sol3/papers.cfm?abstract_id=1815442 (accessed 4 May 2014); see also T. Heller, "An Immodest Postscript" in E. Jensen and T. Heller (eds), *Beyond Common Knowledge: Empirical Approaches to the Rule of Law* (Palo Alto, CA: Stanford University Press, 2003).

20 M. Trebilcock and R. Daniels, *Rule of Law Reform and Development: Charting the Fragile Path of Progress* (Cheltenham, UK and Northampton, MA, USA: Edward Elgar, 2008), chapter 1.

of uncertainty related to the effects of reforms caused by institutional interconnections and path dependence-related factors.

One example of an institutional bypass is a bureaucratic reform in Brazil called *Poupatempo* (Saving Time).[21] In 1997, the government of the state of São Paulo created a one-stop shop for bureaucratic services. In contrast to the pre-existing system, in which government services were accessed by the public at multiple service points, offices of the federal, state and, in some cases, local administration were placed in one location in order to provide easy access to a variety of services, and new staff were hired and trained. Services were provided more quickly than within the pre-existing bureaucracy, disrupting entrenched institutional cultures. *Poupatempo* became the main provider of governmental services within the state shortly after its creation. In 2007, it provided services to an average of 50,000 people a day in the state of São Paulo. In that year, 18 units together serviced 23 million people. *Poupatempo* is an example of a successful institutional bypass because it created a new pathway for the provision of the same services that were being provided by the existing bureaucracy, but in a more efficient fashion.

9.3.5 Decentralization

Another line of thinking in much of the recent public service reform literature emphasizes the virtues of formal decentralization of government functions to sub-national levels of government (regional or local). This is based largely on the theory that decentralization moves the state closer to the people and renders it more responsive to local needs and preferences. While this, in principle, may be true, experience suggests that implementing decentralization strategies poses major design challenges.

First, a careful identification of functions that are better performed at the local rather than national level needs to be determined so as to minimize inter-jurisdictional spillovers (negative or positive externalities) which risk promoting local policies that may be at variance with or antithetical to the national interest. Such spillovers are likely to be pervasive in areas such as infrastructure, healthcare, education, law and order, and environmental degradation, rendering an appropriate division of power between national, regional and local governments a major challenge.

---

21 Prado and Chasin, *supra* note 19.

Second, once a division of functions is determined, a reallocation of financial capacity, commensurate with the reallocation of functions, is required. On the one hand, decentralizing functions without decentralizing financial capacity is likely to degrade the quality of services offered at the local level and is likely to require some form of fiscal equalization to ensure that all regions have reasonably equivalent capacity to deliver basic public services. On the other hand, decentralizing functions and decision-making authority without clearly defined and stable caps on the central government's fiscal responsibilities – through transfers or subsidies, or explicit or implicit guarantees of borrowings by sub-national levels of government – is likely to encourage fiscal irresponsibility by sub-national levels of government, as well as macro-economic instability.

Finally, if decentralization fails to increase local citizens' influence over the public sector, the principal benefits of decentralization will be lost. One of the key determinants of local accountability is the system for electing local officials – governors, mayors and members of sub-national legislatures. Where these regimes of accountability are deficient, decentralization may simply lead to more clientelism, patronage and outright corruption (an outcome, unfortunately, too often borne out by experience).[22] As Atul Kohli points out in an insightful recent article on state capacity for development, countries like India and Brazil often possess competent national bureaucracies – or at least apex economic bureaucracies – but state or local government functions, including the provision of infrastructure and basic education and healthcare, are often mired in incompetence, corruption, patrimonialism or excessive influence by wealthy local elites (explaining, in part, high levels of inequality in access to these services).[23]

---

22 See W. Dillinger and M. Fay, "From Centralized to Decentralized Governance" (1999) 36 *Finance and Development* 19; World Bank, *World Development Report: 1999–2000: Entering the 21st Century* (New York, NY: Oxford University Press, 1999), chapter 5; D. Halberstam, "Federalism: Theory, Policy, Law" in M. Rosenfeld and A. Sajo (eds), *Oxford Handbook of Comparative Constitutional Law* (Oxford, UK: Oxford University Press, 2012); S. Choudhry and N. Hume, "Federalism, Devolution, and Secession: From Classical to Post-conflict Federalism" in T. Ginsburg and R. Dixon (eds), *Research Handbook on Comparative Constitutional Law* (Cheltenham, UK and Northampton, MA, USA: Edward Elgar, 2012).

23 See A. Kohli, "State Capacity for Development" (2010) UNDP, Global Event Working Paper.

9.3.6   Building on social capital

A variant on formal decentralization strategies is to emphasize the potential for informal collaborative arrangements between the public and private sectors – in particular the realization of synergies between contributions by government and those by community or civil society organizations (intermediaries between government and individual citizen) that are able to deploy significant forms and levels of "social capital" amongst their members in collaborative enterprises for mutual benefit. Peter Evans argues that synergies may be realized because of the differences in comparative advantage between the state and civil society organizations in the provision of different inputs to joint projects and the greater potential for embeddedness that such projects permit in terms of civil servants engaging with the concerns of local communities.[24]

By way of examples, Evans points to successful cases of rural irrigation project developments in Taiwan, condominium sewer developments in urban areas of Brazil, and some of Tendler's case studies (for example, her study of the provision of agricultural extension services), as well as the dense public sector-private sector business networks that are often claimed to have been important ingredients in the industrialization of the high-performing East Asian economies. Tendler also argues that, from this perspective, public sector unions can be seen in a more sympathetic light than they are often portrayed in the development literature, where they are often seen as self-interested defenders of a dysfunctional status quo in public administration.

However, the East Asian example (amongst others) provides some basis for caution in assigning an indiscriminately large role to civil society in the development equation. What was once seen as an important strength of governments in the high-performing East Asian economies – extensive public sector-private sector networks – quickly became derided by many commentators during and after the Asian financial crisis in the late 1990s as symptomatic of "crony capitalism" –

---

24 P. Evans, "Government Action, Social Capital and Development: Reviewing the Evidence on Synergy" (1996) 25 *World Development* 1119; P. Evans, *Embedded Autonomy – States and Industrial Transformation* (Princeton, NJ: Princeton University Press, 1995); see also M. Woolcock, "Social Capital and Economic Development: Towards a Theoretical Synthesis in Policy Framework" (1998) 27 *Theory and Society* 151; C. Grootaert and T. van Bastelaer (eds), *The Role of Social Capital in Development: An Empirical Assessment* (Cambridge, UK and New York, NY: Cambridge University Press, 2002).

patronage and corruption in the allocation of credit, licenses and government contracts.[25]

9.4 Conclusion

While perhaps not as obvious as the design of political institutions and related constitutional frameworks, law and legal institutions do, in fact, play an important part in structuring the public administration in most countries. Public sector employment laws and collective bargaining regimes, grievance procedures, anti-discrimination or affirmative action laws (often enforced by courts, arbitral bodies or specialized human rights agencies), and specialized administrative agencies charged with overseeing recruitment and promotion (such as public service commissions) all play a central framework role in structuring the performance of a country's public service. Any major set of reforms to the public service must address reforms to this legal framework. In the case of specialized administrative agencies performing regulatory functions (discussed in Chapter 4), administrative law principles and judicial review potentially have a large area of application in ensuring transparency, impartiality and due process in their functioning.[26]

---

25 See, for example, D.C. Kang, *Crony Capitalism: Corruption and Development in South Korea and the Philippines* (Cambridge, UK: Cambridge University Press, 2002).

26 See S. Rose-Ackerman, *From Elections to Democracy: Building Accountable Government in Hungary and Poland* (Cambridge, UK and New York, NY: Cambridge University Press, 2005).

10 Corruption and development

Corruption affects most countries around the world but the problem is especially acute, and indeed pervasive, in many developing countries. The cost of corruption is high for developing countries, because it has a negative impact on a country's economy (impairing growth), its politics (affecting governmental regulation and policy decisions), its international relations (affecting FDI and diverting foreign aid from its intended purposes), and its society (worsening the distribution of wealth). The World Bank has identified "corruption as among the greatest obstacles to economic and social development".[1]

10.1 Defining corruption

Although there are many definitions of corruption, we use the term to refer to "the use of public office for private gain" – that is, corruption of or by public officials (political or bureaucratic).[2] This includes both "behaviour which deviates from the normal duties of a public role",[3] and "the violation of the formal rules governing the allocation of public resources".[4] However, in some countries there may be a lack of formal rules governing official behaviour, or the normal duties of an official may include behaviour that would qualify as corruption in

1 World Bank, "Fraud and Corruption", available at http://web.worldbank.org/WBSITE/EXTERNAL/ EXTSITETOOLS/0,,contentMDK:20147620~menuPK:344192~pagePK:98400~piPK:98424~theSit ePK:95474,00.html (accessed 4 May 2014).

2 C.W. Gray and D. Kaufmann, "Corruption and Development" (March 1998) 35 *Finance and Development* 1; P. Bardhan, *Scarcity, Conflicts, and Cooperation: Essays in the Political and Institutional Economics of Development* (Cambridge, MA: MIT Press, 2005) at 138.

3 J. Nye, "Corruption and Political Development: A Cost–benefit Analysis" (1967) 61 *American Political Science Review* 2.

4 M.H. Khan, "Patron-client Networks and the Economic Effects of Corruption in Asia" (1998) 10:1 *European Journal of Development Research* 15–39.

other countries, such as accepting gifts. This complicates comparison between countries.[5]

Generally, corruption entails an "exchange of government property for personal gain".[6] More often than not, economic gains are the goal of corrupt behaviour, but the term can also encompass the use of public office to obtain non-economic gains (political or personal). Although corruption comes in many forms, the common element is that an agent (usually a government official) pursues personal gain by bargaining away an item or benefit over which he or she has discretion, but which belongs to a principal (usually the public).[7] Corruption involving large sums of money is often referred to as "grand corruption", in contrast to those acts of corruption that involve smaller sums, which is known as "petty corruption". Grand and petty corruption have distinct consequences for a country's legal, political and economic systems, raising different types of concerns.[8]

Two of the most important types of corruption for economic gain are embezzlement and bribes. While embezzlement entails the misappropriation of public funds, bribes, in contrast, involve the appropriation of private funds by public officials. Officials might ask for bribes to perform their functions (for example, a city official asking for money to issue a permit that a citizen would otherwise be entitled to), not to perform their functions (for example, a police officer asking for money not to issue a ticket to the driver of a speeding vehicle), or not to perform acts that are not part of their functions but which they can threaten to perform through abuse of power (for example, a police officer asking for money not to torture a prisoner, or a tax official demanding a bribe to forgo an audit). Decisions can be "sold wholesale, as when government policies are distorted to benefit a specific interest group who has bribed policy-makers or retail, as is the case when public employees personally collect a payment for the granting of a permit or a license".[9]

Forms of corruption that involve non-economic benefits, clientelism or patronage take place where public resources and political processes

---

5   M. Johnston and A.J. Heidenheimer (eds), *Political Corruption: Concepts and Context* (New Brunswick, NJ: Transaction Publishers, 2001) at 26.

6   A. Shleifer and R.W. Vishny, "Corruption" (1993) 108:3 *Quarterly Journal of Economics* 1.

7   R. Klitgaard, *Controlling Corruption*, (Berkeley, CA: University of California Press, 1988) at 69–74.

8   G. Moody-Stuart, *Grand Corruption in Third World Development* (Oxford, UK: Worldview Publishing, 1997).

9   M. Naim, "Corruption Eruption" (Summer 1995) 2:2 *Brown Journal of World Affairs*, 245–61.

are manipulated to increase personal power. This entails a political exchange between a politician or public official, the "patron", who gives patronage in exchange for the vote or support of a "client". This is a form of "institutional corruption", which generates gains in a way that benefits officials in their capacity as public officials rather than in their personal life (individual corruption).[10] For example, an elected official may offer high-ranked and well-paid jobs in the bureaucracy in exchange for political support, rather than hiring based on merit.[11]

When patronage is applied to personal relationships, often referred to as "nepotism", it results in personal gains for elected officials who use public office to provide benefits and grant privileges to people with whom they are personally affiliated in some way. In this case, public office is used to create benefits for people who belong to a particular social network to which a public official also belongs (extended family, political party or ascriptive group, such as clan, ethnic or religious group).

10.2   Measuring corruption

The absence of an authoritative and universally applicable definition of what constitutes corruption limits the development of a measurement tool. This is further complicated by the absence of "direct, simple and easily contrastable indicators". Because it is a clandestine activity, corruption measurement requires "much more elaborated constructions, subject to complex and, often, subjective inputs".[12] Another problem is that the collection of data only started with the relatively recent attention to corruption in the development literature, resulting in an absence of data from before 1980.[13] Thus, there is limited capacity to analyse how corruption has evolved over longer periods of time.

Most assessments of corruption use one of three methods: (1) gathering the perceptions of stakeholders and individuals; (2) national

---

10 Johnston and Heidenheimer (eds), *supra* note 5, at 42.

11 J.A. Robinson and T. Verdier, "The Political Economy of Clientelism" (2003) Center for Economic Policy Research Discussion Paper No. 3205.

12 F. Javier-Urra, "Assessing Corruption – An Analytical Review of Corruption Measurement and its Problems: Perception, Error and Utility" (May 2007), E.A. Walsh School of Public Service, Georgetown Washington, available at http://unpan1.un.org/intradoc/groups/public/documents/apcity/unpan028792.pdf (accessed 4 May 2014).

13 A. Williams and A. Siddique, "The Use and Abuse of Governance Indicators" (2008) *Economics of Governance* 9.

institutional profiles which function as a proxy for corruption (budget management or procurement practices); and (3) auditing individual projects as a sample of likely national practices. None of these assessments is a direct measure of corruption. The most direct corruption indicators gather survey information on the real experiences of individuals and businesses of corruption and paying bribes.[14]

The most recent development in corruption measurement is the emergence of "second-generation"[15] or "aggregate indicators",[16] which combine several primary measurements. The most widely used measurements are the Corruption Perception Index, developed by Transparency International, and two indices developed by the World Bank: the Business Environment and Enterprise Survey and the World Governance Indicators (WGI).

The Corruption Perception Index incorporates a list of sources which have undertaken their own assessments of levels of corruption, such as the World Business Environment Survey or Freedom House, which are each given a weighting to yield an average corruption ranking. The major advantage of these indices is that they take an average rating, therefore avoiding biases in individual sources and measurement errors.[17] For example, the WGI expresses its rankings with larger confidence intervals for countries for which they have fewer primary sources.

Criticisms of these measures reveal the complicated challenge of measuring corruption. These measures primarily focus on expert assessments, such as elite business panels, rather than local household or business sector perceptions. They have been criticized for excluding the experiences of the poor or the informal sector, while focusing too heavily on the perspectives of multinational organizations.[18] Further, a significant gap has been found between perceptions and actual levels of corruption.[19]

---

14 See, for example, M. Seligson, "The Impact of Corruption on Regime Legitimacy: A Comparative Study of Four Latin American Countries" (2005) 64 *Journal of Politics* 408.

15 M. Johnston, "Measuring the New Corruption Rankings: Implications for Analysis and Reform" in Johnston and Heidenheimer (eds), *supra* note 5.

16 D. Kaufmann, A. Kraay and P. Zoido-Lobaton, "Aggregating Governance Indicators" (1999) World Bank Policy Research Working Paper No. 2195.

17 D. Kaufmann and A. Kraay, "On Measuring Governance: Framing Issues for Debate" (2007) Issues Paper for 11 January 2007, Roundtable on Measuring Governance, World Bank Institute and the Development Economics Vice-Presidency of the World Bank.

18 Williams and Siddique, *supra* note 13.

19 D. Treisman, "What Have We Learned about the Causes of Corruption from Ten Years of Cross-National Empirical Research?" (2007) 10 *Annual Review of Political Science* 211 at 215.

Perceptions have been found to overestimate local experiences of corruption when compared to survey evidence of real experiences of corruption.[20] However, even if more objective data regarding government practices is used, it is still likely to obscure the real situation because of the difficulty of obtaining accurate measurements of a secret activity.

10.3   Consequences of corruption

How does corruption negatively affect development prospects? The misappropriation of public funds for private use has a clear and direct effect on the amount of government finances available to be spent on development-related projects and services. Bribes, in contrast, raise more complicated questions.[21]

In the past, some authors have suggested that bribery can positively influence government functioning and development. Bribes have been considered to be supplementary to a bureaucrat's salary, and thus are similar to the government raising taxes and increasing the remuneration of public servants.[22] This would be especially true if bribes are being paid for these servants to perform their functions or to overcome bureaucratic hurdles (a form of piece-work or performance-based compensation).[23] Some scholars have argued that using bribery to fund the bureaucracy instead of taxes may reduce the tax burden paid by businesses that do not use the government service calling for these bribes, and these lower taxes may be beneficial for growth.[24]

It has also been claimed that bribery can help to overcome institutional shortcomings and foster efficiency. For example, Huntington has argued that bribery could enhance efficiency by "oiling" the ineffective

---

20 M. Razafindrakoto and F. Roubaud, "How Far Can We Trust Expert Opinions on Corruption? An Experiment Based on Surveys in Francophone Africa" in *Global Corruption Report* (London/Ann Arbor: Transparency International, Pluto Press, 2005).

21 Gray and Kaufmann, *supra* note 2.

22 B. Weder, "Institutions, Corruption, and Development and their Ramifications for International Cooperation" in H. van Ginkel, B. Barrett, J. Court and J. Velasquez (eds), *Human Development and the Environment: Challenges for the United Nations in the New Millennium* (New York, NY: United Nations University Press, 2002) 149–59.

23 Of course, the argument does not apply if the bribe was being paid to stop acts in which officials are abusing their powers and positions, such as police officers who ask for bribes not to torture prisoners.

24 G.S. Becker and G.J. Stigler, "Law Enforcement, Malfeasance, and Compensation of Enforcers" (1974) 3 *Journal of Legal Studies* 1.

mechanisms of a poorly functioning government, thus improving governance through an informal mechanism.[25] Bribes have also been described as an allocative mechanism that allows for a kind of bidding contest for government services, which may result in an efficient allocation of resources.[26]

These arguments in favour of bribery are not persuasive. A major difference between taxes and bribery is the cost of keeping corruption secret to avoid detection and punishment, with the result that corruption is more distortionary than taxation.[27] There is also evidence that suggests that the cost of capital for organizations tends to be higher where bribery is more prevalent.[28] Moreover, there is a high degree of uncertainty in corruption practices: a private party will never be sure if a corrupt official will keep his promises.

The negative impact of bribes on economic development was first demonstrated empirically by Mauro in a 1995 article "Corruption, Country Risk and Growth".[29] In a business environment with substantial unpredictable costs, businesses will be reluctant to invest. The more variable the rates of corruption, the more negative the effect on foreign investment.[30] Instead, public investment is often increased, as larger budgets and bureaucratic structures of government provide more ample opportunities for corruption and misappropriation.[31] The argument that claims that corruption is efficiency-enhancing assumes that red tape is an exogenous factor, and ignores the fact that bribes might become an incentive for the creation of pervasive and cumbersome regulation, thus exacerbating rather than solving the problem of inefficient governance.[32] Corruption may also create incentives to

---

25 S.P. Huntington, *Political Order in Changing Societies* (New Haven, CT: Yale University Press, 1968).

26 N.H. Leff, "Economic Development through Bureaucratic Corruption" (1964) 8:3 *American Behavioral Scientist* 8–14.

27 Bardhan, *supra* note 2, at 139–40.

28 *Ibid.*, at 146.

29 P. Mauro, "Corruption, Country Risk and Growth" (1995) 110 *Quarterly Journal of Economics* 681.

30 S.-J. Wei, "Why is Corruption so Much More Taxing than Tax? Arbitrariness Kills" (1997) National Bureau of Economic Research Working Paper 6255 (Cambridge, MA).

31 V. Tanzi and H. Davoodi, "Corruption, Public Investment, and Growth" (1997) International Monetary Fund Working Paper, 97/139.

32 V. Tanzi, "Corruption around the World: Causes, Consequences, Scope and Cure" (1998) 45 IMF Staff Papers 4; Gray and Kaufmann, *supra* note 2, at 8; Bardhan, *supra* note 2, at 141.

preserve the existence of a burdensome regulatory framework, given that interest groups that benefit from the status quo will resist any type of reform aimed at reducing red tape.

Empirical evidence shows that in countries where bribery is common the amount of time private enterprise representatives spend with public officials is higher than in less corrupt countries, reflecting an inefficient use of resources that are wasted on courting political connections.[33] Moreover, those best able to utilize bribery are often not the socially optimal service recipients:

> The grease argument is particularly troublesome in this context [where laws and regulations serve productive social objectives, such as building codes, environmental controls, and prudential banking sector regulations] since bribes can override such regulations and cause serious social harm, such as illegal logging of tropical rain forests or failure to observe building codes designed to ensure public safety.[34]

Corruption negatively affects the ability of the government to regulate market activity effectively by distorting the decision-making process of government officials. Anti-corruption detection and punishment efforts are also costly for the state. Finally, the distributive effect of corruption is negative: while a tax system can have progressive features, bribery-driven bureaucracies inherently disadvantage the poor, increasing inequality and perpetuating vested interests. Corruption increases levels of inequality by limiting access to beneficial government activities to an already privileged group.[35] In sum, corruption is a major obstacle to development.

While corruption has negative consequences for economic growth it is not fully clear whether causality between corruption and development runs in only one direction. Corruption can reduce GDP per capita, but at the same time poorer countries have fewer resources to fight corruption, and the lack of resources creates more incentives to be corrupt,[36] which suggests that growth may reduce corruption.

---

33 R. Fisman and R. Gatti, "Bargaining for Bribes: The Role of Institutions" (2006) Discussion Paper No. 5712, CEPR.

34 Gray and Kaufmann, *supra* note 2, at 8–9.

35 J.-S. You and S. Khagram, "A Comparative Study of Inequality and Corruption" (2005) 70:1 *American Sociological Review* 136–57.

36 See Mauro *supra* note 29 and J.G. Lambsdorff, "Consequences and Causes of Corruption – What Do We Know From a Cross-section of Countries?", in S. Rose-Ackerman (ed.), *International*

Another set of consequences of corruption has recently received increased attention. Transparency International has declared that "in low-income countries, rampant corruption jeopardizes the global fight against poverty, threatening to derail the United Nations Millennium Development Goals". For instance, countries with higher levels of corruption have higher maternal mortality rates and lower levels of education. These results are not directly correlated with countries' GDP per capita. This has prompted calls to include anti-corruption measures in the post-2015 global development agenda.[37]

10.4   Causes of corruption

Corruption has not always been a prominent issue on the development agenda. Until recently, there was resistance to discussing the prevalence of corruption in developing countries because this could suggest that it was part of the culture of these countries – a claim that could be perceived as racist, discriminatory or morally patronizing.[38] Some studies have linked levels of corruption to such factors as more hierarchical social structures or social embeddedness, which can be detrimental to individual civic engagement – a factor which should help to reduce corruption.[39] Although culture may not be able to explain fully the presence of corruption in developing countries, it is clear that reforms targeting corruption must take cultural factors into account.[40]

The importance of culture has been documented in a study by Raymond Fisman and Edward Miguel.[41] They measured how likely it was for

---

Handbook on the Economics of Corruption (Cheltenham, UK and Northampton, MA, USA: Edward Elgar, 2006).

37 P. Garson, "Push to Tackle Corruption in Post-2015 Agenda" (4 October 2013) IRIN, available at http://www.irinnews.org/report/98876/push-to-tackle-corruption-in-post-2015-agenda_(accessed 4 May 2014). See also S. Gupta, H. Davoodi and E. Tiongson, "Corruption and the Provision of Health Care and Education Services" (2000) IMF Working Paper WP/oo/116, at 24–5.

38 R. Klitgaard, *supra* note 7, at 208–9.

39 R. La Porta, F. Lopez-De-Silanes, A. Shleifer and R.W. Vishny, "The Quality of Government" (1999) 15:1 *Journal of Law, Economics and Organization* 222–79; Lambsdorff, *supra* note 36; A. Licht, C. Goldschmidt and S. Schwartz, "Culture Rules: The Foundations of the Rule of Law and other Norms of Governance" (2007) 35 *Journal of Comparative Economics* 659.

40 B. Husted, "Wealth, Culture, and Corruption" (1999) 30:2 *Journal of International Business Studies* 339–60.

41 R. Fisman and E. Miguel, "Corruption, Norms and Legal Enforcement: Evidence from Diplomatic Parking Tickets" (2007) 115 *Journal of Political Economy*, 1020–48.

diplomats from different countries working for the United Nations in New York to comply with parking rules. These diplomats have immunity and therefore cannot be fined when they park illegally (they can be issued tickets, but they do not have an obligation to pay them). Their study shows that diplomats from corrupt countries are more likely to park illegally and, whenever fined, these same diplomats are less likely to pay these fines than diplomats from less corrupt countries. The lesson, as Fisman and Miguel put it, is "that reformers of government institutions – whether local officials or World Bank hotshots – must be aware that values and social norms can undermine their attempts at change. In other words, altering the law is unlikely to be sufficient in the presence of a pervasive culture of corruption".[42]

Corruption is more commonly explained as rampant in developing countries "not because their people are different from people elsewhere, but because conditions are ripe for it".[43] Institutional arrangements (such as low civil service salaries, monopoly rents in regulated industries, discretion of public officials, and poorly defined and ever changing rules and regulations) create opportunities and incentives for corruption, making the problem more pervasive in these nations.[44]

Poor government quality can be either a cause or a consequence of corruption. Sometimes they reinforce each other and the causal arrow runs in both directions. There are, however, certain institutional arrangements that are more often correlated with higher levels of corruption, as Lambsdorff shows in a detailed review of the literature.[45] Centralized states seem to be more corrupt than federal states with a high level of fiscal decentralization. This seems especially true if decentralization reforms take place in countries that have civic cooperation, trust among people, and well-developed sub-national units. The relationship between democracy and corruption is non-linear: democratic practices inhibit corruption after a country has a robust, fully functional democratic regime; however, corruption in medium-democratic regimes is higher than in authoritarian countries. Within democracies, smaller voting districts, proportional representation and presidential systems are correlated with higher levels of corruption.[46]

---

42 R. Fisman and E. Miguel, *Economic Gangsters: Corruption, Violence, and the Poverty of Nations* (Princeton, NJ: Princeton University Press, 2008) at 102.

43 Gray and Kaufmann, *supra* note 2.

44 *Ibid.*, at 9.

45 Lambsdorff, *supra* note 36.

46 *Ibid.*

It is not very often, however, that reformers find themselves in a position to change a country's political regime. The windows of opportunity for state-building exercises are rare and more often than not reformers will be able to do little to change the political institutions along the lines implied by Lambsdorff. With this in mind, we turn to potential reform options that take into account the fact that the reformers are not writing on a blank slate.

10.5   Potential cures

Institutional reforms can reduce the opportunities and incentives to use public office for private gains and therefore have significant potential to reduce overall levels of corruption. In this regard, Susan Rose-Ackerman provides the following categories of reform strategies that are available for tackling corruption:

1. the redesign of government programmes to limit the underlying incentives for corruption by limiting the pay-offs available from corruption;
2. increasing accountability and transparency of government actions to increase the likelihood of preventing corruption;
3. more radical reforms of government structure, such as constitutional re-engineering, to limit opportunities for corruption.[47]

In addition to these strategies, a common proposal is the creation of anti-corruption watchdog bodies, such as the Hong Kong Independent Committee against Corruption (ICAC), which was created in 1974 in response to perceived high levels of corruption in Hong Kong society.[48] This body conducts high-profile investigations and prosecutions, which have led to a significant decrease in corruption levels since its creation.[49] The results have been particularly striking in the Hong Kong Police Department, where the ICAC, operating completely separately from regular law enforcement bodies, was able to launch a strong anti-corruption offensive, including the investigation, arrest and interroga-

---

47 S. Rose-Ackerman, *Corruption and Government: Causes, Consequences and Reform* (Cambridge, UK: Cambridge University Press, 1999) at 26.

48 D. Kaufmann, "Revisiting Anti-Corruption Strategies: Tilt towards Incentive Driven Approaches?" in UNDP, *Corruption and Integrity Improvement Initiatives in Developing Countries* (New York, NY: UNDP, 1998).

49 B. de Speville, *Hong Kong: Policy Initiatives against Corruption*, (OECD Development Centre Publishing, 1997).

tion of police management and officers. The success of these efforts was largely as a result of maintaining routine investigations, regardless of the presence of specific reports of corruption.[50]

As well as focusing on enforcement and prevention, the ICAC also included mass public education campaigns, which informed citizens about the role of the ICAC, and the illegality of corruption and what this comprised. Reporting of corruption was also encouraged, and this served to increase social disapproval of corrupt activities. This fundamental change in the attitudes of the Hong Kong community was coupled with the institutional changes necessary to increase public perceptions of corruption control, especially within the police.[51] The results of these efforts were the eradication of syndicated police corruption by the end of the 1970s, and a clear reduction in corruption in government by the late 1980s.[52] This created "a new equilibrium of clean government", and the public expectation that this should remain the norm.[53]

It is important to acknowledge, however, that the creation of an anti-corruption body alone is unlikely to be an effective measure to tackle corruption. Since the 1990s, more than 30 countries have established some form of anti-corruption agency (ACA), but, "almost two decades later, ACAs are struggling to show a clear and significant impact on corruption and are generally not regarded as an effective policy tool against corruption".[54] Monitoring bodies will only be as effective, independent and capable as the overseers who run them.[55] Moreover, as in other cases of reform, there are important institutional interconnections that require more than stand-alone reforms. For instance, there is little that a watchdog can do without strong anti-bribery legislation

---

50 M. Manion, *Corruption by Design: Building Clean Government in Mainland China and Hong Kong* (Cambridge, MA: Harvard University Press, 2004) at 41.

51 *Ibid.*, at 44.

52 *Ibid.*, at 72.

53 *Ibid.*

54 F. Recanatini, "Anti-Corruption Authorities: An Effective Tool to Curb Corruption?" in S. Rose-Ackerman and T. Soreide, (eds) *International Handbook on the Economics of Corruption* (Cheltenham, UK and Northampton, MA, USA: Edward Elgar, 2011, 2nd edn) 528–9. See also A. Doig, D. Watt and R. Williams, "Measuring 'Success' in Five African Anti-Corruption Commissions: The Cases of Ghana, Malawi, Tanzania, Uganda and Zambia" U4 Research Report (Bergen: Chr. Michelsen Institute, 2005).

55 S. Rose-Ackerman and R. Truex, "Corruption and Policy Reform" (2012), Working Paper, Copenhagen Consensus Project, 21, available at http://www.copenhagenconsensus.com/sites/default/files/Working%2Bpaper_Corruption.pdf (accessed 4 May 2014).

and an effective independent court system to enforce the applicable sanctions.[56] There is also a more indirect connection between reform success and incentives and opportunities for corruption. Some reforms may increase the risk of punishment, but they are less likely to be effective if strong incentives and opportunities for corruption remain. Indeed, a great deal of the Hong Kong experience is also based on a variety of specific institutional reforms including, for instance, the legalization of off-track betting, which eliminated an opportunity for police officers to extract bribes from citizens.[57]

Another challenge for institutional reforms is that they need to account for self-reinforcing mechanisms in corruption practices. As Bardhan explains, adopting a game theoretic approach, social norms can settle in multiple equilibria, making the problems of corruption relatively rare, widespread or systemic.[58] The basic assumption is that expected gains from corruption depend on the number of other people who are expected to be corrupt. In this context, there are three possible equilibria: (1) nobody is corrupt, and it does not pay to be corrupt; (2) everyone is corrupt, and it does not pay to be non-corrupt; (3) there are both corrupt and non-corrupt officials, who are indifferent between being corrupt or non-corrupt. While the first and the second equilibria are stable, the third is not: if more and more officials decide to be corrupt, this can tip the equilibrium to one where everyone is corrupt.[59] Self-reinforcing mechanisms will be an obstacle for institutional reform in cases in which there is an equilibrium where everyone is corrupt and these social norms are very stable.

In cases "where there is systemic corruption, the institution's rules and norms of behaviour have already been adapted to a corrupt modus operandi, with bureaucrats and other agents often following the predatory examples of, or even taking instructions from, their principals in the political arena".[60] On the other hand, small changes in an unstable equilibrium can tip the balance in the opposite direction, towards the point where nobody is corrupt. In this regard, reformers can use self-reinforcing mechanisms to move the equilibrium towards lower levels of corruption. For instance, the functions of an anti-corruption watch-

---

56 See, for example, M.M. Taylor and T.J. Power (eds) *Corruption and Democracy in Brazil* (Notre Dame, IN: University of Notre Dame Press, 2011).

57 Klitgaard, *supra* note 7, at 116.

58 Bardhan, *supra* note 2, at 152.

59 *Ibid.*, at 154.

60 Gray and Kaufmann, *supra* note 2, at 8.

dog can be reinforced by the creation of various kinds of accountability mechanisms, such as "an independent office of public auditing, an election commission to limit and enforce rules on campaign contributions in democratic elections, citizens' watchdog committees providing information and monitoring services, a local ombudsman's office with some control over the bureaucracy. . .".[61]

In addition to institutional interconnections and self-reinforcing mechanisms, there is yet another similarity between reforms to tackle corruption and other pro-development institutional reforms: the problem of an uncongenial political economy in which interest groups that benefit from corruption are likely to resist reform.[62] Systemic corruption means that many powerful groups are likely to fall in this category, making it difficult to identify the possible beneficiaries from reform who might be mobilized to promote the necessary changes. In these cases, for example, it might be necessary to wait for a window of opportunity where a dramatic change in political regime or a major public scandal makes it politically feasible to promote reform.[63]

In the case of bribery, one possible solution is to promote reform focused on multinational companies based in developed countries, but which operate within developing countries, often engaging with corrupt governments. Bribes involve two parties: the public official demanding the bribe (the demand side) and the private party willing to pay for it (the supply side). Thus, in addition to reforms that reduce opportunities and incentives for corruption among public officials, it is also possible to reduce opportunities and incentives for corruption among multinational corporations, thus reducing the supply side. These companies can be controlled by extra-territorial legislation in their countries of origin, which would also govern their acts outside the home country's territory. This would overcome some of the institutional complexities of promoting reform in developing countries.

One of the first countries to enact legislation against these practices was the United States. The 1977 Foreign Corrupt Practices Act (FCPA)

---

61 P. Bardhan, *The Role of Governance In Economic Development: A Political Economy Approach* (OECD, 1997) at 35. Also see F.T. Lui, "A Dynamic Model of Corruption Deterrence" (1986) 31 *Journal of Public Economics* 215.

62 See Chapter 3, section 3.5.

63 W. Dillinger and M. Fay, "From Centralized to Decentralized Governance" (1999) 36 *Finance and Development* 4.

forbids American companies from bribing foreign officials, or from knowingly arranging for a bribe through an intermediary.[64] However, there are limitations to its scope: the Act does not forbid payments to speed up bureaucratic processes (facilitation or "grease payments") and in 1988 the Act was amended to expand the list of what qualifies as facilitation. This list now includes "all payments to foreign officials to expedite procedures, such as customs procedures or permits, that would otherwise occur without a bribe, but more slowly".[65] It also exempts payments to family members. The Act applies to all United States' nationals, or entities established under United States' law or operating principally in the United States. The FCPA's books and records provisions also apply to all issuers, thus covering all entities that hold securities registered with the Securities and Exchange Commission (SEC), or that are required to file periodic reports with the SEC. In other words, foreign companies trading shares in the United States can also be held liable under the FCPA. Since the enactment of the FCPA, the United States has put considerable pressure on other countries to follow its actions.

In 1997, the OECD promulgated the first multilateral convention to combat bribery of foreign officials – the OECD Anti-Bribery Convention – which was also signed by Argentina, Brazil, Bulgaria, Chile and the Slovak Republic.[66] Currently it has 40 signatories, accounting for 80 per cent of the world's exports and 90 per cent of outward FDI.[67] The Convention closely follows the basic principles of the anti-bribery provisions of the FCPA. The Convention also includes the provisions of the 1995 Recommendation on the Tax Deductibility of Bribes of Foreign Public Officials – which recommended that member countries make bribes paid to foreign officials no longer tax deductible as a business expense – which has since been implemented by all signatories.[68] Although the implementation of the Convention has been heralded as significant progress in advancing anti-corruption efforts, its efficacy is limited by the allocation of minimal resources in many countries to monitoring compliance and enforcement, and often limited incentives to undertake such actions against a state's own businesses competing with foreign

64 Foreign Corrupt Practices Act, 15 U.S.C.78 m, 78dd-2, 78dd-3, 78ff.

65 A. Cuervo-Cazurra, "The Effectiveness of Laws against Bribery Abroad" (2008) 39:4 *Journal of International Business Studies* 636.

66 OECD Convention, OECD Doc. DAFFE/IME/BR(97)20, reprinted in 37 I.L.M. 1 (1998).

67 OECD Working Group on Bribery, Annual Report 2013 7 (10 June 2013).

68 OECD Convention, OECD/C(96)27/Final, (1996), reprinted in 35 I.L.M. 1311 (1996).

businesses for contracts in other countries.[69] Also, major foreign investors such as China are not signatories; this creates collective action problems. Thus it may be a weak substitute for domestic institutional reform.

The recent Extractive Industries Transparency Initiative (EITI) is an attempt to reduce the supply of bribes from multinational companies (MNCs) in natural resource extraction sectors. Such bribes enable MNCs to gain control of the desired resource without paying the country the full value it would have received in a fair and competitive market.[70] The EITI involves a coalition of governments, companies, civil society groups, investors and international organizations.[71] Governments and companies that sign the EITI do so voluntarily, and are then bound to publish all payments made, or payments received, which are independently verified by a multi-stakeholder group ("Publish What You Pay"). In line with this, both the United States and the European Union have enacted regulations requiring public (and, in the case of the European Union, large private) companies to report publicly how much they pay for oil, gas, and minerals on a country-by-country and project-by-project basis. Canada is considering similar regulations.[72]

10.6   Conclusion

Corruption is a complex phenomenon, but academic research has shown that some of the underlying causes of corruption are institutional.[73] Based on this assumption, we have assessed the prospects

---

69 F. Heimann and G. Dell *Exporting Corruption? Country Enforcement of the OECD Anti-Bribery Convention Progress Report 2012* (Transparency International, 2012, 2nd edn), available at http://issuu.com/transparencyinternational/docs/2012_exportingcorruption_oecdprogress_en?e=2496456/2042485_(accessed 4 May 2014).

70 J. Stiglitz, *Making Globalization Work* (New York, NY: W.W. Norton & Co., 2006) at 140–41.

71 Extractive Industries Transparency Initiative, "What is the EITI?", available at http://eiti.org/eiti (accessed 4 May 2014).

72 See *Disclosure Rules: US and EU Standards* (Revenue Watch Institute), available at http://www.revenuewatch.org/sites/default/files/EU-US-rules.pdf (accessed 4 May 2014) and see "Background to Recommendations on Mandatory Disclosure of Payments from Canadian Mining Companies to Governments" (The Resource Revenue Transparency Group, 14 June 2013), available at http://www.revenuewatch.org/sites/default/files/RRTWG%20Background%20-%20June%202013.pdf (accessed 4 May 2014).

73 Rose-Ackerman, *supra* note 47, at 226.

for anti-corruption reforms. Combating corruption requires a complex plan of action, which must be adapted to the particular circumstances of each country, and needs to take into account institutional interdependencies, self-reinforcing mechanisms that generate path dependence and political economy problems. In sum, anti-corruption reforms face similar challenges to other institutional reforms analysed in this book.

11 State-owned enterprises, privatization and public-private partnerships[1]

11.1 Introduction

Infrastructure is a critical driver of economic growth and can significantly raise living standards. In the developing world, where basic infrastructure such as transportation networks, electricity generation and distribution, water distribution, and telecommunication systems are often lacking, infrastructural investment is widely viewed as an urgent priority. For developing country governments, infrastructural projects test government budgetary, technological and institutional capacity.

The most recent estimate for Africa pegs infrastructural needs at US$93 billion per year, or 15 per cent of the continent's annual GDP – more than double the current rate of investment. Just under half of the need is in the electricity sector, followed by water and sanitation.[2] The Middle East and North African region faces an annual infrastructural need of US$206 billion (close to 7 per cent of GDP), mainly in transportation and electricity.[3] Meeting the infrastructural gap in Latin American and the Caribbean would require countries in the region to boost investment as a share of GDP from the current rate of 2 per cent to 5.2 per cent (principally in the transportation and water

---

1 Portions of this chapter are adapted and updated from three previous publications by one of the authors: D. Andrew, C. Smith and M.J. Trebilcock, "State-owned Enterprises in Less Developed Countries: Privatization and Alternative Reform Strategies" (2001) 12 *European Journal of Law and Economics*; R.J. Daniels and M.J. Trebilcock, "The Private Provision of Public Infrastructure: An Organizational Analysis of the Next Frontier" (1996) 46 *University of Toronto Law Journal* 393; and M. Trebilcock and M. Rosenstock, "Infrastructure Public-Private Partnerships in the Developing World: Lessons from Recent Experience" (forthcoming).

2 V. Foster and C. Briceno-Garmendia (eds), *Africa's Infrastructure: A Time for Transformation* (Washington, DC: The World Bank/Agence Français de Développement, 2010), Table 1.2 at 47.

3 A. Estache, E. Ianchovichina, R. Bacon and I. Salamon, *Infrastructure and Employment Creation in the Middle East and North Africa* (Washington, DC: The World Bank, 2013) at 16.

infrastructure sectors).[4] Electricity and transportation represent the bulk of infrastructural needs in Asia, which total over US$825 billion annually.[5] Across the developing world, electricity and transport make up over 80 per cent of infrastructural needs.

How might these infrastructural needs be met? In the 1980s and 1990s a wave of privatizations swept the world as the answer to these problems. State-owned enterprises (SOEs) in many countries were sold to private investors in sectors as varied as steel, mining, banking, telecommunications, electricity and water. From 1977 to 1999 there were 2,459 privatization deals in 121 countries.[6] Privatization, together with a number of other reforms that constituted the so-called "Washington Consensus",[7] was part of an internationally accepted strategy for fostering economic growth.

Privatizations came to replace the strategy so far adopted to deal with infrastructure – SOEs. SOEs traditionally played a prominent role in delivering infrastructural services in some developed and most developing countries. Thus, governments performed many of the economic functions pursued by the private sector in other countries. Privatization reforms were driven by the assumption that these functions could be more efficiently performed by the private sector. However, the results have been mixed.

Over the past two decades, developing country governments have increasingly turned to PPPs to build and operate infrastructure, with the goal of delivering timely, cost-effective and efficiently run projects and to meet governments' budgetary constraints. PPPs have gained prominence on the development agenda by offering a compromise between the two solutions previously proposed. On the one hand, SOEs may provide social and political benefits to a country, but these may come at significant economic and fiscal costs because of operational inefficiencies. On the other hand, private companies may be able to deliver essential and basic services, such as electricity or telecommunications, but there are significant challenges in ensuring that these

---

4 "'The Economic Infrastructure Gap in Latin America and the Caribbean': Facilitation of Transport and Trade in Latin America and the Caribbean" (2011) FAL Bulletin, Issue No. 293 at 6.

5 B.N. Bhatacharwy, "Financing Infrastructure for Connectivity: Policy Implications for Asia" (2011) Asian Development Bank Institute Research Policy Brief 33, at 5–6.

6 B. Bortolotti, M. Fantini and D. Siniscalco, "Privatization around the World: Evidence from Panel Data" (2003) 88 *Journal of Public Economics* 305.

7 See Chapter 2.

companies will provide universal service and foster other social and political goals. Reducing the inefficiencies of state-owned companies can provide infrastructure for other economic activities, thus fostering economic growth. However, this goal cannot be decoupled from alleviating poverty and providing universal access to essential services. This is especially true in developing countries. While PPPs may offer a compromise between the two alternatives of direct state intervention (SOEs) and privatization, many challenges remain in designing PPPs to achieve these objectives effectively.

This chapter analyses the arguments for and against state-owned companies, reviews the evidence from the most recent privatization experiences around the world, discusses possible reasons for multiple failures, assesses whether PPPs offer an alternative strategy, and concludes with a discussion of new forms of state intervention in a market economy. The conclusion is that there is a strong institutional component in all of these arrangements. The success or failure of SOEs, privatization or PPPs is connected both with a country's broader institutional environment (a healthy private sector, effective regulation, lack of corruption and a stable political system). Thus, reforms to improve the delivery of basic services in developing countries are intrinsically connected to the reforms discussed in other chapters of this book.

11.2   State-owned enterprises (SOEs)

11.2.1   Rationales for SOEs

SOEs emerged in the developing world for a mix of political, ideological and economic reasons. They were often formed (and subsequently expanded) to marshal support for new and fragile governments in developing countries: the larger an SOE sector, the larger a government's direct influence over its economy. Developing country governments were also often influenced by the spread of socialist ideology following World War II, which dictated that the state should control the "commanding heights" of its economy.[8] Nationalism, often in the form

---

8 See, for example, M. Haririan, *State-Owned Enterprises in a Mixed Economy: Micro versus Macro Economic Objectives* (London: Westview Press, 1989) at 10; R. Muir and J.P. Saba, *Improving State Enterprise Performance: The Role of Internal and External Incentives* (Washington, DC: World Bank, 1995) at 11; M. Gillis, "The Role of State Enterprises in Economic Development" (1980) 47:2 *Social Research* 248, at 263.

of sovereignty concerns following decolonization, similarly fuelled the desire for developing countries to control the strategic sectors of their economies. SOEs were also advocated as a workable method of income redistribution – for example, by reducing prices of goods primarily consumed by the poor – especially in developing countries with large informal sectors in which income redistribution could not practically be accomplished through a progressive tax system. Profitability was often not the most important goal behind their creation.

The primary economic motivation behind SOEs was increased capital investment. Several constraints hindered capital investment in developing countries in the years following World War II, the most important of which was low domestic savings rates. Developing countries also often lacked the institutions, such as effective financial intermediaries, necessary to facilitate allocative efficiency in capital markets. Moreover, developing countries suffered from market failures, such as low-level investment traps and a lack of basic infrastructure. In addition to ostensibly addressing these problems, SOEs also served other economic purposes, including combating inflation, controlling industries susceptible to natural monopolies, protecting fragile developing country economies from external shocks, and promoting regional development within a developing country. Thus, SOEs were not created exclusively to generate revenue for the nation state but were also intended to yield economic and social benefits above and beyond any financial reforms.[9] When assessing the success of SOEs, particularly in comparison to private enterprises, it is important to evaluate an SOE in light of its putative social purposes.

11.2.2 The cost of poor SOEs' performance

Over the 1980's, an increasing number of SOEs in developing countries were unable to generate the resources needed to finance their operations, expansion and the servicing of their debts.[10] Financing came from borrowed money that led to persistent deficits of SOEs, which in turn triggered derivative social costs. First, SOEs received a dispropor-

---

9 For some less developed countries (LDCs), SOEs operated as an institutional bypass, as these countries suffered from a lack of bureaucratic capacity, more specifically an inability to tax and regulate private enterprise at arm's length, and state ownership offered an alternative means of taxation: World Bank, *World Development Report 1991: The Challenge of Development* (New York, NY: Oxford University Press, 1991) at 130.

10 The World Bank, *Bureaucrats in Business: The Economics and Politics of Government Ownership* (Washington, DC: World Bank, 1995) at 42–3.

tionate amount of domestic investment, significantly increasing the cost of capital for private enterprises in developing countries. More generally, inefficient levels of production in SOEs resulted in the withdrawal of resources from areas of the economy in which they might be more productively employed.[11] Second, developing country governments, which are often reluctant to cut social expenditures, tended to cut expenditures with long-term benefits (such as infrastructure) in order to finance SOE deficits. The direct and indirect losses attributable to poor SOE performance have been estimated at between 5 and 8 per cent of GDP in the typical developing country and, where an SOE sector is relatively large, as high as 8 to 12 per cent of GDP.[12] In many developing countries, SOEs' operating subsidies could have at least doubled education and healthcare expenditures.[13]

SOEs have often not delivered the social benefits they were intended to achieve.[14] For example, notwithstanding that one of the key economic rationales behind the creation of SOEs was an increase in capital investment in infrastructure so as to make private investment in developing countries more attractive, the World Bank estimates that the poor quality of utilities and infrastructure adds 10 to 25 per cent to a firm's costs in sub-Saharan Africa.[15] If SOEs do provide positive social externalities (a benefit not necessarily specific to public enterprise), they do so at a significant cost to organizational efficiency.

11.2.3   The causes of SOEs' poor performance

Academics have argued that there are two key factors that can potentially explain SOEs inefficiency: (1) the ownership effect and (2) the competition effect.

---

11 An SOE sector typically represents about 11 per cent of GDP in developing economies, rising to an average of 14 per cent in the poorest developing countries. The SOE share of gross domestic investment (GDI) is generally much higher: in 1991 accounting for about 18 per cent of GDP in developing economies and about 27 per cent in low-income countries. By way of contrast, SOE sectors typically represented about 8 per cent and 13 per cent of GDI respectively in high-income economies in 1988, which is now much lower as a result of privatizations (*ibid.*, at 33–4).

12 Muir and Saba, *supra* note 8, at vii.

13 World Bank, *supra* note 10.

14 V.V. Ramanadham, *The Economics of Public Enterprise* (New York, NY: Routledge, 1991).

15 World Bank, *Private Sector Development in Low-Income Countries* (Washington, DC: World Bank, 1995) at 39.

In the modern large corporation, there is a division between principals (the owners or shareholders) of the organization and the agents (the management and employees). The governance structure of the corporation is designed to ensure that the principal has effective control over the agent's actions, and the interests of the agent are aligned with those of the principal so that agency costs are minimized. In addition, the market creates further managerial incentives to improve the organization's performance, as it rewards proven management skills and punishes inadequate performance through product markets, markets for corporate control, markets for managerial talent and bankruptcy laws.[16] In the context of SOEs, however, often both the governance structure of SOEs and the market have a much more attenuated impact on managerial performance. This is because SOE managerial appointments are often made on the basis of politics rather than merit, and because SOEs are not subject to traditional market risks such as takeovers or bankruptcy. In the private sector, shareholders often monitor the activities of a corporation, because they expect returns from their investments in monitoring. In the case of SOEs, the owner is the state and thus, in some sense, each citizen can be considered a shareholder. However, since these ownership interests are not transferable, the returns to any one citizen as a result of monitoring will never be greater than the opportunity cost of the time invested in such activities and citizens face major collective action problems in coordinating their monitoring efforts. Further, unlike private corporations, SOEs often face multiple economic and non-economic objectives. This makes it difficult for SOE monitors to properly assess the performance of managers, who can blame poor enterprise financial performance on non-commercial objectives. This is not to say that such control is impossible, but well-managed SOEs tend to be the exception, rather than the rule.

Another possible explanation for the inefficiencies of SOEs is the fact that, in the absence of a natural monopoly, private enterprise encourages competition, whereas government ownership tends to encourage monopoly. Competition engenders allocative efficiency by removing the ability to set prices from the monopolist and placing it in the market. In theory, competition also engenders productive efficiency by encouraging producers to minimize costs. Where cost reductions permit producers to earn economic profits, new producers will enter

---

16 See J. Vickers and G. Yarrow, *Privatization: An Economic Analysis* (Cambridge, MA: MIT, 1998).

the market, once again driving prices down to the marginal cost of supply. In these circumstances, constant attention to productive efficiency becomes a matter of an organization's very survival. In contrast, state-protected monopolists are not faced with the threat of being priced out of the market place, and so do not have the same incentives to increase productive efficiency.

11.3 Privatization

The term "privatization" is often used ubiquitously to cover a wide range of different policy options. However, generally speaking, it refers to the transfer of productive assets from the state sector to the private sector that came of age as a broad-based economic policy under the United Kingdom Thatcher administration during the 1980s. Between 1979 and 1997, the Conservative government reduced the SOEs' share of GDP from approximately 10 per cent to nearly nothing. In the 1990s, privatization programmes outside the United Kingdom also began to accelerate. As a result, privatization represented a major policy change in the economies of the world: from 1980 through 1999, governments throughout the world generated over US$1 trillion in revenue from privatization.[17] Depending on the way it is implemented, privatization may be one, but not the only, solution to the sizeable social costs inflicted by poor SOE performance.

11.3.1   The rationale and the evidence for privatization

The theory behind SOEs holds that the ownership and competition effects undermine the performance of SOEs. However, it is important to examine the empirical evidence to test whether these theoretical conjectures are borne out in practice, first by comparing the relative performance of SOEs and private organizations in the same sectors, and then comparing pre- and post-privatization performance.

Most sectoral studies involving developing countries have focused on reform in utilities, particularly telecommunications.[18] While there are some differences between the specific conclusions of the numerous

---

17 W.L. Megginson and J.M. Netter, "From State to Market: A Survey of Empirical Studies on Privatization" (2001) 39:2 *Journal of Economic Literature* 321 at 326.

18 See D. Parker and C. Kirkpatrick, "Privatisation in Developing Countries: A Review of the Evidence and the Policy Lessons" (2005) 41 *Journal of Development Studies* 4, at 519.

studies, researchers have mostly found that privatization impacted positively on the telecommunications industry in terms of teledensity levels (service coverage), decreases in service costs and profitability.[19] Perhaps more importantly, however, some of the studies also concluded that privatization alone was insufficient to yield such benefits: to improve organizational performance privatization must be combined with other structural changes, notably effective competition or effective and independent sectoral regulation. While there is a need for more detailed research on the various sectors undergoing privatization, the results from the telecommunications industry suggest that divestiture, coupled with the necessary institutional reforms, is likely to result in improvements in terms of organizational profitability and efficiency.

A number of studies have compared the pre- and post-privatization performance of a variety of divested SOEs. The results of these studies largely support the argument that privatization generally increases social welfare when implemented in the appropriate environment. However, where such an environment is absent, privatization offers greatly reduced social benefits.[20] This implies that privatization may offer substantial social welfare improvements to middle- and upper-middle-income developing countries, but they are much less significant in low-income and lower-middle-income countries.

In sum, there seems to be a connection between the benefits of privatization and the broader institutional environment of the country conducting the reforms, such as incentive and contracting issues, hardened budget constraints, removal of barriers to entry, an effective legal and regulatory framework, as well as the introduction of new management.[21] Further, the results of these studies suggest that unless

---

19 *Ibid.*, see also D. Petrazzini and T.H. Clark, "Costs and Benefits of Telecommunications Liberalization in Developing Countries" (1996) Working Paper, Hong Kong: Hong Kong University of Science and Technology; A.J. Ros, "Does Ownership or Competition Matter? The Effects of Telecommunications Reform on Network Expansion and Efficiency" (1999) 15 *Journal of Regulatory Economics* 65; S.J. Wallsten, "An Econometric Analysis of Telecom Competition, Privatization and Regulation in Africa and Latin America" (2001) 43 *Journal of Industrial Economics* 1, at 1 and 33; B. Bortolotti, J. D'Souza, M. Fantini and W.L. Megginson, "Privatization and the Sources of Performance Improvement in the Global Telecommunications Industry" (2002) 26 *Telecommunications Policy* 243.

20 Megginson and Netter, *supra* note 17; A. Galal, L. Jones, P. Tandoy and I. Vogelsang, *The Welfare Consequences of Selling Public Enterprises: Case Studies from Chile, Malaysia, Mexico and the UK* (New York, NY: Oxford University Press, 1994) at 22–3.

21 Megginson and Netter, *supra* note 17. See also C. Zinnes, Y. Eilat and J. Sachs, "The Gains from Privatization in Transition Economies: Is 'Change of Ownership' Enough?" (2001) IMF Staff

privatization is coordinated with significant private sector reform (including the regulation of anti-competitive behaviour), the lack of competition in low-income economies may ensure privatized SOEs (and the individuals and corporations who control them) monopoly profits; society will gain little or nothing.

Building institutions, however, is not an easy task, as we have suggested earlier in this book. Establishing competition and securing an effective regulatory framework, for instance, depends on a non-corrupt bureaucracy and competent regulatory agencies. Similarly, broader institutional reforms, such as judicial and bureaucratic reforms and anti-corruption policies, seem to be relevant in transition economies and low-income countries contemplating privatization, reinforcing the importance of institutions in this process.

11.3.2   The pre-conditions for effective privatization

In addition to a country's institutional environment, certain conditions and prerequisites are necessary for privatization not only to improve economic efficiency within a given undertaking or industry, but for it to contribute positively to long-term and sustainable economic and social development. These pre-conditions are not only country-specific, but also industry-specific. The four primary and interconnected prerequisites are: (1) a healthy private sector; (2) effective regulatory structures; (3) macro-economic stability; and (4) an absence of corruption.

First, privatizing SOEs into a non-competitive environment may result in economic losses, including deadweight losses associated with monopoly pricing and possibly the further crowding out of the indigenous private sector as private monopolists exploit their economic power. One solution to the absence of a competitive private sector, especially in the case of natural monopolies, is regulation. The absence of effective regulation has been a major cause of mediocre post-privatization performance in lower-income developing countries.[22] While designing an effective regulatory regime is an extremely

---

Papers, Vol. 48 – Transition Economies: How Much Progress? 146–70; and C. Zinnes, Y. Eilat and J. Sachs, "Benchmarking Competitiveness in Transition Economies" (2001) 9 *Economics of Transition* 315.

22 N. Boubraki and J.-C. Cosset, "The Financial and Operating Performance of Newly Privatized Firms: Evidence from Developing Countries" (1998) 53 *Journal of Finance* 1081; C. Kirkpatrick, D. Parker and Y. Zhang "An Empirical Analysis of State and Private-Sector Provision of Water Services in Africa" (2006) 20:1 *World Bank Economic Review* 143.

complex exercise that is dependent on context, it is recommended that these regulatory arrangements should be finalized prior to divestiture. Changes in the regulatory structure following privatization undermine the government's credibility with potential investors, and thus impact negatively on levels of investment.

With respect to macro-economic instability, the dangers of privatizing in a crisis are obvious. Macro-economic instability increases economic uncertainty and therefore investment risk, and thus results in decreased interest by domestic and foreign investors in the SOEs of a developing country. Perversely, developing country governments often face increased incentives to privatize in times of economic crisis as a result of a dire need for revenue. With severely constrained bargaining power, such developing countries may be forced to accept terms that are far less attractive than they could have achieved in the absence of a crisis. Moreover, in order to maximize revenue from privatization, developing countries may be tempted to turn public monopolies into private monopolies. Decisions to privatize should be made on the basis of an analysis of the long-term social benefits of a given divestiture, not the state's need for immediate revenue.

The final economic prerequisite is the absence of corruption. Prima facie, one might think that corruption in the public sector would make privatization desirable. However, privatizing SOEs in developing countries with highly corrupt public sectors can greatly increase the costs of such corruption. These include the more obvious costs such as kickbacks in the privatization process, but also involve problems such as officials making and implementing privatization decisions on the basis of personal or political gain rather than social benefit (which, arguably, militates in favour of a centralized, specialized agency with well-developed protocols for privatization), or the fact that widespread corruption undermines investor confidence. Moreover, corruption may not only impede original investment in SOEs, but may also impede subsequent investment in the divested enterprise, thereby destroying one of the key benefits promised by privatization: increased capital investment.

These prerequisites are institutional in nature because they depend on a complementary set of private and public sector institutions. For instance, a healthy private sector requires a functioning financial system, an appropriate regulatory framework depends on a functioning bureaucracy, and a stable macro-economic environment depends on a functional and competent central bank (amongst other things).

11.3.3   Political obstacles to privatization reforms

Even where a developing country has the institutions in place to make privatization welfare-increasing, privatization will only succeed if it is politically practicable. This involves two considerations: (1) whether key policy-makers in developing countries are desirous of implementing privatization; and (2) if so, whether privatization can succeed in the face of political opposition.

A study examining the success of SOE reform in 12 developing countries, found that both political desirability and political feasibility were necessary elements of SOE reform.[23] However, privatization will be politically desirable in only two circumstances: (1) where a developing country government has experienced a change in leadership and the new leader is not dependent on SOE interests for his or her support; and (2) where privatization is demanded by an economic crisis.[24] Although this study argues that an economic shock alone is insufficient, another study – covering SOE reform attempts in 15 less-developed countries (LDCs) over the period 1972 to 1991 – found that 19 of the 24 reform attempts studied were preceded by a crisis (although this involves the serious dangers of privatizing in a crisis noted above).[25] In terms of political feasibility, often this not only includes placating opposition parties, but also garnering the support of the affected workforce.[26]

Political economy concerns more generally can be conceived of as raising the following three policy dilemmas for governments of developing countries contemplating privatizing one or more of their SOEs:

1. *When* to privatize (in good economic times or in bad)?
2. *What* to privatize (winners that may attract higher sales prices but offer fewer prospects of substantial performance improvements, or losers that may sell for little more than their break-up value)?
3. *How* to privatize (by tender offer or auction to the highest bidder, domestic or foreign; or by an initial public offering with restrictions on foreign shareholdings that may yield a much lower price and diffuse ownership that may exacerbate agency problems; or by

---

23 World Bank, *supra* note 10, at 175–6.
24 *Ibid.*, at 178–9.
25 J.E. Campos and H.S. Esfahani, "The Political Foundations of Public Enterprise Reform in Developing Countries" (World Bank, 1994, unpublished) at 23.
26 *Ibid.*, at 9.

partial privatization with the state retaining a significant interest, which may be unattractive for private investors and hence reduce the sale price)?

11.3.4 Privatization strategies

In determining how to shift from an economy dominated by SOEs, there are two primary schools of thought: the shock therapists and the gradualists.

Shock therapy is based on the premise that both markets and market institutions will quickly and spontaneously appear with rapid economic liberalization. Rapid reform advocates consider a gradual approach to transition to be needlessly costly, both in terms of time and lost output. In part, this set of economic prescriptions has been predicated on a set of political assumptions – a kind of political Coase theorem of privatization: (1) the initial owners of privatized assets do not matter much as the market will soon reallocate the assets to efficient owners; and (2) appropriate laws and legal institutions will follow private property rather than the other way around. This view assumes a critical interaction between economic and political reforms – namely, that economic reforms create pressure for political reforms and that business pressures are likely to play a critical role in political and consequential legal reforms. The underlying presumption is that such pressures did not exist before the economic reforms.[27]

By contrast, gradualists caution that rapid liberalization will be impractical to implement because privatization requires a broad social consensus, and generating such consensus is a long-term process.[28] Gradualists tend to favour an extended period of state intervention: price and wage controls, fixed exchange rates, gradual privatization and nurturing of market institutions are key elements of this process. Gradualists also tend to emphasize the importance of the institutional infrastructure of a market economy, including competition, entrepre-

---

27 A. Shleifer and R. Vishny, *The Grabbing Hand: Government Pathologies and Their Cures* (Cambridge, MA: Harvard University Press, 1998), chapter 11.

28 See, for example, J.E. Stiglitz, "The Insider" (17 April 2000) *The New Republic*; J.E. Stiglitz, "Whither Reform? Ten Years of the Transition" World Bank Annual Bank Conference on Development Economics, Washington, DC, 28–30 April 1999; J.E. Stiglitz, *Globalization and Its Discontents* (New York, NY: W.W. Norton & Co., 2002); K. Arrow, "Economic Transition: Speed and Scope" (2000) 156 *Journal of Institutional and Theoretical Economics* 9.

neurship, regulation of financial markets, social capital and a strong legal system.[29]

Both shock therapists and gradualists claim that the performance of transition countries proves the relative success of their reform agenda. Poland, Kyrgyzstan, the Czech Republic and the Baltic states, as radical liberalizers, have grown faster than "go-slow" countries such as Belarus and Ukraine.[30] On the other hand, China has created its own path of gradual transition from a planned to a market economy, and has enjoyed enormous economic success. Russia's economic decline in the period following the break-up of the Soviet Union is cited by both sides to prove their point: gradualists argue that the Russian experience proves that shock therapy was seriously misconceived, while advocates of shock therapy reclassify Russia as a go-slow reformer because they believe reforms were partial at best.

11.4   Public-private partnerships (PPPs)

PPPs is a term that exhibits a high degree of ambiguity in common usage, but it is often used to refer to projects in which the private sector designs and builds new, or refurbishes and expands existing infrastructure, provides project financing, manages the asset and operates the service. In other words, for our purposes, the arrangement typically involves "bundling" – or vertical integration – in the form of a consortium that brings together project designers, managers, construction companies, engineers, and financiers.[31] PPPs recover their costs through user fees, government payments, or both. Whether the asset reverts to the public sector at the end of the contract depends upon the terms of the contract. Most PPPs implemented to date provide that ownership in the asset is retained by, or will revert to, the public sector.

11.4.1   The advantages and disadvantages of PPPs

PPPs are promoted on several grounds. The bundling aspect of PPPs incentivize the builder-operator to incorporate long-term operating cost considerations in the design and construction phases of the

---

29 Stiglitz, "Wither Reform?" *supra* note 28.

30 Shleifer and Vishny, *supra* note 27, at 228.

31 R. J. Daniels and M.J. Trebilcock, "Private Provision of Public Infrastructure: An Organizational Analysis of the Next Privatization Frontier" (1996) 46 *University of Toronto Law Journal* 375, at 390.

project, and arguably also reduces the coordination costs that would otherwise be faced by various departments or agencies of government in undertaking all of the functions performed by a vertically integrated consortium.[32] Similarly, as the PPP transfers to the builder-operator the financial risks associated with design, construction and operation, there is a heightened incentive to mitigate cost and time overruns. PPPs have also been viewed by some governments as a means of shifting spending off balance sheet or circumventing legislative budgetary limits. Clearly, this is problematic, as masking government liabilities does not reduce them nor is it transparent.[33]

PPPs are typically highly leveraged. The identity of the lenders is an important aspect of project finance, particularly for developing world PPPs. Lenders in developing world PPP projects often include national or international development banks, whose strong credit ratings allow projects in developing countries to obtain a lower cost of capital, and institutional lenders, such as banks, insurance companies and pension funds (although there is ongoing debate about whether private debt associated with PPPs drives up total costs relative to public borrowing). Lenders have a strong incentive to take an active role in project monitoring with a view to moving to operations and a revenue stream as soon as possible. A special purpose vehicles (SPVs) consortia is typically established to contract with government. SPVs insulate the members of the consortium from separate liability for contractual defaults, and ensure that the assets that are to be constructed pursuant to a PPP, as public assets, may not readily be collateralized as security against default (rendering project revenues the principal source of debt repayment).

However, PPP contracts pose special problems of contractual design, monitoring, and enforcement. Typically, they involve large investments in durable, transaction-specific assets of the kind that Nobel Laureate Oliver Williamson describes as raising a bilaterally dependent contractual relationship between the parties.[34] That is, while governments may have some choice among competing consortia *ex ante*, once they "lock into" a long-term relationship with a single consortium, there are significant risks of mutual opportunism or "hold-ups". The consortium will

---

32 J. Delmon, *Private Sector Investment in Infrastructure* (The Hague: Kluwer Law International, 2009) at 10.

33 OECD, *Public-Private Partnerships: In Pursuit of Risk Sharing and Value for Money* (Paris: OECD, 2008) at 21.

34 O.E. Williamson, "The Logic of Economic Organization" (1988) 4 *Journal of Law, Economics and Organizations* 65, at 71.

be concerned that the government may use threats of expropriation or changes in tax or regulatory policies to obtain better *ex post* terms after initial construction costs are sunk. On the other hand, the government is dependent on the firm's technical knowledge required to operate the asset, faces political ramifications for contract failure, and reputational damage in terms of the government's ability to attract FDI in the future. There are also costs and delays associated with tendering and negotiating another PPP. All these factors may give a consortium an incentive to bid low to win a contract and then exert undue leverage in subsequent contract renegotiations to secure better terms.

11.4.2   PPP experience in the developing world

Across the developing world, private participation in infrastructure, beyond design-build, accounts for less than 20 per cent of infrastructural investment and thus remains a relatively small share of total investment. Nevertheless, the World Bank's Private Participation in Infrastructure database shows that total investment committed through PPPs in the developing world reached US$145 billion in 2011 distributed over almost 400 projects. Two-thirds of the PPPs are in the electricity and transportation sectors.

Over the past two decades, the majority of PPP projects have taken place in developing countries with relatively high incomes. Just under 60 per cent of total projects were undertaken in upper-middle-income countries and 37 per cent in lower-middle-income countries. Only 4 per cent of projects took place in low-income developing countries, although this latter number may under-estimate the true extent that PPPs are used in low-income countries, especially in sub-Saharan Africa, given the increasing number of "resources for infrastructure" exchanges between Chinese SOEs and sub-Saharan African countries (although because the Chinese firms are often SOEs these are not strictly public-private partnerships).

A recent statistical analysis by the International Monetary Fund (IMF) found that after adjusting for population, PPP concentration was more likely in larger markets with a stronger rule of law, political stability, administrative capacity, greater consumer demand and macro-economic stability.[35]

---

35 M. Hammami, J.-F. Ruhashyankiko and E.B. Yehoue, "Determinants of Public-Private Partnerships in Infrastructure" (2006) International Monetary Fund Working Paper 06/99, at 15.

11.4.3 Evaluating PPP performance

A number of studies have attempted to evaluate the relative operating efficiencies of PPPs. Some of these studies have found that service quality and reliability has often improved and that labour productivity has greatly increased through substantial reductions in public sector employment.[36] The effect of PPPs on user fees yields more mixed results.[37] As predicted by Williamson, renegotiation rates of PPPs even early in their contractual terms, is strikingly large. An equally striking finding is the limited impact of PPPs on improving access to infrastructure relative to a continuation of the status quo. Often very poor consumers see relatively few benefits from a PPP and continue to rely on the relatively expensive informal sector, for example, for access to potable water.[38] In terms of expanding access to essential infrastructure, such as water distribution or electricity, developing country governments need to build stronger incentive mechanisms in PPP contracts to provide such access, or alternatively to subsidize low-income consumers directly.

11.4.4 Potential solutions

Institutional limitations or weaknesses weigh on developing countries governments that, even in the absence of any such constraints, already face inherently complex challenges throughout the planning, bid evaluation, negotiation, monitoring, and enforcement phases of PPPs. The creation of specialized and experienced PPP units within central government administrations (for example, the Ministry of Finance) helps to ensure an equal footing with the consortia when negotiating complex PPP arrangements.[39] Addressing weaknesses in administrative capacity at the sub-national levels of government is also critical,

---

36 L.A. Andres, J.L. Gausch, T. Haven and V. Foster, *The Impact of Private Sector Participation in Infrastructure: Lights, Shadows and the Road Ahead* (Washington, DC: The World Bank, 2008); P. Marin, *Public-Private Partnerships for Urban Water Utilities* (Washington, DC: The World Bank, 2009) at 29.

37 *Ibid.*, at 110; Andres *et al.*, *supra* note 36; C. Kirkpatrick, D. Parker, and Y. Zhang, "An Economic Analysis of State and Private-Sector Provision of Water Services in Africa" (2006) *World Bank Economics Review* 143.

38 Marin, *supra* note 36, at 64–5; see for example, A. Estache, "PPI partnerships versus PPI divorces in LDCs" (2005) World Bank Policy Research Working Paper 3470, at 1.

39 OECD (2008), *supra* note 33; "PPP Units around the World" The World Bank, available at http://ppp.worldbank.org/public-private-partnership/overview/international-ppp-units#South%20Asia (accessed 4 May 2014); and see "Evaluating the Environment for Public-Private Partnerships in Latin America and the Caribbean: The 2012 Infrascope" (February 2013) *The Economist* at 26, 28.

given their responsibility for certain infrastructural sectors (such as the water distribution sector).

Encouraged by development banks and others, many governments have introduced legislative, regulatory, or policy frameworks for PPPs. These typically guide the steps that must be taken before adopting a PPP: the bidding and selection process, credible independent monitoring and dispute resolution processes. Development banks and other international organizations are also attempting to address poor contract design and related legal and institutional capacities through the dissemination of standardized infrastructure contracts, legislation, regulation, policies, and other templates that allow developing countries to gain access to internationally recognized "best practices" and contractual innovations made by other governments. There are questions, however, as to whether these mechanisms are likely to be effective in institutional environments that are otherwise deeply problematic.

11.5   Conclusion

There are at least three different strategies that developing countries may adopt to deal with the infrastructural deficit described at the beginning of this chapter. First, as discussed in the first part of this chapter, the state can own infrastructure facilities, often through SOEs. Second, the state may choose to privatize the state-owned facilities, by divesting them to private investors, who will own and operate the facilities. PPPs lie between these two models, as the government assumes part of the financial risk but the private sector designs and builds new, or refurbishes and expands existing, infrastructure, provides project financing, manages the asset and operates the service. Each one of these options is likely to be more or less effective depending on the broader institutional environment in which it is operating. In sum, any discussion about these solutions cannot be detached from the issues raised in the other chapters of this book.

The rise of PPPs around the world also raises a broader theoretical question on the role of the state in promoting economic growth and improving development indicators. While the Washington Consensus policies (and most privatization processes) were based on the premise that a reduced role for the state is desirable, there is today greater acceptance in many developing countries of state intervention in the economy. Unlike the state interventionism that existed before, however, this recent trend contemplates both a strong state and a strong market and it is not confined to infrastructural projects. These new forms of state intervention and government involvement in market economies have been labelled "state capitalism", and have been particularly pronounced in Brazil and China. State capitalism involves governmental attempts to promote national industry champions in many sectors of the economy and state support to private companies through state-owned banks, especially national development banks.[40]

This new trend has been labelled the "New Developmental State" by Trubek, Garcia, Coutinho and Santos,[41] in reference to the concept coined by Chalmers Johnson to describe Japanese industrial policy from 1925 to 1975.[42] The original concept of developmental state suggested that there can be a type of economy which is capitalist but is not based on free-market economics. In this economy state intervention does not translate into centralized state control over all economic activity, as in socialist economies. Despite focusing on the interventionist policies of the Japanese Ministry of International Trade and Industry (MITI) over a 50-year time-span, Johnson's concept has travelled far in development circles and has been fruitfully used to analyse a wide variety of distinct institutional arrangements of state intervention in the economy. Indeed, the developmental state seems to have existed in one form or another in Asia, Africa and Latin America. It is not fully clear whether the so-called, "New Developmental State", as defined by Trubek et al., exists beyond Latin America, or even beyond Brazil. This is especially true if we consider that their definition of the "New Development State" also encompasses social policies that seek to reduce inequality, such as conditional cash transfers. Nonetheless, the hybrid forms of state and market arrangements, such as PPPs, are a growing trend among developing nations. If such hybrid forms expand further or into other areas, we may soon need to abandon the sharp dichotomy between state and market that have informed the development field to date.

---

40 A. Musacchio and S.G. Lazzarini, *Reinventing State Capitalism: Leviathan in Business, Brazil and Beyond* (Cambridge, MA: Harvard University Press, 2014). See also "The Rise of State Capitalism" *The Economist*, 21 January 2012.

41 D. Trubek, H.A. Garcia, D.R. Coutinho and A. Santos (eds), *Law and the New Developmental State: The Brazilian Experience in Latin American Context* (Cambridge, UK: Cambridge University Press, 2013).

42 C.A. Johnson, *MITI and the Japanese Miracle* (Stanford, CA: Stanford University Press, 1982).

PART V

INTERNATIONAL ECONOMIC RELATIONS, LAW
AND DEVELOPMENT

12 International trade

In this chapter and the following two chapters, we address features of the international economic order that bear importantly on the economic prospects of developing countries: international trade; FDI; and foreign aid, with a particular focus in each case on how these external sources of financial flows, and conditions attaching thereto, either facilitate or impede domestic institutional reforms in developing countries.

Export earnings are by far the most important source of external revenues for developing countries, followed by FDI flows, with foreign aid a very small percentage of both these flows. Developing country merchandise exports rose from US$599 billion in 1980 to almost US$5 trillion in 2009. Over this period developing countries' share of world merchandise exports rose from about 29 per cent to 39 per cent. However, this increased relative share of world merchandise exports was largely attributable to China.[1] In 2008, foreign direct investment flows to developing countries reached almost US$520 billion,[2] and official development assistance flows (foreign aid) reached around US$130 billion[3] (with around another US$30 billion from NGOs).[4] Remittances from emigrants from developing countries to relatives and friends in their home countries are currently running at about US$400 billion per year. To complete the picture, one might add portfolio investment flows into developing countries (investments in government and corporate bonds and passive equity holdings), which tend to be

---

1 United Nations Conference on Trade and Development, UNCTAD *Handbook of Statistics* (Geneva: United Nations, 2010).

2 UNCTAD, "Assessing the Impact of the Current Financial and Economic Crisis on Global FDI Flows" 19 January 2009, available at http://unctad.org/en/Docs/webdiaeia20091_en.pdf (accessed 4 May 2014).

3 J. Paul and M. Pistor, "Official Development Assistance Spending" 13 May 2009, Parliamentary Information and Research Service Library of Parliament, available at http://www.parl.gc.ca/Content/LOP/researchpublications/prb0710-e.htm (accessed 4 May 2014).

4 R.C. Riddell, *Does Foreign Aid Really Work?* (Oxford: Oxford University Press, 2007) at 259, 317.

highly volatile, reflecting responses to divergences in interest rates and movements in exchange rates (and are sometimes negative).

12.1   Trade and development[5]

International trade has a long history, both in terms of intellectual thought[6] and in terms of actual practice. Countries, or more accurately merchants in these countries, have been trading with each other for millennia.[7] However, it was not until the Enlightenment and the writings of political economists – such as Adam Smith in *The Wealth of Nations*[8] and David Ricardo in *The Principles of Political Economy*[9] – that the basic economic theory of international trade was first formulated. Adam Smith emphasized the gains from specialization. He pointed out that very few families find it economically rational to produce all the goods and services that they require, but in fact they produce goods or services for some of their needs and otherwise purchase goods or services from others who are better qualified to provide them. Smith argued that, just as this makes sense in the case of the family it also makes sense in the case of a nation. The degree of specialization (or the division of labour) that is possible is limited only by the extent of the market. According to Ricardo's theory of comparative advantage, countries should specialize in exporting goods where their comparative advantage is greatest and import goods where their comparative disadvantage is greatest, implying that all countries will find it advantageous to trade with other countries, even though they may lack an absolute advantage in any product.[10]

It is conventional wisdom amongst trade scholars that a liberal world trading system in which countries are free to exploit or develop distinctive forms of comparative advantage is key to increased produc-

---

5   For an introduction to international trade law, see M. Trebilcock, *Understanding Trade Law* (Cheltenham, UK and Northampton, MA, USA: Edward Elgar, 2011); for a much more detailed exposition, see M. Trebilcock, R. Howse and A. Eliason, *The Regulation of International Trade* (London: Routledge, 2013, 4th edn) esp. chapter 16.

6   See D. Irwin, *Against the Tide* (Princeton, NJ: Princeton University Press, 1996).

7   See N. Chanda, *Bound Together: How Traders, Preachers, Adventurers and Warriors Shaped Globalization* (New Haven, CT: Yale University Press, 2007); W.J. Bernstein, *A Splendid Exchange: How Trade Shaped the World* (New York, NY: Atlantic Monthly Press, 2008).

8   A. Smith, *The Wealth of Nations* (London: Methuen & Co Ltd, [1776] 1904, 5th edn).

9   D. Ricardo, *On the Principles of Political Economy* (London: John Murray, 1817).

10 See generally E. Helpman, *Understanding Global Trade* (Cambridge, MA: Harvard University Press, 2011).

tivity, economic growth and development. This thinking was evident in the original Bretton Woods Agreement (1944), which gave birth to the post-war international economic architecture, including the IMF, the World Bank and the General Agreement on Tariffs and Trade (GATT). In other words, conventional economic thinking was that, with the emergence of a liberal world trading system, a rising tide would lift all boats. Unfortunately, this has not proven to be the case.

A number of developing countries have successfully integrated themselves into the world trading system and have benefited enormously from it (especially in Asia, the most prominent contemporary examples being China and India). Many other developing countries, however, have largely been left behind by the process of globalization. In *The Bottom Billion*, Paul Collier documents the stagnation or absolute decline in real incomes of a number of very poor countries around the globe:[11] most are concentrated in sub-Saharan Africa, but a number are located in Central Asia and Latin America. These countries – about 60 on Collier's count – are home to the bottom billion of the world's population living on less than one dollar a day. They comprise almost a third of the countries in the world (mostly small) and one-sixth of the world's population. While foreign aid sometimes mitigates their economic decline, minimal exports and foreign direct investment preclude significant growth. According to Collier, these countries are caught in various traps – the conflict trap, the natural resource trap, the landlocked-with-bad-neighbours trap, and the bad governance trap.

The multilateral trading system has not been oblivious to the special economic challenges facing developing countries. Almost from the beginnings of the GATT in 1947, developing countries were accorded a form of exceptionalism in terms of the application of standard GATT disciplines (referred to as "special and differential treatment" – SDT). While SDT takes many forms, it can be broadly conceived in two branches. The import branch of SDT provides policy flexibility for developing countries with respect to multilateral trade disciplines governing imports. The export branch of SDT provides for the possibility of enhanced preferential non-reciprocal market access for developing countries' exports to developed country markets.

Article XVIII of the GATT, in the form that emerged after a review of the Agreement in 1954–55, contains detailed provisions regarding

---

11 P. Collier, *The Bottom Billion* (New York, NY: Oxford University Press, 2007).

developing country members. These provisions granted developing country members exemptions from their GATT commitments in order to provide the tariff protection required for the establishment of a particular industry. These countries are allowed to promote specific domestic industries through ISI (infant industry) policies, and to restrict imports in order to address balance of payment difficulties. In 1965, Part IV of the GATT was added, which focuses on expanding developing country access to developed country export markets. Part IV urged developed countries to make tariff concessions to developing countries on a non-reciprocal basis on products of export interest to them, although most of the commitments in Part IV are merely exhortatory and non-binding on developed country members.

The most substantive measures taken to address the plight of developing countries were two waivers adopted in 1971. One waiver provided an exception to the Most-Favoured Nation (MFN) obligation, allowing developed countries to grant preferential tariff treatment to developing countries (known as the Generalized System of Preferences – GSP). The second waiver to the MFN principle permits developing countries to exchange such preferences amongst themselves, without satisfying the conditions of Article XXIV (relating to customs unions and free trade areas). These waivers were formalized as a permanent part of the GATT in 1979 through the Enabling Clause, which authorizes preferential tariff reductions towards developing countries on a "generalized, non-reciprocal, and non-discriminatory basis". Pursuant to the initial waivers and the subsequent Enabling Clause, most developed countries have adopted GSP programmes, which unilaterally extend preferential terms of trade to many developing countries.

The two limbs of special and differential treatment need to be seen as inherently inter-related. The much greater policy flexibility extended to developing countries on the import side necessarily implies that in securing better access to developed country markets for their exports, they cannot be expected to offer reciprocal trade concessions without undermining their policy flexibility on the import side. Hence the second limb of SDT contemplates non-reciprocal and preferential treatment of exports from developing countries by developed countries. While it was assumed that this combination of policies would substantially enhance the economic prospects of developing countries, this assumption has come under increasing scrutiny in academic research.

12.2   Import substitution policies

Extensive dispensations from GATT disciplines on infant industry or ISI rationales were justified by many developing countries, many mainstream development economists in developed countries, and international agencies in the early years of the GATT on various grounds:

1. Developing countries often inherited truncated economies from their colonial overseers. They had been largely restricted economically to the role of "hewers of wood and drawers of water", leaving them with large, traditional and inefficient agricultural sectors where the marginal product of labour was often thought to be negligible or even zero. As with most developed countries earlier in their histories, a major transformation in developing country economies was called for in reallocating resources from traditional agricultural sectors to industrial or manufacturing sectors. To facilitate this, it was argued that at least temporary protectionism was required for these fledgling manufacturing industries, in order to enable them to achieve minimum efficient scale and become competitive in both domestic and export markets.

2. Many developed countries early in the process of their economic development, including the United States, Canada, Germany, and many other currently developed economies, aggressively pursued infant industry protectionism. Developing countries that found themselves at similar stages of development in their early post-independence history should not be denied similar policy flexibility.

3. Due to low levels of education, poor physical infrastructure, weakly developed financial credit and insurance markets, and inadequate or non-existent social safety nets, many developing countries were likely to face adjustments costs in moving to a fully open international trading regime that were much more severe than those faced by developed countries embarking upon a similar strategy of liberalization.

4. At least for smaller and poorer developing countries, their share of world trade, and in particular imports, was typically so small that protectionist policies on their part were likely to have negligible adverse impacts on world prices in the commodities affected by these policies. Hence, any terms of trade externalities from the pursuit of such policies were likely to be small to non-existent.

The efficacy of infant industry or ISI policy continues to be hotly debated in scholarly literature and policy circles. Proponents of a liberal trading regime argue that such policies often hurt developing countries by promoting permanently inefficient industries that require continuing protection and also encourage rampant rent seeking and corruption in the highly discretionary policies associated with this strategy. They also point to the impressive growth performance of a minority of developing countries that have adopted export-led growth policies, including the so-called East Asian miracle economies and more recently China, as well as Chile in Latin America and Botswana and Mauritius in Africa.[12]

Proponents of infant industry or ISI policies point out that even these economies did not adopt unconstrained free trade early in their development trajectories, but highly selective forms of intervention designed to promote the transformation of their economies from predominantly agricultural in nature to predominantly manufacturing and service-oriented. Those who take this view criticize classical conceptions of comparative advantage as being much too static and argue that if countries such as Korea had applied such theories early in their development, they would have been encouraged to become, for example, better rice growers, rather than espousing an activist set of development policies designed (successfully) to transform the Korean economy into a high technology manufacturing-based economy.[13]

Proponents of such policies criticize the current multilateral system for limiting the policy space and flexibility open to developing countries. The Uruguay Round agreements that came into force in 1995, such as the Agreement on Trade Related Intellectual Property Rights (TRIPS), the Agreement on Trade Related Investment Measures (TRIMs), the Agreement on Subsidies and Countervailing Measures (SCM Agreement), the Agreement on the Application of Sanitary and Phytosanitary Measures (SPS Agreement), the Agreement on Technical Barriers to Trade (TBT Agreement), and the General Agreement on Trade in Services (GATS), constrained the policy space and flexibility available to developing countries to pursue more activist development policies. In some cases, they imposed on these countries

---

12 Writing in 2002, J. Williamson reports that the World Bank has conducted over 41 studies of developing countries and contrasted the performance of relatively open and relatively closed economies, concluding that trade openness and growth are positively correlated: see J. Williamson, "Winners and Losers Over Two Centuries of Globalization" (September 2002) NBER Working Paper No. W9161, at 9.

13 J. Lin, *The Quest for Prosperity: How Developing Economies Can Take Off* (Princeton, NJ: Princeton University Press, 2012).

burdensome domestic institutional reform obligations, especially with respect to intellectual property rights and domestic health and safety regulatory regimes.[14]

12.3   Export limb of special and differential treatment

Much recent research suggests preferences on the export side have not proved as valuable to developing countries as they had hoped, for the following reasons:

1. The benefits of the preferences seem to be concentrated on a relatively small number of developing countries, many of whom needed them least. For example, under the US African Growth and Opportunity Act of 2003 just three of the 33 eligible sub-Saharan countries (Nigeria, South Africa and Gabon) account for 86 per cent of preferential imports under this scheme.
2. GSP market access preferences tend to become much less valuable as margins of preference have been eroded through successive negotiating rounds, which have reduced MFN tariff levels.
3. Preferences are not durable, since they have often been tied to the level of a country's economic development; countries that are successful in increasing their per capita incomes are often graduated out of the programmes.
4. Donor countries often reserve the right to withdraw preferences if import volumes threaten domestic producers.
5. Many imports of major export interest to development countries have been excluded from GSP schemes, for example, textiles, clothing, footwear, and various agricultural products.
6. Preferences have increasingly been subject to various forms of conditionality such as human and labour rights, environmental standards, and ideological or geo-political factors.
7. Complex rules of origin have often diluted the value of GSP preferences, preventing developing countries from producing goods most efficiently.
8. Preferences cause trade diversion from non-preference recipient

14 See D. Rodrik, *One Economy, Many Recipes: Globalization, Institutions and Economic Growth* (Princeton, NJ: Princeton University Press, 2007); D. Rodrik, *The Globalization Paradox: Democracy and the Future of the World Economy* (New York, NY: W.W. Norton & Co., 2011); J. Stiglitz, *Making Globalization Work* (New York, NY: W.W. Norton & Co., 2006); H. Chang, *Bad Samaritans: The Myth of Free Trade and the Secret History of Capitalism* (New York, NY: Bloomsbury Press, 2008).

developing countries to preference recipients, which may benefit some developing countries in the short run but are unlikely to benefit developing countries overall, and may create inducements to distort comparative advantage, which puts the preference recipients at risk if and when preferences are withdrawn.

9. Because these preferences are non-reciprocal, developing countries have forsaken significant bargaining leverage in negotiations with developed countries – without a *quid*, there is often a very meager *quo*.

The future scope of special and differential treatment for developing countries has become a major fault line between developing and developed countries in the current Doha Round of World Trade Organization (WTO) negotiations, and in part explains the dramatic proliferation of Preferential Trade Agreements (PTAs) in recent years, in many cases between or among developing countries. However, such agreements do not enhance access by developing countries to the economies of large developed countries, while bilateral PTAs between poor developing countries and large developed countries may entail burdensome additional commitments that reflect unequal bargaining power.[15] In the case of large, rapidly growing and highly competitive developing countries, such as China, India, and Brazil, it is difficult to imagine major developed countries, especially in today's global economic environment, being prepared to expand SDT treatment to them, hence implying a need (going forward) to differentiate among developing countries.

In our view, in future multilateral negotiations, member countries should agree to provide immediate, unconditional and non-reciprocal duty-free access to their markets for all exports (without exceptions) from the least-developed countries that are the focus of Collier's concerns. Developing countries in higher income tranches, in contrast, should follow a different path. It is likely to be in their long-term interests to phase out reliance on SDT and bargain reciprocally for enhanced access to developed countries' markets, albeit with longer transition periods. This implies a need for more gradual reductions in trade barriers, more expansive safeguard protections, and cross-issue bargaining, where reductions in developed country trade barriers can be exchanged not only for reductions in developing country trade barriers but also for a relaxation of restrictions on foreign direct investment and services. In addition, specialized agreements like TRIPS and

---

15 See Trebilcock, Howse and Eliason, *supra* note 5, chapter 3.

TRIMs should in future generally be plurilateral rather than multilateral in nature (as they were prior to the Uruguay Round), leaving more policy flexibility for developing countries on the scope and timing of commitments beyond the general GATT principles.

12.4   Institutional implications of trade policy

A growing body of literature finds a positive two-way relationship between trade policy and domestic institutional quality: countries with better domestic institutions (especially legal institutions) tend to be more successful exporters (especially of more complex products) because of credible commitments they can offer to their customers.[16] In turn, more open trade policies tend to strengthen domestic institutions because of the ability of traders to vote with their feet if the domestic institutional environment is not conducive to trade (thus enhancing inter-jurisdictional competition). The evidence once again places a premium on domestic institutional quality – this time in external economic relations.

The positive feedback effects of more open trade policies on domestic institutions suggest a case for general orientation to trade openness. However, even with such an orientation, domestic institutional capacity constraints argue for less developed countries placing a priority on enhancing their bargaining power (often in coalitions with larger, more sophisticated developing countries) in the multilateral trading system rather than attempting to negotiate and administer a plethora of bilateral PTAs. Such constraints also suggest that, to the extent that developing countries feel a need to protect various economic sectors from international competition, a premium should attach to very simple, broad gauge policies – a common tariff across all such sectors, for example, rather than a highly calibrated tariff structure that lends itself to rent seeking and corruption in its formulation and administration.

Professor Gerald Helleiner, a distinguished development economist, in his 2000 Praul Prebisch lecture[17] argued that developing countries,

---

16 D. Dollar and A. Kraay, "Institutions, Trade and Growth" (2003) 50 *Journal of Monetary Economics* 133; D. Berkowitz, J. Moenius and K. Pistor, "Legal Institutions and International Trade Flows" (2004) 26 *Michigan Journal of International Law* 163.

17 G. Helleiner, "Markets, Politics, and Globalization: Can the Global Economy be Civilized?" 10th Praul Prebisch Lecture, Geneva, 11 December 2000.

accounting for over 85 per cent of the world's population, are severely under-represented in current governance arrangements for the global economy. Decision-making on key global economic issues remains highly concentrated in the major industrial powers and the major international financial institutions, which they control. The selection processes for the leadership of key multilateral financial institutions demonstrate no regard for the principles of due process, with the presidencies of the IMF and the World Bank vested permanently with the European Union and the United States respectively. Groups such as the G7 countries entirely exclude developing countries from their membership. Even the G20, which includes some larger developing countries, entirely excludes smaller and poorer developing countries. Whereas developed countries account for only 17 per cent of voting strength in the United Nations and 24 per cent in the WTO, they account for almost three-quarters of total World Bank membership, where they hold 40 per cent of total votes.[18]

In the case of the WTO, at least in principle, decision-making authority is distributed equally, with each of the 158 member countries entitled to one vote (from smallest to largest), and most major decisions taken by consensus. However, the reality has been that negotiations in the late and critical stages of previous negotiating rounds under the GATT, and more recently the WTO, have typically been dominated by the so-called triad – the United States, the European Union and Japan – and the results of their three-way negotiations in the so-called "Green Room" simply presented to other countries largely as a fait accompli. According to Stiglitz, developed countries impose far higher – on average four times higher – tariffs against developing country imports than imports from other developed countries; rich countries have cost poor countries three times more in trade restrictions than they give in total development aid.[19]

While it is hard to support the idea that all or most of the problems that afflict poor countries are attributable to the international economic system (as dependency theorists, discussed in Chapter 2, tend to argue), it is easy to be persuaded that substantial reforms are required to this system to more fully integrate developing countries into the global economy, and on a fairer and more efficient basis.

18 The South Centre, "Reform of World Bank Governance Structures" (September 2007), available at http://www.southcentre.int/wp-content/uploads/2013/07/AN_GEG4_World-Bank-Governance-Structures_EN.pdf (accessed 4 May 2014).

19 Stiglitz, *supra* note 14, at 78.

These various asymmetries between developing and developed countries in the institutional arrangements governing international economic relations require urgent attention. However, they should not obscure the imperative that for developing countries to participate effectively even in a fairly designed international economic system and its governance, especially in trade negotiations and formal dispute settlement proceedings, effective domestic institutional capacity that facilitates such participation is an essential pre-condition. In short, fair international institutions and effective domestic institutions are complements, not substitutes.

13 Foreign direct investment

FDI should be distinguished from portfolio investment. FDI typically involves some form of effective control and active management of assets in host countries, while portfolio investment typically involves passive investments in host countries. Over the last several decades, there has been a dramatic increase in FDI around the world, much of it between developed countries, but increasingly developing countries have been major recipients of FDI, including countries such as China, and in some cases have themselves become exporters of FDI (again, China is a prominent example).[1] More than 40 per cent of world FDI inflows are directed to developing countries and FDI flows to developing countries now exceed foreign aid flows by a factor of about 5 to 1.[2]

13.1 Policy concerns

In their early post-independence years, many former colonies viewed FDI with scepticism and, in some cases, outright hostility, as it was perceived to be a new form of economic imperialism (reflecting again dependency theories that were influential in many developing countries in the 1950s and 1960s, as discussed in Chapter 2). More recently, many developing countries have come to see FDI as having at least the potential for making significant contributions to their economies – as a source of investment in infrastructure, as a source of technology transfers and spillovers, as a source of investment in human capital and skills upgrading, as a source of investment in major natural resource

---

1 See D. Brautigam, *The Dragon's Gift: The Real Story of China in Africa* (Oxford and New York, NY: Oxford University Press, 2011); M. Klaver and M. Trebilcock, "Chinese Investment in Africa" (2011) 4 *Law and Development Review* 1.
2 UNCTAD, "Assessing the Impact of the Current Financial and Economic Crisis on Global FDI Flows" 19 January 2009 available at http://unctad.org/en/Docs/webdiaeia20091_en.pdf (accessed 4 May 2014).

extraction projects, and as a major source of local employment in low-wage, low-skilled manufacturing activities.[3]

Foreign direct investors, in turn, sometimes see international trade in goods or services and FDI as complements and in other cases as substitutes. Where host countries have large protected domestic markets, FDI may be the most effective way of accessing these markets behind prevailing tariff walls – particularly the case with host countries with large growing populations and hence significant potential demand for the goods or services that foreign investors can produce. In this case, FDI is a substitute for trade (horizontal FDI). In other cases, foreign investors are able to expand their opportunities for international trade in goods or services by accessing lower cost inputs (for example, natural resources or low-cost labour) in host countries and thereby gain a comparative advantage in export markets. In this case, FDI and trade are complementary (vertical FDI).[4]

In principle, the theory of comparative advantage should apply as much to international movements of FDI as to international trade in goods or services – capital is likely to gravitate to where its marginal productivity is greatest. If unqualified, this presumption would suggest the case for an international regime that facilitates the free movement of FDI, and constrains countries from adopting domestic policies designed either to encourage it – for example, through subsidies, tax breaks or tax incentives – or to discourage it – for example, through regulations pertaining to local sourcing, minimum export requirements, restrictions on exports, trade-balancing requirements that restrict the value or volume of imports to the value or volume of exports, technology transfer requirements, and so on. In fact, many countries have adopted a wide range of domestic policies that either encourage or restrict FDI either generally or, more commonly, in particular sectors.

---

3 See, for example, T.H. Moran, "Enhancing the Ability of Developing Countries to Attack and Harness FDI for Development" in Theodore Moran (ed.), *Harnessing Foreign Direct Investment: Policies for Developing Countries* (Washington, DC: Brookings Institution Press, 2006); T.H. Moran, E. Graham and M. Blomstrom (eds), *Does Foreign Direct Investment Promote Development?* (Washington, DC: Peterson Institute, 2005); OECD Report, *Foreign Direct Investment for Development: Maximizing Benefits, Minimizing Costs* (Paris: OECD, 2002). For recent analysis of the benefits of FDI in developed and developing countries see T.H. Moran, *Foreign Direct Investment and Development: Launching a Second Generation of Policy Research: Avoiding the Mistakes of the First, Reevaluating Policies for Developed and Developing Countries* (Washington, DC: Peterson Institute for International Economics, 2011).

4 See E. Helpman, *Understanding Global Trade* (Cambridge, MA: Harvard University Press, 2011), chapter 6.

Restrictions on FDI by host countries may be motivated by a range of concerns:

1. There are likely to be concerns about foreign investors taking control of activities that raise national security issues – a concern that has been exacerbated by the rapid growth of Sovereign Wealth Funds. Foreign governments who control these funds may gain access to sensitive national security technology or information, through foreign acquisitions.

2. There may be significant practical constraints in the effective application of domestic laws where the bulk of the organization's assets, many of its senior personnel, and much of the information about its activities and decision-making are located abroad.

3. There may be concerns about attempts by home country governments to enforce their laws and foreign jurisdictions through foreign subsidiaries of home country parent corporations – that is, the extra-territorial application of the laws of the home country.

4. There may also be concerns that foreign subsidiaries will be managed in such a fashion as to reflect home country bias in business decisions – for example, by purchasing inputs from home country affiliates or using personnel from home country or other affiliates rather than local personnel. In some cases, this may be motivated by a desire to appear to be a "good corporate citizen" in the home country to maximize political influence in that jurisdiction.

5. There may be concerns that foreign investors will seek to protect their investments in specialized technology and know-how by restricting access to them by domestic organizations or individuals in the host country, thereby reducing the benefits of technological spillovers and human capital enhancements in the host country.

6. There may be cultural and political sovereignty concerns with permitting FDI in certain sectors such as the print and electronic media sectors.

Foreign direct investors, in turn, are likely to confront their own set of concerns in contemplating investments in a foreign country. These may include political and policy instability (including macro-economic instability). Where investments are sunk, subsequent governments may have incentives to behave opportunistically towards foreign direct investors who lack direct political voice in host countries by unilateral *ex post facto* re-specification of the terms on which the initial investment was made. Other concerns include weak protection of private property rights; ineffective enforcement of contracts; law and order; and corruption in the administration of state functions (including legal functions).

13.2   Multilateral regulation of foreign direct investment[5]

Historically, the GATT was almost exclusively focused on international trade in goods, and not international trade in services or international movement of capital.

At the beginning of the Uruguay Round in 1986, the United States proposed that the multilateral negotiating agenda should include a comprehensive agreement on foreign investment. The agreement on TRIMs that emerged from the round is, in fact, much more modest than the initial United States' proposals and focuses mostly on trade-distorting policies, for example, local sourcing or trade-balancing requirements.

Disaffected with this modest outcome from the Uruguay Round, the United States and other developed countries sought to shift the venue for multilateral negotiations on a comprehensive investment treaty from the WTO to the OECD. It was assumed that the predominance of developed countries in the OECD would yield a readier consensus on liberalizing restrictions on FDI than the WTO, where the preponderance of developing country members with more sceptical, or at least more cautious, views of the merits of FDI was likely to preclude achievement of a consensus on a more ambitious set of international disciplines. The expectation was that non-OECD members would be able to accede to any resulting treaty, and that there would be strong inducements to do so in order to compete effectively for FDI.

From 1996 through to 1998 negotiations on a multilateral agreement on investment (MAI) proceeded within the OECD, but negotiations were non-transparent, even clandestine. The leaking of a draft of the agreement to various NGOs precipitated an international firestorm of criticism of the draft agreement and the process by which it was being

---

5 See generally M. Sornarajah, *The International Law on Foreign Investment* (Cambridge, UK: Cambridge University Press, 2010).

negotiated. The principal criticism was that it would confer extensive rights on foreign direct investors but with few, if any, concomitant obligations on their part to host countries or their citizens, for example, with respect to technology transfer, health and safety, the environment, labour standards and international human rights. In the face of these criticisms, the MAI negotiations were formally abandoned in December 1998. Proposals to include negotiations over FDI in the Doha Round of the WTO were also abandoned at the Cancun Ministerial in September 2003 in the face of opposition from developing countries.

13.3   Bilateral investment treaties

While attempts at negotiating a comprehensive multilateral treaty on FDI appear to have been abandoned, at least for the time being, a notable contrasting phenomenon has emerged: the dramatic proliferation in the number of bilateral investment treaties (BITs) or international investment agreements (IIAs) – from just over 400 in 1990 to about 3,000 today.[6] The primary impetus behind this proliferation of BITs appears to be that in the competition for foreign direct investment many countries, especially developing countries, feel obliged to provide investors with certain legally enforceable protections for their investment. However, BITs are not limited to developed–developing country dyads (only about 40 per cent are between developed–developing countries, while about a quarter of all BITs are between pairs of developing countries).[7]

BITs typically include provisions on the scope and definition of foreign investment; admission of investment; national and MFN treatment; fair and equitable treatment; guarantees and compensation in respect of expropriation and compensation for war and civil disturbances; guarantees of free transfer of funds and repatriation of capital and profits; and dispute settlement, both state-to-state and investor-to-state (typically by international arbitration, most often the International Centre for the Settlement of Investment Disputes (ICSID) affiliated with the World Bank).

---

6 See G. Van Harter, *Investing Treaty Arbitration and Public Law* (Oxford: Oxford University Press, 2008), chapter 2; S. Schill, *The Multilateralization of International Investment Law* (Cambridge, UK: Cambridge University Press, 2009).

7 UNCTAD, "Recent Developments in International Investment Agreements" IIA Monitor No. 3 (2009).

The proliferation of BITs has raised a number of controversies:

1. The "fair and equitable" standard of investment protection lacks precision and consistent interpretation or clearly articulated exceptions or qualifications for measures by host countries to address health, safety and environmental concerns or financial crises, which has led to criticisms of BITs as unduly constraining the political sovereignty of host countries.

2. The expropriation provisions in most BITs also lack clear definition and may be interpreted as extending beyond outright transfer of title to foreign investors' assets or physical dispossession of those assets to various forms of regulatory "takings" that can be viewed as significantly impairing the value of these assets. This is criticized for constraining or "chilling" legitimate spheres of regulatory autonomy relating to, for example, the regulation of health, safety and environmental hazards.

3. Given that many countries have signed multiple BITs with various other countries, each of which typically contains a MFN clause, major disputes have arisen as to when foreign investors are able to invoke ("cherry pick") either substantive or procedural provisions in BITs other than the BITs to which their home country is a party (which are more favourable to their claims than their own BITs).

4. The National Treatment principle, which is contained in most BITs, also gives rise to ambiguity as to when foreign investors have been treated less favourably than domestic investors in "like circumstances".

5. The international arbitral dispute resolution system has been criticized as lacking transparency, consistency and scope for effective third-party (amicus) interventions, and in general being biased towards the interests of foreign investors.[8]

6. It is argued that BITs largely remove foreign investors as a political constituency for domestic legal reform in host countries by providing them with privileged supra-national legal protections.[9]

---

8 For a review of many of the foregoing critiques, see D. Schneiderman, *Constitutionalizing Economic Globalization: Investment Rules and Democracy's Promise* (Cambridge, UK: Cambridge University Press, 2008).

9 T. Ginsburg, "International Substitutes for Domestic Institutions: Bilateral Investment Treaties and Governance" (2005) 25 *International Review of Law and Economics* 107. For a contrary view, see S. Franck, "Foreign Direct Investment Treaty Arbitration and the Rule of Law" (2007) *Pacific McGeorge Global Business and Development Law Journal* 337.

A new generation of BITs attempts to strike a finer balance between the interests of investors and the interests of host countries by adding interpretive provisions, general exceptions clauses, and new preambular language as to the purpose of the agreements.[10] However, it remains to be seen how arbitrators will interpret such provisions and whether they are effectively justiciable in a consistent and credible manner.

The argument that BITs actually increase FDI flows to host countries has yielded a rather mixed body of empirical evidence.[11] The most recent and comprehensive study finds (contrary to some earlier studies) that BITs do promote FDI flows to developing countries, although yielding declining marginal impacts as more BITs are signed.[12] BITs may even substitute for weak domestic institutions, though probably not for unilateral measures such as opening up previously restricted industries, removing foreign ownership restrictions, promotional efforts and tax and fiscal inducements.

Nevertheless, the extent to which BITs can substitute for weak domestic institutions is limited because arbitral awards still need to be enforced in the domestic courts of host countries, and purely private disputes may still need to be resolved in these courts unless the parties have contracted out of the jurisdiction through (increasingly common) choice of law and choice of forum clauses – although even in these cases foreign judgments or arbitral awards need to be enforced in host countries' courts.[13] It needs to be acknowledged more generally that the empirical evidence on how important a host country's legal system is as a determinant of FDI is contested terrain, with scholars pointing, as counter-evidence, to the case of large recent inflows of FDI into China, despite relatively weak legal institutions, at least on conventional criteria.[14]

---

10 See S. Spears, "The Quest for Policy Space in a New Generation of International Investment Agreements" (2010) 13 *Journal of International Economic Law* 1037; see also P. Muchlinski, "Holistic Approaches to Development and International Investment Law: The Role of International Investment Agreements" in J. Faundez and C. Tan (eds), *International Economic Law, Globalization and Developing Countries* (Cheltenham, UK and Northampton, MA, USA: Edward Elgar, 2010).

11 For a review of this evidence, see A. Lehavi and A. Licht, "BITs and Pieces of Property" (2011) 36 *Yale Journal of International Law* 115, at 126–8.

12 M. Busse, J. Koniger and P. Nunnenkamp, "FDI Promotion through Bilateral Investment Treaties: More than a Bit?" (2010) 146 *Review of the World Economy* 147.

13 See J. Dammann and H. Hansmann, "Globalizing Commercial Litigation" (2008) 94 *Cornell Law Review* 1.

14 See A. Perry, "Effective Legal Systems and Foreign Direct Investment: In Search of the Evidence" (2000) 49 *International and Comparative Law Quarterly* 779; cf. A. Benassy-Quere, M. Coupet

13.4   Conclusion

The proliferation of BITs stands in stark contrast to successive failures to negotiate a MAI. However, BITs entail a risk of collective action problems and a race to the bottom among host countries (especially developing countries). This argues for a further attempt at negotiating a multilateral agreement, probably under the aegis of the WTO (where coalition bargaining is possible), building on the new generation of BITs that attempt to strike a better balance between the interests of foreign investors and host countries.

---

and T. Mayer, "Institutional Determinants of Foreign Direct Investment" (2007) 30 *The World Economy* 5.

14 Foreign aid

14.1 Introduction

Foreign aid flows to developing countries are substantially smaller than the other major sources of international financial flows, namely trade and FDI (as discussed in the previous two chapters). In recent years, most developed countries have officially committed themselves to increasing levels of foreign aid to 0.7 per cent of gross national product (GNP). On average, aid levels (about US$130 billion per year) are currently running at about half of this number.[1]

Who gives aid and who receives it? About 70 per cent of aid is provided on a bilateral basis and 30 per cent on a multilateral basis.[2] About 70 per cent of all official development assistance is provided directly to recipient governments. NGOs account for about another US$30 billion in development assistance, and emergency and humanitarian aid for about another US$15 billion a year, on average.

Should we be giving aid? Assessments by long-time aid practitioners of the efficacy of foreign aid in promoting long-term economic development support a generally pessimistic view, in large part because foreign aid (which is mostly government-to-government) has done little or nothing to transform dysfunctional institutions in developing countries and may indeed have helped to perpetuate them,[3] leading to what some commentators have called an "aid-

---

1 D. Moyo, *Dead Aid: Why Aid is Not Working and How There is a Better Way for Africa* (New York, NY: Farrar, Strauss, Giroux, 2009) at 10.

2 OECD, Development Co-operation Directorate, "Reference DAC Statistical Tables", available at http://www.oecd.org/dac/stats/data.htm (accessed 4 May 2014).

3 See T. Carothers and D. de Gramont, *Development Aid Confronts Politics: The Almost Revolution* (Washington, DC: Carnegie Endowment for International Peace, 2013); M. Andrews, *The Limits of Institutional Reform: Changing Rules for Realistic Solutions* (Cambridge, UK: Cambridge University Press, 2013); L. Pritchett, M. Woolcock and M. Andrews, "Looking Like a State: Techniques of Persistent Failure in State Capability for Implementation" (2013) 49 *Journal*

institutions paradox".[4] In contrast, more optimistic views of the contribution that foreign aid can make to improving human well-being stress the substantial convergence that has occurred, through the dissemination of technologies and ideas, over the post-war years between many developed and developing countries on various social indicators, such as life expectancy, fertility rates, infant and maternal mortality rates, literacy rates, school attendance rates, and gender equality. This optimistic view acknowledges growing divergences on measures of material well-being, such as inequalities in income per capita, and the marginal contributions of foreign aid to long-term sustainable economic growth (on the determinants of which there are no robust, general theories).[5]

This chapter will review the debates around foreign aid, focusing on the connections between aid and domestic institutions.

14.2   Debates over the efficacy of foreign aid

Foreign aid programmes in the post-war period find their genesis and inspiration in the Marshall Plan mounted by the United States to reconstruct the war-torn economies of Europe, complemented by similar forms of assistance to Japan during the period of United States' occupation. In both cases, this assistance contributed to a rapid and dramatic reconstruction of many of these economies, with Germany and Japan quickly emerging as major economic powers in the post-war era. However, these two countries possessed highly educated work forces, well-developed infrastructure, high levels of technological sophistication, and well-established institutional and organizational capacity in the public and private sectors. Very few of these conditions were replicated in developing countries, many of whom were granted independence by their former colonial powers (sometimes with very

of Development Studies; A. Chakravarti, Aid, Institutions and Development (Cheltenham, UK and Northampton, MA, USA: Edward Elgar, 2005); M. Shirley, Institutions and Development (Cheltenham, UK and Northampton, MA, USA: Edward Elgar, 2008), chapter 4.

4 See T. Moss, G. Pettersson and N. van de Walle, "An Aid-Institutions Paradox? A Review Essay on Aid Dependency and State-Building in Sub-Saharan Africa" in W. Easterly (ed.), Reinventing Foreign Aid, (Cambridge, MA: MIT Press, 2008).

5 See C. Kenny, Getting Better: Why Global Development is Succeeding and How We can Improve the World Even More (New York, NY: Basic Books, 2011); A. Deaton, The Great Escape: Health, Wealth, and the Origins of Inequality (Princeton, NJ: Princeton University Press, 2013); E. Helpman, The Mystery of Economic Growth (Cambridge, MA: Harvard University Press, 2004).

little in the way of advance preparation or transition), beginning in the mid-1950s.

Moreover, the motivations of developed countries in providing foreign aid to developing countries were subject to a number of serious distortions. First, with the onset of the Cold War in the late 1940s, many developed countries were inclined to provide aid at levels and in forms that reflected judgments about the ideological affinities of recipient states with either communism or capitalism, or other geo-political considerations, irrespective of whether this aid well served basic development priorities. Second, many developed countries, in their aid policies, showed strong preferences for their former colonies, reflecting historical ties, again according secondary importance to whether the aid was being effectively utilized by the recipient countries. Third, many donor countries saw aid partly as an export promotion strategy through "tied aid" conditions. Thus, evaluations of the efficacy of foreign aid to developing countries over the post-war period range from mixed to disappointing.[6]

A number of major controversies surround the foreign aid–development nexus, as illustrated by a spirited (and at times vitriolic) debate between two leading contemporary development economists, Jeffrey Sachs and William Easterly. Sachs argues for a much more expansionary foreign aid policy (in fact, a trebling of aid over the next two decades) and that the limited efficacy of aid to date has been largely a function of its limited scale.[7] William Easterly, in turn, argues that foreign aid in the past has done little to improve the long-term well-being of the citizens of developing nations (beyond short-term emergency or humanitarian aid, which itself has been subject to trenchant criticism for often being afflicted by a lack of coordination amongst multiple donors and corruption in its delivery).[8] Thus, without a major re-orientation in aid strategies, there is no reason to suppose that a dramatic expansion of aid is likely to have a larger impact in the future. Easterly favours bottom-up, rather than top-down approaches to aid ("searchers" rather than "planners").[9] Sachs regards Easterly as "notori-

---

6 For a comprehensive and balanced description and evaluation of the history and efficacy of foreign aid in the post-war period, see R.C. Riddell, *Does Foreign Aid Really Work?* (Oxford: Oxford University Press, 2007).

7 J. Sachs, *The End of Poverty: Economic Possibilities for Our Time* (New York, NY: Penguin Group, 2005).

8 See L. Polman, *War Games: The Story of Aid and War in Modern Times* (London: Viking, 2010).

9 W. Easterly, *The White Man's Burden: Why the West's Efforts to Aid the Rest Have Done So Much Ill and So Little Good* (Oxford: Oxford University Press, 2006); W. Easterly, *The Tyranny of*

ous as the cheerleader for can't-do economics", while Easterly portrays Sachs as a hopelessly utopian global central planner.[10]

More recently, Dambisa Moyo has joined the debate, taking an even more critical view of aid in the case of Africa.[11] She suggests that foreign aid has undermined development by providing external funding for developing country political regimes, which has propped up venal, repressive or incompetent governments by rendering them unaccountable to their citizens for their tax and expenditure policies.[12]

These authors represent three fundamental perspectives which frame more specific debates about foreign aid: Sachs advocates substantially increased aid; Easterly is critical of increasing aid, at least without a major re-orientation of current aid strategies; while Moyo believes aid is damaging and should be eliminated completely.

14.3   Which countries should receive aid

If one takes the view that an expansion in levels of aid should be predicated on reasonable assurances of efficacy, it is then appropriate to consider whether some aid environments are more supportive of effective foreign aid than others. In a widely cited World Bank study reviewing the post-war aid experience,[13] the authors conclude that aid works best in good policy and institutional environments. This conclusion seems intuitively compelling, although it has been challenged empirically.[14] Even if well-founded, it raises a major foreign aid dilemma: developing

---

Experts (NY: Basic Books, 2013); see A. Sen, "The Man Without a Plan", *Foreign Affairs*, March/April 2006, for a review of *White Man's Burden*.

10 See N. Munk, *The Idealist: Jeffrey Sachs and the Quest to End Poverty* (Toronto: McClelland & Stewart, 2013).

11 For an example of this debate, see J. Sachs, "Aid Ironies" Huffington Post (24 May 2009), available at http://www.huffingtonpost.com/jeffrey-sachs/aid-ironies_b_207181.html (accessed 4 May 2014); D. Moyo, "Aid Ironies: A Response to Jeffrey Sachs" Huffington Post (26 May 2009), available at http://huffingtonpost.com/dambisa-moyo/aid-ironies-a-response-to_b_207772.html (accessed 4 May 2014); W. Easterly, "Sachs Ironies: Why Critics Are Better for Foreign Aid than Apologists" Huffington Post (25 May 2009), available at http://www.huffingtonpost.com/william-easterly/sachs-ironies-why-critics_b_207331.html (accessed 4 May 2014).

12 Moyo, *supra* note.

13 D. Dollar and L. Pritchett, *Assessing Aid: What Works, What Doesn't and Why* (Oxford: Oxford University Press, 1998).

14 See W. Easterly, "Can Foreign Aid Buy Growth?" (2003) 17 *Journal of Economic Perspectives* 23; and Riddell, *supra* note 6, at 232.

countries with good policy and institutional environments will often have less pressing claims for aid, as measured on many common economic and social indicators, than developing countries that lack these environments.[15] As Moises Naim puts it (rather too dramatically), "the paradox is that any country capable of meeting such stringent requirements is already a developed country".[16] Failed or fragile states present this dilemma in its most acute form, but many developing countries exhibit a mix of good and bad policies and good and bad institutions.

According to Paul Collier, foreign aid should be concentrated on the 60 or so developing countries comprising the poorest billion citizens of the world and suffering from one or more of the various traps that Collier describes – the natural resource trap, the landlocked-with-bad-neighbours trap, the civil conflict trap, and the bad governance trap.[17] But, of course, these countries are precisely those where the good aid environment described by the World Bank generally does not exist. For multilateral, regional and bilateral aid agencies already facing a significant level of public scepticism in donor countries as to the efficacy of aid, this may be viewed as an extremely high-risk aid strategy. Thus, the aid-institutions paradox: providing aid to countries that need it most is unlikely to have the desired effects because of institutional and policy failures.

14.4   Coordination of foreign aid

Coordination problems manifest themselves in a wide range of dimensions in the foreign aid field. First, within large multilateral aid organizations – such as the World Bank and a plethora of United Nations' agencies, and replicated to some extent in regional and bilateral aid agencies – personnel and budgets are typically organized into various subject area groupings (for example, rural development, infrastructure, governance reform, sustainable development and gender issues), which in turn are overlaid by geographic groupings by country or region. Aid dispensers experience strong incentives to disburse money quickly, as a readily observable measure of activity, while resist-

---

15 See J. Svensson, "Absorption Capacity and Disbursement Constraints" in Easterly (ed.), *supra* note 4.

16 M. Naim, "Washington Consensus or Washington Confusion" *Foreign Policy* (Spring 2000) 87, at 96.

17 P. Collier, *The Bottom Billion: Why the Poorest Countries are Failing and What Can Be Done About It* (New York, NY: Oxford University Press, 2007).

ing both independent evaluations of outcomes and acknowledgements of failure (from which lessons for the future may be learned).[18]

Within recipient governments, there is a somewhat parallel set of organizational issues, with various line ministries of government – for example, health, education and infrastructure – often in some tension with central ministries, such as finance, in competing for donors' assistance. There are also similar incentives to "move the money", while avoiding honest and rigorous evaluations of results.

On the donor side of the equation, these problems are compounded horizontally by donor proliferation, where many donor agencies (recalling that most aid is bilateral) are active in the same subject areas and countries or regions, each reflecting its own citizens' or taxpayers' preferences or priorities[19] (or else there would be only one global aid agency). Each country's aid agency has strong political incentives to "plant the flag" on as many visible projects as possible, and in many cases in as many countries as possible, even though the result is often dozens or even hundreds of donors or their agents involved in various aid projects in a given developing country.[20] Each aid recipient country receives official development assistance from an average of 26 different official donors and upwards of 30 substantial NGOs.[21] Donor agencies are often unaware of the multiple donor agencies working on similar projects and thus make aid allocation decisions with imperfect information about the overall funding going to a particular sector.

On the recipient side, disbursing aid from multiple sources burdens recipient governments with high transaction and managerial costs in complying with each donor's reporting and accountability requirements, over-extending general governmental capacity and undermining the government's ability to attend to basic functions. Problems of horizontal coordination on the recipient side are compounded when sub-national levels of government, community organizations, local or

---

18 See L. Pritchett, "It Pays to be Ignorant: A Simple Political Economy of Rigorous Program Evaluation" in Easterly (ed.), *supra* note 4; Shirley, *supra* note 3.

19 See B. Ramalingam, *Aid on the Edge of Chaos: Rethinking International Cooperation in a Complex World* (Oxford: Oxford University Press, 2013); R. Reinikka, "Donors and Service Delivery", S. Knack and A. Rahman, "Donor Fragmentation" and B. Martens, "Why Do Foreign Aid Agencies Exist?" in Easterly (ed.), *supra* note 4.

20 See Polman, *supra* note 8.

21 Riddell, *supra* note 6, at 52, 54; A. Ghani and C. Lockhart, *Fixing Failed States: A Framework for Rebuilding a Fractured World* (New York, NY: Oxford University Press, 2008), chapter 5.

foreign NGOs, or "ring-fenced" aid projects are involved in the aid delivery process (such problems are often further compounded by "poaching" by these organizations of some of the most knowledgeable employees of the host government at much higher salaries).

Individual donor agencies also face problems of vertical coordination, when aid is delivered through a chain of contracts and sub-contracts with local or foreign contractors or NGOs. There would seem to be obvious gains in aid effectiveness to be realized by bilateral aid agencies developing substantial expertise in a few sectors in a few developing countries (and hence achieving a comparative advantage in these sectors and countries). However, there appear to be powerful institutional and political incentives driving in the opposite direction, such as a desire for donor visibility within many recipient countries and the international aid community.[22]

Here, again, we confront the "aid-institutions" paradox identified earlier in this discussion of foreign aid. While Peter Singer (like Sachs) argues for greatly expanded aid flows, he favours bypassing developing country governments and channelling these funds mostly through local and international NGOs and charities.[23] However, bypassing governments in recipient countries (even those with weak governments) poses various risks. Many charities and NGOs suffer from their own problems of transparency, accountability and effectiveness and moreover are not well-equipped to undertake many large-scale long-term development projects.[24] Setting up a composite body of government, donor and NGO representatives ("independent service authorities") in recipient countries to address the problems of coordination (as Collier and Riddell propose)[25] raises similar issues of transparency and accountability, as well as the risk of dysfunctional internal politics within such bodies and the creation of a parallel *de facto* government that further undermines the legitimacy and effectiveness of the *de jure* government.[26] However, channelling all aid through weak

---

22 D. Goldfarb and S. Tapp, "How Canada Can Improve its Development Aid: Lessons from Other Agencies" (Toronto: CD Howe Institute, Commentary No. 232, April 2006); J. Richards, "Can Aid Work? Thinking about Development Strategy" (Toronto, CD Howe Institute, Commentary No. 231, April 2006).

23 P. Singer, *The Life You Can Save: Acting Now to End World Poverty* (New York, NY: Random House, 2009).

24 See Polman, *supra* note 8 and Shirley, *supra* note 3.

25 Collier, *supra* note 17, at 118–20; Riddell, *supra* note 6, at 396.

26 See Reinikka, *supra* note 19 and Shirley, *supra* note 3.

governments – in its purest form, simply enhancing the central government's budgetary capacity – runs its own set of risks: the risk of gross misallocation, even misappropriation, of aid resources and, even in more favourable circumstances, being unappealing to donor countries whose domestic political constituencies may be unimpressed by the seeming irresponsibility of writing blank cheques to foreign governments in developing countries without visible projects to point to as the result of aid expenditures.

14.5   Aid conditionality

An attempt to address the conflicting relationship between the interests of aid donors and those of developing country governments is the use of conditionality in the terms on which aid is provided to encourage recipient governments to comply with donor interests or expectations. Some forms of aid conditionality are, on their face, quite perverse from a development perspective. In particular, tied aid – whereby donors require recipient governments to commit to purchasing inputs, goods or services from firms in donor countries – has been found to diminish the value of aid by 15 to 30 per cent relative to what the amount of aid could purchase on the open market. This also freezes out local suppliers in developing countries from the growth opportunities that arise from participating in the aid delivery process. Tied aid still accounts for a significant percentage of bilateral aid (approximately 50 per cent), although substantial progress has been made in recent years, through the OECD, in reducing this percentage.[27]

In other cases, aid conditions reflect what donor agencies believe recipient countries should accord a high priority to in development objectives, regardless of whether these priorities are shared by the population or governments of the recipient countries. Just as there are problems of non-alignment of preferences among donors, there are often problems of non-alignment of preferences between donors and recipients; these problems reflect broken information (accountability) feedback loops where citizens/taxpayers in donor countries are ill-informed as to the effects of aid in recipient countries, and citizens in recipient countries have no political voice in donor countries.[28]

---

27 See Riddell, *supra* note 6, at 100–101.
28 See Martens, *supra* note 19; Svensson, *supra* note 15.

If governments in recipient countries are weak, incompetent, corrupt or unaccountable to their citizens, there may be reasons for circumspection about recipient governments' articulation of aid priorities. Thus, in many cases, governments in developing countries are the problem, not the solution. In such cases, aid conditions should ideally be informed by some broader canvassing of priorities amongst representative groups of citizens of the developing countries in question if the problem of broken information (accountability) feedback loops is to be mitigated. This is not easy for external donor agencies to orchestrate in the absence of established broadly based consultative mechanisms, and in the face of potential resistance from the recipient country's government itself. Thus, in many cases, aid conditions are routinely violated or imperfectly followed by the governments of recipient countries, and almost as routinely ignored by many donor agencies facing imperatives to continue to disburse the aid to meet expenditure commitments, regardless of the unmet conditions.[29]

This phenomenon is exacerbated by the problem of conditions imposed by different donors at cross-purposes with one another, and by the problem of effective monitoring of compliance with aid conditions because of the fungibility of money. For example, if a country commits itself to allocating aid that it receives to primary school education, it may simply reallocate resources of its own that it would otherwise have spent on primary school education to other purposes (military expenditure, for example), while claiming that the aid received has been allocated to its intended purpose. In some cases, aid conditionality, particularly when a new reform-oriented government in a recipient country has taken office, can serve the useful function of providing a credible commitment to an agreed agenda of policy and institutional reform, as well as sending credible signals to domestic and foreign economic agents (including foreign investors) that the new government is committed to a well-defined, long-term development strategy. These cases, however, seem very much the exception rather than the rule.

---

29 J. Svensson, "Why Conditional Aid Does Not Work and What Can Be Done About It?" (2003) 70 *Journal of Development Economics* 381.

14.6   Foreign aid and institutional reform

It is useful to place the institutional capacity issues noted above primarily in the context of the Sachs–Easterly debate about foreign aid. Sachs, in arguing for a "big push" on foreign aid, largely ignores these institutional issues, rather casually pointing to the fact that there are several governments in sub-Saharan Africa that possess the institutional competence and integrity to use more aid effectively (leaving as an unanswered mystery what should happen in the many other cases). Easterly, on the other hand, in the face of these institutional dysfunctions, seems largely to throw up his hands in despair and resign himself to aid being deployed on the margins of the development enterprise in small, incremental, local initiatives (such as drilling wells for local villages, providing mosquito nets, vaccinating against various tropical diseases or providing vouchers to citizens for necessary goods or services). For Moyo, aid has mostly pernicious effects, so the less aid the better, making irrelevant any question of how to reform aid policies. While Singer, like Sachs, favours greatly expanded aid flows, he largely side-steps the challenges of institutional reform by "privatizing" the recipients of aid.

The enormous challenge, largely unaddressed by these authors, is whether limitations on institutional capacity and legitimacy can be addressed effectively so that a much larger volume of aid can responsibly be provided to developing countries with some reasonable confidence in its likely efficacy.[30] Setting these institutional issues to one side – or treating them as of second-order importance – in debates over foreign aid is largely to condemn aid to ineffectiveness in precisely those environments where citizens are the victims of the most severe forms of deprivation and misgovernment. However, confronting these issues requires donors to forgo the illusion that aid is a largely technocratic rather than political exercise[31] and that tensions with traditional Westphalian notions of state sovereignty can be avoided. We can no longer persist with the fallacy that poorly performing governments in developing countries simply lack information, technical expertise and resources (which aid can provide), but are otherwise well motivated towards their citizens.[32]

---

30 See Riddell, *supra* note 6, at 373–7.

31 See Carothers and de Gramont, *supra* note 3.

32 See Chakravarti, *supra* note 3.

A promising starting point is to acknowledge that aid agencies require, as committed clients, self-identified agents of institutional reform with self-identified agendas for reform supported by significant and broadly representative constituencies within developing countries. In some cases this may be the government itself, but is often likely to be pockets of reformers within agencies of government, or constituencies outside government, who are committed to an institutional reform agenda. This agenda cannot be imposed from outside by pretending that "Djibouti is Denmark" or by "skipping straight to Weber",[33] but requires an authentic domestic political constituency with a reform agenda that is sensitive to the particularities of its country's context, history, politics and culture.

Given such a reform constituency, foreign aid donors can provide both financial and technical support to such constituencies to assist them in pressing their reform agenda and also exert leverage on government and its agencies by withholding or terminating government-to-government aid for failure to respond to this reform agenda against well-specified milestones. Increasing the percentage of aid channeled through multilateral institutions is likely to increase this leverage (although at the risk of larger systemic policy errors and less policy experimentation at the level of the individual donor). Reforming the governance structures of multilateral institutions to make them more fairly representative of the developing and developed world is also likely to enhance the legitimacy of exerting such leverage. Invoking accession negotiations for membership of trade or broader economic cooperation regimes, offering valuable long-term benefits (as the European Union has done with some success with new member countries from Central and Eastern Europe) to extract, monitor and enhance meaningful institutional reform commitments that enjoy support from substantial domestic constituencies is an analogous strategy that has some promise (but has been insufficiently exploited more generally).[34]

---

33 L. Pritchett and M. Woolcock, "Solutions Where the Solution is the Problem: Arraying the Disarray in Development" in Easterly (ed.), *supra* note 4.

34 M. Trebilcock and R. Daniels, *Rule of Law Reform and Development: Charting the Fragile Path of Progress* (Cheltenham, UK and Northampton, MA, USA: Edward Elgar, 2008), chapter 10.

14.7   Conclusion

If one believes that institutions matter to development, to give up on foreign aid as an important agent of institutional change is to condemn the citizens of many of the world's poorest and most misgoverned countries to a future of more or less perpetual deprivation. Rethinking the most effective bundle of "carrots and sticks" to drive institutional change is the central unmet challenge on the foreign aid agenda. Until this "aid-institutions" paradox is unlocked, foreign aid will largely fail to advance long-term economic development objectives.

15 Conclusion

This book has sought to provide a concise introductory survey of the current state of scholarly knowledge about the relationship between law, institutions and development. We conclude this enterprise by identifying some of the theoretical, methodological and practical issues that scholars confront today in the field of law and development and institutional theories of development.

Perhaps the most pressing issue is the possibility of a universal theory. One can investigate the field of development under the assumption that, despite the numerous particularities of different countries, there is a common set of factors that will determine a country's development prospects. For example, most theories of development discussed in Chapter 2 share this assumption, ascribing development to a particular cause (the economy, geography, culture or a country's institutional arrangements). There are, however, scholars who argue that the search for a general theory of development is futile as a country's fate will be determined by a series of factors that are quite unique and particular to that country. We should instead be discussing separately the particular circumstances of, for example, Brazil, China and the Sudan.

This divergence of views regarding the existence of a "universal theory" of development can also be found in microcosm in institutional theories of development. Some scholars believe that it is possible to conceive of a general theory of institutional development or institutional change.[1] In contrast, strong scepticism is espoused by those who see the institution-building exercise as a complex and dynamic phenomenon, informed by a variety of societal factors – such as politics and culture – that are beyond the reformers' (or perhaps anyone's) knowl-

---

1 The most emblematic example would be the work of D. North, founder of the NIE. For a more detailed discussion of this work, see Chapter 3.

edge or control.[2] While the first view subscribes to the idea that we can collectively engage in a common intellectual exercise to understand the institution-building process, the second view either sees this exercise as unique and particular to each country or each institution, or it rejects altogether the idea that it is possible to conceive of "institution building"; institutions grow organically and cannot be intentionally created or modified.

Other scholars take positions somewhere in between these two extremes. Dani Rodrik argues that we may have universal tools to identify problems, such as welfare economics, but that institutional reforms and economic policies to address such problems need to be adapted to particular contexts.[3] Prado and Trebilcock, in turn, have argued for middle-level generalizations.[4] They reject the idea that every single institution emerges and evolves according to a universal pattern, but believe that there may be useful commonalities that can be found among institutions performing similar functions, such as police forces, educational systems, courts, etc.[5] This is especially true when the political, social and economic circumstances under which these institutions are operating are very similar.[6] In a similar fashion, David Trubek has argued for "horizontal learning" in law and development, which can be described as networking among developing countries to share experiences that can inform and inspire legislative reform and policy experimentation.[7]

Another strand of research has addressed this challenge in a different way: instead of theorizing about institutions, it seeks to identify

---

2 B.Z. Tamanaha, "The Primacy of Society and the Failure of Law and Development" (2011) 44 *Cornell International Law Journal* 209.

3 D. Rodrik, *One Economics, Many Recipes: Globalization, Institutions and Economic Growth* (Princeton, NJ: Princeton University Press, 2007). See also D. Rodrik, *The Globalization Paradox: Democracy and the Future of the World Economy* (New York, NY: W.W. Norton & Co., 2011).

4 M.M. Prado and M. Trebilcock, "Path Dependence, Development and the Dynamics of Institutional Reform" (2009) 59:3 *University of Toronto Law Journal* 341.

5 M. Trebilcock and R.J. Daniels, *Rule of Law Reform and Development: Charting the Fragile Path of Progress* (Cheltenham, UK and Northampton, MA, USA: Edward Elgar, 2008) M.M. Prado, M. Trebilcock and P. Hartford, "Police Reform Violent Democracies in Latin America" (September 2012) 4:2 *Hague Journal on the Rule of Law* 252. L.D. Carson, J. Noronha and M. Trebilcock, "Picking Up Big Bills from the Sidewalk: The Supply of and Demand for Quality Basic Education in Brazil and India" (October 2013, University of Toronto) (unpublished manuscript).

6 M. Trebilcock and M.M. Prado, *What Makes Poor Countries Poor? Institutional Determinants of Development* (Cheltenham, UK and Northampton, MA, USA: Edward Elgar, 2011), Conclusion.

7 D. Trubek, "Scan Globally, Reform Locally: The Horizontal Learning Method in Law and Development" ABDI Conference, Law School of the Getulio Vargas Foundation in São Paulo, São Paulo, Brazil (2–4 November 2010).

commonalities in the process of institutional change.[8] While institutional design may need to be adapted to each particular context, there may be clear and common patterns in the process through which institutions change. One example of this type of analysis is Milhaupt and Pistor's case studies of legal responses to corporate governance crises in six developed and middle-income countries, which are used to trace different methods of legal adaptation, finding commonalities in diverse contexts.[9]

The second issue is methodological. If we are to use empirical data to test theoretical claims, is there a preferable method? Scholars have engaged and analysed at length the value and adequacy of two of the most widely used empirical methods: quantitative and qualitative analyses. Examples of quantitative analyses include the Global Governance Indicators Project at the World Bank and the legal origins literature.[10] By consulting the most comprehensive empirical evidence available, these analyses assess the validity of theoretical generalizations and possibly limit their scope. This type of analysis has great potential, but it also has important shortcomings when applied to legal institutions. Statistical tools cannot prove causality between institutional design and development outcomes because it is difficult to ensure that there is not an omitted variable bias.[11] Moreover, they are typically too coarse-grained to yield useful operational implications.[12]

Qualitative analyses, also known as case studies, also offer valuable insights.[13] First, while quantitative data will confirm *whether* or not a certain theoretical claim is true and can be generalized, case studies

---

8   K. Davis and M.M. Prado, "Law, Regulation and Development" in B. Currie-Adler, R. Kanbur, D.M. Malone and R. Medhora (eds), *International Development: Ideas, Experience and Prospects* (New York, NY: Oxford University Press, 2014) (calling this shift of focus a change from a search for principles to a search for metaprinciples).

9   C.J. Milhaupt and K. Pistor, *Law & Capitalism: What Corporate Crises Reveal about Legal Systems and Economic Development around the World* (Chicago, IL and London: University of Chicago Press, 2008).

10 These are discussed in Chapters 3 and 4, respectively.

11 J. Klick, "The Perils of Empirical Work on Institutions" (2010) 166 *Journal of Institutional and Theoretical Economics* 166.

12 M.M. Shirley, *Institutions and Development: Advances in New Institutional Development* (Cheltenham, UK and Northampton, MA, USA: Edward Elgar, 2008) at 4 (indicating how cross-country analysis of institutions offers little guidance to reformers).

13 *Ibid*. See also D. Rodrik, *In Search of Prosperity: Analytical Narratives of Economic Growth* (Princeton, NJ: Princeton University Press, 2003).

(qualitative data) are likely to illuminate *why* that claim is not true or cannot be generalized. Thus, case studies are helpful in illuminating under which circumstances middle-level generalizations are possible or not.[14] Second, case studies may help to inform what kinds of cultural, political and economic factors are likely to interact with formal institutions and under which circumstances. In this regard, sociological, anthropological and political studies may be an additional tool that can help scholars to understand the context, fully capture what has transpired in a particular country, and analyse to what extent this can yield lessons that are applicable to countries that face similar conditions. Third, case studies that analyse the historical evolution of a certain institutional arrangement can also indicate the relevance of institutional interconnections and sequencing, and may call attention to the different possible configurations that an institutional reform may take, and the possible outcomes that each of these configurations is likely to generate. The limitation of case studies is that they are not easily generalizable and therefore do not provide a solid basis for broader claims or theoretical formulations.

More recently, the field of economic development has been disrupted by a new methodological approach: the use of randomized controlled trials (RCTs) to test policy outcomes in developing countries.[15] Similar to medical trials, where RCTs have been known as the gold standard for scientific research, subjects are randomly assigned to either a group that is subjected to the intervention, the "treatment group", or a group that has not been subjected to the intervention, the "control group". The intervention (a particular development policy) is presumed to be the cause of different outcomes (if any) between the treatment group and the control group.

Some legal scholars have also argued in favour of using RCTs to evaluate legal reforms in developed countries.[16] However, practical, legal and ethical problems limit the scope for experimenting with legal

---

14 For an interesting on-the-ground experience, see UNDP, Making the Law Work for Everyone: Report of the Commission on Legal Empowerment of the Poor, Vol. I (New York, NY: United Nations, 2008) at 87.

15 A. Banerjee and E. Duflo, *Poor Economics: A Radical Rethinking of the Way to Fight Global Poverty* (New York, NY: Public Affairs, 2011). See also D. Kaplan and J. Appel, *More than Good Intentions: How a New Economics is Helping to Solve Global Poverty* (New York, NY: Dutton, 2011).

16 M. Abramowicz, I. Ayres and Y. Listokin, "Randomizing Law" (March 2011) 159:4 *University of Pennsylvania Law Review* 929.

norms. As Davis and Prado highlight, these problems can be especially acute in developing countries:

> Where is a government to find people with the expertise and integrity to design, conduct and interpret the results of these kinds of experiments in good faith? Do they have legal authority to apply legal norms selectively? Is it ethical to experiment with the welfare of people on the brink of subsistence? Without answers to these questions it is hard to determine the extent to which this type of experimentalism will help the field of law and development move forward.[17]

In sum, each of these three methods has advantages and disadvantages. The field is likely to benefit from the information generated by these methods in different ways, but for that it is necessary that both producers and consumers of these studies be aware of the methods' potentials as well as limitations.

The third issue is practical. What is the best strategy to translate the knowledge acquired in scholarly investigation into concrete institutional and legal reforms for development? It seems intuitive that one could look at successful practices and functional institutions in other countries and try to mimic them. The idea seems to work for some public policies and anti-poverty programmes, such as microcredit and conditional cash transfers.[18] Best practices or blueprints, however, have not been so successful with institutional reforms.[19] Scholars have claimed that the main reason for this is the complex interactions between formal and informal institutions (often referred to as "culture"). This interaction does not leave room for blueprints or justify assumptions that transplanted institutions are likely to work in the same fashion as they do in their country of origin.[20] Due to this uncer-

---

17 Davis and Prado, *supra* note 8.

18 M. Yunnus, *Banker to the Poor: Micro-Lending and the Battle against World Poverty* (New York, NY: Public Affairs, 2003); A. Fiszbein and N. Schady, "Conditional Cash Transfers: Reducing Present and Future Poverty" *World Bank Research Reports*, 2009.

19 M. Trebilcock and R. Daniels, "The Political Economy of Rule of Law Reforms in Developing Countries" (2004) 26 *Michigan Journal of International Law* 99.

20 See, for example, A.N. Licht, C. Goldschmidt and S.H. Schwartz, "Culture Rules: The Foundations of the Rule of Law and Other Norms of Governance" (2007) 35:4 *Journal of Comparative Economics* 659; L.E. Harrison and S.P. Huntington (eds), *Culture Matters: How Values Shape Human Progress* (New York, NY: Basic Books, 2000); L.E. Harrison, *The Central Liberal Truth: How Politics Can Change a Culture and Save It from Itself* (Oxford: Oxford University Press, 2006); L.E. Harrison and J. Kagan, *Developing Cultures: Essays on Cultural Change* (London and New York, NY: Routledge, 2006).

tainty, in borrowing ideas and insights from successful experiences in other countries or contexts, reformers should be mindful of the fact that institution building requires a great deal of adaptation to the particular conditions of each country.[21]

The question, then, is how best to proceed with this adaptation process? This is a fiercely debated matter. On the one hand, some argue that institutional interconnections are likely to render ineffective partial or piecemeal reforms.[22] As institutions depend on each other to function effectively, reforms are unlikely to be effective unless they are all-encompassing and comprehensive. In sum, reformers need to "think big". In contrast, there are those who are sceptical about the possibility of promoting all-encompassing reforms.[23] As a result of path dependence, political economy and other obstacles to institutional reform, some scholars believe that it is not possible to promote an institutional overhaul that will amount to something that we call "good governance" or the "rule of law". Instead, reformers should confine their agenda to one institution at a time. For these scholars, the assumption is that "thinking small" is the most promising strategy to making a particular institution functional.[24]

There are scholars who do not subscribe to either of these extreme positions. Charles Sabel, for instance, supports experimentalism in governance of developing countries. This experimentalism can be implemented on a small or large scale. Small-scale experimentalism can take place in clusters of industries and some government branches that are isolated from national dysfunctional institutions.[25] Large-scale experimentation is what Sabel has termed democratic experimentalism, which seeks to create (in an incremental manner) new forms of

---

21 See also K.E. Davis, "Legal Universalism: Persistent Objections" (2010) 60:2 *University of Toronto Law Journal* 537.

22 See, for example, R.E. Kranton and A.V. Swamy, "The Hazards of Piecemeal Reform: British Civil Courts and the Credit Market in Colonial India" (1999) 58 *Journal of Development Economics* 1; W.C. Prillaman, *The Judiciary and Democratic Decay in Latin America: Declining Confidence in the Rule of Law* (Westport, CT: Praeger, 2000).

23 Prado and Trebilcock, *supra* note 4; M. Prado, "The Paradox of Rule of Law Reforms: How Early Reforms can Create Obstacles to Future Ones" (2010) 60:2 *University of Toronto Law Journal* 555.

24 We are using here the term coined by J. Cohen and W. Easterly (eds), *What Works in Development? – Thinking Big and Thinking Small* (Washington, DC: Brookings Institution, 2009).

25 C. Sabel, "Bootstrapping Development: Rethinking the Role of Public Intervention in Promoting Growth" in V. Lee and R. Swedberg (eds), *On Capitalism* (Stanford: Stanford University Press, 2007) 305–41.

law making and administration. Sabel uses this to describe elements of the regulatory experiences in the European Union as well as in the United States.[26]

The most pressing question for the field of law, institutions and development is how to account for the particularities of different countries, while at the same time sustaining the idea that there are some common elements in this intellectual inquiry that can be used across time, places and contexts. As discussed in this chapter, this is still an open question from a theoretical, methodological and practical perspective. Thus, the future of the field remains largely unchartered terrain.

---

26 See C. Sabel and J. Zeitlin, "Learning from Difference: The New Architecture of Experimentalist Governance in the EU" in C. Sabel and J. Zeitlin (eds), *Experimentalist Governance in the European Union: Towards a New Architecture* (Oxford: Oxford University Press, 2010) 10; C. Sabel, "Dewey, Democracy and Democratic Experimentalism" (August 2012, Columbia Law School, unpublished manuscript), available at http://www2.law.columbia.edu/sabel/papers/Dewey,%20Democracy%20 and%20Democratic%20Experimentalism.pdf (accessed 4 May 2014).

Index